HIP-HOP JAPAN

ian condry

HIP-HOP

Duke University Press   Durham and London   2006

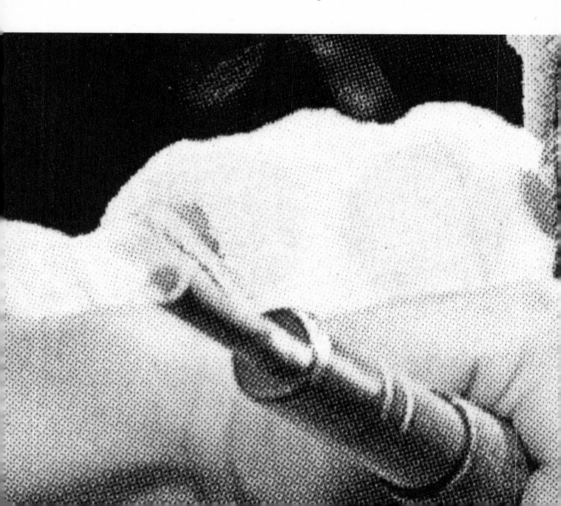

JAPAN

RAP AND THE PATHS OF CULTURAL GLOBALIZATION

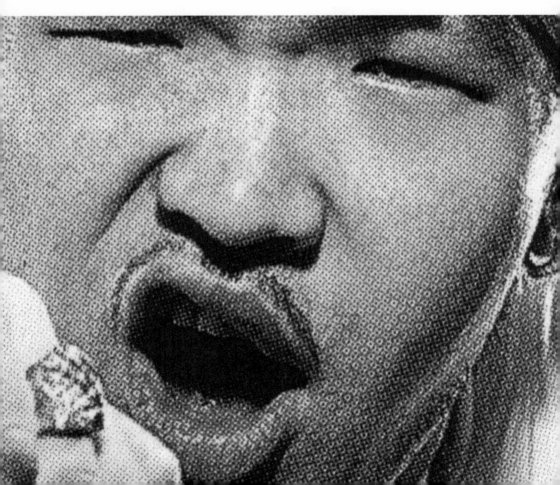

for Margot

CONTENTS

ACKNOWLEDGMENTS

Much props to the Japanese artists, fans, writers, promoters, and record-company people who took the time to explain to me what hip-hop music and the culture means to them. This book captures only a small slice of the many fascinating stories that go into the history of hip-hop in Japan, but I would like to thank all those who helped make sense of things to the gaijin with a notepad. I especially acknowledge the help of the musicians Umedy (Umehara Masaru), Utamaru (Sasaki Shirō), and the writer Furukawa Kou, who spent hours and hours over the years discussing with me the faces of hip-hop in Japan.

I have also been blessed with the assistance of countless colleagues, friends, and critics who have helped me push forward this project with their thoughtful reactions, insights, and advice. I can acknowledge only a fraction of them here, and for the rest I hope that you can recognize your own ideas in the text that follows. A few names, however, deserve special mention. I gratefully acknowledge the support of my colleagues in MIT's Foreign Language and Literature section who both supported my project and provided critical feedback. I particularly appreciate Jing Wang's incisive suggestions during my revisions. I also appreciate the encouragement and advice of Ken Wissoker at Duke University Press. Thanks go to three anonymous reviewers of earlier versions of the manuscript as well.

Financial support for the project came from the Japan-US Educational Commission (Fulbright), Yale University's East Asia Prize Fellowship, and from Union College and MIT.

I am especially grateful for the superb guidance and teaching of William W. Kelly, who balanced critical comments with support for this project throughout the process. I would also thank the Japan Ethnography Reading Group at Yale, who gave the book a careful reading at critical stages in the process of revising the book. Finally, I would like to acknowledge the unwavering support of my wife. Margot, your insights, incredible energy, and love make everything worthwhile.

NOTE REGARDING TRANSLATIONS, JAPANESE NAMES, AND WORDS

All translations are by the author. All interviews were conducted in Japanese by the author, unless otherwise noted. Japanese names are given in the Japanese order, that is, family name followed by given name (e.g., Sasaki Shirō), except in cases where a Japanese scholar publishes in English, in which case the Western form is followed (given name then family name). Song information is written in the form "Song title" *Album title*. Please be aware that Japanese words usually take the same form whether in singular or plural. Thus, the term *kimono* can refer to one or more pieces of clothing.

It was a revolution. Scratching
two records to make one music.
. . .
That energy came from the Bronx,
where hip-hop was first discovered,
from there across the ocean to Japan,
a spark flew and caught fire.
Yes, it is the beginning of the legend.

—ECD "Intro" on *Big Youth*

Kakumei datta. Nimai no rekōdo o
hikkaite hitotsu no ongaku o tsukuridasu.
. . .
Sono kakki wa buronkusu, tsumari
hippu hoppu ga saisho ni hakken sareta basho,
soko kara umi o koe nihon ni mo
tobihi shita no de aru.
Sō, densetsu no hajimari da.

INTRODUCTION

HIP-HOP, JAPAN, AND CULTURAL GLOBALIZATION

With these words, the Japanese rapper ECD uses the image of a spark to reflect on the ways hip-hop crosses borders and sets the world alight.[1] He gives credit to the New York City pioneers—Grandmaster Flash, Kool Herc, Rakim, KRS-One—and the energy of the Bronx that started the movement, but he also reminds us that while origins are important, hip-hop depends on the people who keep the fire going wherever they might be. *Hip-Hop Japan* analyzes the paths these sparks took as the music and culture spread from a small, underground scene in the eighties and early nineties, largely dismissed by Japan's major media companies, to become a mainstream pop culture phenomenon today. Hip-hop was a revolution, as ECD says, because it provided a particular means for youth to express themselves through rhythm and rhyme, sampling and remixing, and battling with one's skills. As the flames spread in the late nineties, Japanese hip-hop became more commercialized, but that commercialization developed alongside a widening and diversifying underground scene, encompassing artists and fans from a broader range of socioeconomic backgrounds and from throughout Japan, from Hokkaido in the north to Okinawa in the south.

Hip-hop caught on because it spread through the smoky bowels of Tokyo's underground club scene. There one can experience the ways Japanese hip-hop draws inspiration from American artists while at the same time integrating the language and everyday understandings of Japanese youth. In this book, I focus on these sites of performance, what artists and fans call the *genba*, or actual site, of the Japanese hip-hop scene, referring to the all-night dance clubs where the combined efforts of artists, fans, and promoters fed the fire.[2] I use the concept of *genba* to draw attention to the ways hip-hop is constantly made and re-made in specific locations through local dialects and for particular audiences. These clubs were pivotal sites of performance, socializing and networking that form the dynamic links between the global and Japan.

The evolution of the Japanese hip-hop scene reveals a path of globalization that differs markedly from the spread of cultural styles driven by major corporations such as Disney, McDonald's, or Wal-Mart. Indeed, hip-hop in Japan is illuminating precisely because it was initially dismissed as a transient fad by major corporations and yet ultimately took root as a popular style nevertheless. This shows that globalization is not driven solely by powerful media companies, but travels through alternative paths as well. This ethnography aims to give an insider's view of what the music means to young Japanese, but I would argue that the lessons of this case study are more far-reaching, providing insight into how culture is changing worldwide today. In particular, the book offers two general conclusions. First, localization of cultural forms can, and at times does, proceed simultaneously with an increasing global sharedness, thus showing that the opposition between local and global can be a false dichotomy that hides more than it reveals. Second, I propose a method for understanding how the forces driving new cultural styles emerge from the interaction among diverse actors—media industries, artists, fans, writers, and so on—in a way that requires grasping the connections (rather than oppositions) between culture industries on one hand, and creative artists and active fans on the other. Attending to *genba* of cultural production provides immediate access to the intersecting power lines that produce transnational popular culture, while at the same time allowing us to consider the mutual construction of what are often viewed as dichotomous analytical categories (global/local, producer/consumer, complicit/resistant, etc.).

With these larger issues in mind, this book attempts to capture and make sense of the ways hip-hop is lived in late-twentieth-century, early-twenty-first-century Japan, at a time when youth face an increasingly uncertain economic future, and when the nation as a whole is struggling to adjust to its shifting position vis-à-vis Asia and the West. Among the rappers discussed in these pages are those who challenge government whitewashing of the World War II military atrocities, question racism in Japan, criticize the nation's sex industry, rap about teenage bullying-victims-turned-schoolyard-murderers, and ask whether a job as a salaryman is anything but acquiescence to a life of quiet desperation. Far from being a straightforward example of Americanization, hip-hop in Japan includes rap songs that question the US government's reaction to 9/11 and the reasons for the Iraq war. Understanding the impact of this diversity of messages requires attention not only to the words, but also to the contexts in which they are performed and heard.

To understand these contexts, I have organized the book such that each successive chapter details hip-hop's development in Japan in terms of a central analytical theme: race, battling, performance, fans, language, gender and the market. Although break-dancers, deejays (DJs), and graffiti artists all figure importantly in the story of hip-hop in Japan, I concentrate on Japanese rappers and their lyrics, in part because rap has become the most commercially successful aspect of hip-hop, and because rap, more than dance, graffiti art, or deejaying, is most deeply intertwined with the Japanese language, and therefore provides particularly interesting insights into Japaneseness and its interaction with global flows.[3] How is hip-hop changing as it gets relocated, re-interpreted, transformed and commodified in new settings? Are we witnessing the emergence of a what might be called a global hip-hop nation, or is hip-hop simply the latest foreign cultural style to be seamlessly integrated into Japanese culture? Does Japanese hip-hop resist entertainment-industry capitalism, or has it simply been gobbled up by the omnivorous J-Pop world? Does hip-hop promote deeper connections with African American culture or is it primarily a vehicle for superficial fashion encoded with offensive stereotypes? What drives the spread of these styles, and to what extent is it top-down or bottom-up? (Indeed, what is the top? America? Media conglomerates? The super-producer Dr. Dre?) To answer these questions, we must begin in the *genba*, where the huge sound, the intensely focused artists, the energized fans, the committed promoters, the critical writers, and the business-minded executives each bring particular energy, interests, and expertise to the movement.

Going to a Club

About a quarter mile from Tokyo's Shibuya station, the aptly named club Cave represented an important location for hip-hop in 1996. There I attended about a dozen rap performances and deejay scratch contests. To find out about an event at one of Tokyo's clubs, whether at Cave, Harlem, Family, Web, The Room or countless others, one could start by checking for flyers in Tokyo's so-called record town (*reco mura*), an area in Shibuya that boasts what may be the world's most extensive collection of new and used vinyl record stores.[4] Although the flyer may read "doors open at 10 p.m.," few people arrive before midnight, and the action picks up an hour or two after that. Arriving at a small office building's back door, you find no sign, but are likely to see a few clubbers in hip-hop gear outside talking on cell phones. Head down the narrow staircase, and at a ticket window you are charged about $25 (¥3000) for the night's entrance fee, which many clubbers think inexpensive, given that a movie costs about $15 (¥1800). Unlike most clubs in the mid-nineties, Cave would ask for ID to confirm that clubbers were at least twenty years old, the legal drinking age in Japan. A heavy door prevents seeing or hearing inside before paying. You receive two tickets each good for a beer or rail drink.

Inside the club, the air is warm and thick, humid with the breath and sweat of dancing bodies. Head left, and you will enter the cramped bar area with a graffiti-painted wall reading "Vortex," the record label associated with the club. Here, hip-hop artists meet before their shows to plan upcoming recording projects and live events, to pass on demo tapes from friends, and to gossip. Back through a narrow hallway, past filthy bathrooms covered with street promotion stickers, you arrive at the upper level dance floor. When Takagi Kan spins as a deejay, a group of disciples stand at the deejay booth, watching mix techniques and trying to read the artist and song names off the spinning vinyl. They never speak to him, nor does he acknowledge them. Standing on the dance floor, you feel the bone-thudding bass lines thump out of enormous speakers. There is the scritch-scratch of a deejay doing his turntable tricks, and the hum of friends talking, yelling really, over the sound of the music. The lighting is subdued, much of it coming from a mirrored ball slowly rotating on the ceiling. The smell of stale beer is mostly covered by the cigarette haze, but it is best not to look too closely at what is making the floor alternately slippery and sticky. At a couple of times throughout the night, a break-dance circle will open up, as the rest of us peer over shoulders to catch the good moves.

In 1996, groups that would later become staples on music television shows performed before small crowds between 1 a.m. and 4 a.m. in a downstairs space that could hold only about a hundred people. It was a veritable firetrap with only a bare light bulb shining on the emcees rapping from the cramped deejay booth. I remember seeing Zeebra's head brush against the ceiling as he rapped to the underground crowd in his early days. During scratch solos, if you look at the hands of the assembled fans, you will see the would-be deejays doing "air mixer," wiggling their mixer fingers back-and-forth in time to the scratches, a contemporary equivalent to a bygone era's air guitar. The darkness, low ceiling, black walls, and smoky murk create a space both intimate and claustrophobic. The loud sound and drunken revelry give clubs an atmosphere of excitement that culminates with the live show and often a freestyle session afterwards. But an important part of clubbing is also the lull before and after the live show, when deejays work their crates, and everyone else circulates among the crowd, flirting, networking, gossiping, dancing, or simply checking out the scene. Clubs are spaces where the diffuse network of hip-hop fans, artists, organizers, producers, and entrepreneurs gather, and where work and pleasure mix. The nightclubs produce the hip-hop scene in a way that extends beyond the performances on stage. In this sense, *genba* are the crucibles where "hip-hop" and "Japan" merge to form the shape-shifting amalgam "hip-hop Japan."[5]

Fieldwork to Study Global Popular Culture

I came to this project as a graduate student in cultural anthropology interested in the intersection of global and local cultures (and also as a fan of American hip-hop). After listening to some albums by the Japanese groups Rhymester and Scha Dara Parr, I was struck by what unique perspectives they brought to their society. I decided that depicting what Japan looked like from the perspective of a Japanese rapper would add something I had yet to see in my years of studying Japanese culture. But when I began fieldwork in the fall of 1995, the number of potential sites was daunting. There were the places where the music was produced: record companies, recording studios, home studios, and in some cases on trains (some artists programmed beats using portable, handheld synthesizers). There were the places where the music was promoted: music magazines, fashion magazines, TV and radio shows, nightclubs, and record stores. There was also the interaction between musicians and fans to be observed at live shows or in mediated form on cassettes, CDs, and twelve-inch LPs. Besides, hip-hop includes not only rap music but also breakdancing, deejaying, and graffiti, and all of these aspects took their own shape in Japan. One of the tenets of anthropological fieldwork is that you cannot understand a people without being there, but in the case of hip-hop, where is "there"?

As I began interviewing rappers, magazine writers, and record company people, the term *genba* kept coming up. Even among those who were skeptical about hip-hop in Japan, everyone agreed that to understand Japanese rap music it was necessary to go to the *genba*, that is, nightclubs. The clubs (also called *kurabu*) provided a space where the gamut of participants met, and provided an entry point for grasping the experiential pleasures within a variety of business practices. The idea of *genba* can be applied broadly to sites that become a focus of people's energies and where something is produced. Live shows are central for understanding the paths that Japanese hip-hop has taken, and they also constitute the events around which many musicians' lives revolve, at least, the musical parts of their lives.

At the same time, artists, magazines and, of course, record companies also measured productivity in terms of CD releases. After attending various events for several months, and as the artists became aware of my interests, some musicians invited me to observe recording sessions. Recording studios offered a different but also revealing *genba* of performance and networking. There, performance is turned into a material object and a commodity. Studios also prove important sites for teaching musicians what a company expects from a professional. In recording studios, the intense focus on the sound and the repetition involved in getting it right illustrates the on-going processes of pre-production, demos, rehearsal, writing, recording, mixing, and promoting that constitute other sides of hip-hop performance. Recordings also remain the best opportunity for widespread success, both in terms of getting paid and getting props. In these ways, recording studios serve as another central research *genba*, though they figure less prominently, compared to clubs, in the narrative that follows.

In some respects, this book is an experiment aimed at exploring what sites of cultural production can teach us about the intersecting forces that produce global hip-hop. My fieldwork assumes an ethnographic approach that is performative rather than place-based. I did not focus on a single club, but attended a variety of different clubs to establish a comparison. I spent five weeks in Tokyo during the summer of 1994 to begin research for this project. My intensive fieldwork was conducted between September 1995 and February 1997. I have made brief return trips almost every year since then, most recently in July 2005. In all, I have attended more than 120 club events, mostly in Tokyo, but also some in outlying suburbs. I have also witnessed over fifty recording sessions in venues ranging from small home studios to multimillion-dollar studios.[6] *Genba* research in clubs and recording studios offered opportunities for interviews with musicians, fans, event organizers, record company executives and club owners. Eventually, I visited the homes of several musicians and met with some of their parents as well. I supplemented this fieldwork with interviews with record company representatives, record store owners, and music magazine writers.[7] I continue to follow the scene by reading magazines and Web sites, through contacts by e-mail, and, during my return trips, by meeting with friends, artists, and writers to go to clubs and to record stores.

Of course club performances do not generate a singular or even converging approach to combining Japan and hip-hop, but rather constitute a complex and evolving scene has arisen out of a range of competing approaches. To get a small sense of this variety, we need to step out of clubs to visit an event at which a wider range of artists battled for attention at one of Japan's cornerstone hip-hop events.

B-Boy Park 2001

In August 2001, I attended a four-day festival in Tokyo called B-Boy Park that provided an overall snapshot of Japanese hip-hop as it entered the new millennium. Organized by Japanese hip-hop pioneer Crazy-A, the festival began on Thursday and Friday with competitions in freestyle rapping, breakdancing and battle deejaying, events that were the culmination of regional competitions held throughout Japan. The finals of the freestyle competition drew upwards of a thousand fans to watch the emcees compete on a boxing-ring-style stage at On Air East, a big box live space in Shibuya. The six expert judges— writers, rappers, producers—voted after each head-to-head round, but they relied on the screaming fans to decide all ties. In the end, Kreva (of Kick the Can Crew), battled to victory, winning his third straight title with his pointed dis raps and clever rhymes. The break-dance and deejay competitions drew audiences in the hundreds as well.

On Saturday and Sunday, the performances took place at the outdoor stage in Yoyogi Park. Nestled between the youth shopping districts of Shibuya and Harajuku and adjacent to the Meiji Shrine with its giant wooden torii gates and nationally famous iris gardens, the park constitutes a space between traditional Japan and the youth consumer culture that symbolizes the present day. Since the 1980s, the park has been a gathering point for street musicians on Sundays. It was here in 1984 that the first Japanese break-dancers started practicing. Crazy-A and his brother Naoya were among the people who first performed there, and later DJ Krush, the group B-Fresh, and others joined in the fray. In the 1980s, when hip-hop was just beginning in Japan, small-scale gatherings nurtured the first generation of artists as groups of friends shared what little information was available about hip-hop while experimenting with the new style.

In 2001, B-Boy Park illustrated the long way hip-hop in Japan had come.

The variety of groups and activities at B-Boy Park also embodied a movement caught between pressures of commercial media, diverse aesthetic approaches, and an array of political messaging. In the early afternoon on Saturday, a panel discussion featuring rappers, writers, and radio personalities, took questions from the audience and discussed the state of Japanese hip-hop, with particular attention to the dangers associated with rap's on-going commercialization in mainstream media. On Saturday afternoon, several independent record labels sponsored a "new talent" showcase, featuring two dozen up-and-coming groups, including then new-face teams Gagle and Torikabuto. B-Boy Park culminated in an all-day free concert on Sunday, featuring over forty of the leading Japanese rap groups and break-dance teams, including Crazy-A's outfit Rock Steady Crew Japan. The capstone event drew an audience of upwards of eight thousand people, and constituted the largest hip-hop show up until that time.

Wandering around Yoyogi Park during the final day's performances, you could see all manner of Japan's hip-hop fans. Some of the men were dressed in the latest thug fashion, with bandanas, do-rags, and platinum chains. Some of the fans had tanned skin, dread hair, or even beauty-salon-styled Afros to go with their NBA jerseys or FUBU wear, but overall the darkened-skin fans were few and far between. More common were simply baggy pants, baseball caps, Kangol hats, and Nike sneakers along with a variety of more normal, everyday Tokyo youth fashion (i.e., jeans and a T-shirt that none of your friends have). The audience was weighted 60-40 toward men, with most listeners in their teens and early twenties. The musicians tended to be a little older, in their early- to late-twenties.

The performances on stage paid homage to hip-hop's four elements (yon yōso) featuring break-dancers, deejays, and rappers, while several graffiti artists produced pieces on both sides of the half-dome stage. The woman graffiti artist Belx2, for example, made a manga-inspired piece, namely, a big eyed, bare breasted woman giving the finger (see figure 1) while another artist next to her depicted rappers with their microphones and iconic images of aerosol artists with face masks and spray cans.

Like other graffiti writers in Japan such as Kazz Rock and Tomi-E, Belx2 does work-for-hire like this, and also bombs outdoor pieces. For example, a wall along the train tracks near Sakuragi-cho station in Yokohama features a mile-long stretch covered with pieces from many of the Kantō area crews (see figure 2).

The rapping, deejaying, breakdancing, and graffiti at B-Boy Park would be instantly recognizable to hip-hop fans worldwide. In a way, it could have been

1. Belx2 working at B-Boy Park 2001. Photo by the author.

a hip-hop event anywhere—until one looked a little more closely at the details. The street vendors, for example, were selling *yakisoba* (fried noodles), *takoyaki* (octopus dumplings), *okonomiyaki* (an omelet-like snack), along with corn dogs, dried squid, and cans of Kirin beer. An undercurrent of eco-friendly activities was noteworthy as well, as some environmental groups had tables set up with information about atomic energy (bad) and beer made with hemp (good). Several times between acts, announcements were made to encourage the tobacco smokers in the crowd to use non-flammable plastic snap-pockets as portable ashtrays to prevent dirtying the park with cigarette butts (and people were actually using them). At the back of the viewing area were garbage cans that required you to separate your trash into six categories for recycling.

But above all it was the Japanese lyrics that marked the event as Japanese. Not only did the day's emcees transform what is often thought of as the subtle and refined language of haiku into a rhythmically pounding flow of rap, but they all rapped about topics that carried a distinctly Japanese flavor. Among the event's peak moments, performances by Rhymester and Zeebra stood out. When one of Rhymester's emcees Utamaru performed a song criticizing the Japanese government, thousands of fans joined him for the chorus, screaming, cheering, taunting, calling on the government to "open the zipper" and lay bare the sordid backroom dealings that were corrupting Japan's

2. Kazz Rock graf piece in Sakuragi-cho, 1999. Photo by the author.

political system. Hip-hop and global politics also intertwined in Zeebra's performance of a song inspired by the Kitano Takeshi film *Brother* (2000). The film portrays an exiled yakuza tough, played by Kitano, taking over the Los Angeles drug trade with the help of his brother and an African American friend. In the song, Zeebra riffs on the idea of Japanese beating Americans at their own game, yet he positions himself not as "representing Japan," but as fighting for himself, "Zeebra the ill skill."

it's true we lost the war	*Tashika ni maketa ze, sensō jya*
but don't dis us now	*da kedo* DISR*arenee, kon no genjō wa*
we're tough, hard internationalists	*orera tafu de, haado na kokusaiha*
the top fighters who made it through	*masa ni erabinukareta toppu faitaa*

—Zeebra feat. Aktion (2001) "Neva Enuf" single (Future Shock, PSCR-5936)

Zeebra's song illustrates how hip-hop, even as a Western form, can be used to challenge Western cultural hegemony. Later in the song, fellow emcee Aktion even brags, "I can't even understand your English—ha ha!" with the implication that knowing English hardly proves necessary to be number one. Utamaru, criticizing the Japanese government, and Zeebra, questioning American dominance, offer two examples of the ways in which hip-hop cannot be seen as straightforward Japanization of a global style, nor as simply Americanization. B-Boy Park 2001 demonstrated that there exists no singular Japanese approach to hip-hop, but rather a wide range of artists competing to promote diverse visions of what hip-hop in a Japanese setting might be.

An explosion of divergent styles in the first years of the twenty-first century shows how different groups of artists, each with somewhat distinct fan bases, use their expressions to draw selectively among competing aspects of hip-hop. The proponents of these different styles—party rap, underground hip-hop, hard core (*haa ko*), conscious rap (*konshasu*), spoken-word rap, free-jazz rap, and rock rap, to name a few—all emphasize different linkages of aesthetics and politics. These choices help us grasp why different club events (*genba* performances) draw different audiences and promote divergent visions of what Japanese hip-hop can be. While some Japanese emcees portray themselves as self-styled thugs cruising Yokohama streets in Southern-California-style lowrider cars, others are featured in music videos fighting ninja with *katana* (samurai swords).[8] The annual event B-Boy Park, which began in 1998, is unusual in the sense that the different groups, each with an individual approach to Japanese hip-hop, tend to segregate themselves through separate late-night events. But the competitive interaction between the groups at the huge festival acts as a metaphor for the competitive dynamic that generated the widening diversity within the overall scene. By the time of B-Boy Park 2001, it was clear that neither the term *localization* (becoming more Japanese) nor the phrase *global homogenization* (becoming more like everywhere else) could characterize that range of stylistic approaches within the scene. It was also a scene that many people had doubted would ever develop at all.

Hip-Hop Endures Despite Doubts

When I began this study of hip-hop during a preliminary research trip to Tokyo in 1994, few would have predicted that an event like B-Boy Park could draw thousands of fans, much less support four days' worth of performances. Up until the mid-nineties, people who worked in the entertainment world pointed to hip-hop's rootedness in African American communities as a reason to doubt its possible takeoff in Japan, where different understandings of race, language, and social class prevail. At the time, when I interviewed Japanese music magazine writers, musicians, and record company representatives, many were skeptical: "Japanese rap is all imitation"; "Japanese youth don't understand where hip-hop is coming from"; "It'll soon disappear"; "Japanese B-Boys are only interested in hip-hop as a fashion statement"; and "The Japanese language just doesn't work with rap." Except for File Records, a small, independent label in Tokyo, few record companies were showing any interest in producing Japanese rap music. The early 1990s constituted a winter for Japanese rap and it was not clear whether warmer times would ever arrive.

Japanese hip-hop reached a tipping point, however, later in 1994 and 1995, when several rap singles sold around a million copies each. In contrast to the United States where Run-DMC's 1986 crossover hit "Walk This Way" hinged on a combination of rock and rap, Japan's mid-nineties crossover moments arrived with songs that combined the *kawaii* (cute) orientation of pop music with rap vocals and deejay textures. Of particular importance were two singles by East End X Yuri (the "X" is read "plus") and a single by the group Scha Dara Parr that featured singer-songwriter Ozawa Kenji. The huge sales drew the attention of major record companies who viewed teenage girls as the linchpin for expanding the genre. Those corporate attitudes angered the more underground rappers, who sought to establish their own legitimacy, their own "street cred," despite selling fewer records. When I returned to Tokyo in September 1995 to begin a year and a half of intensive fieldwork, cute-oriented so-called J-Rap was being covered in music/fashion magazines, while underground artists, still ignored in the mainstream press, stoked the fire in late-night clubs. Years later, some of these underground groups found their way to mainstream recognition.

What was once expected to be an ephemeral, fashion-oriented, transient fad now figures prominently in Japan's popular culture, appearing on television, radio, in magazines, and influencing many areas of Japan's pop music world. In what ways does the view from live performance spaces help us understand hip-hop's longevity, vibrancy, and diversity in Japan? In contrast to symbols of cultural globalization, such as Coca-Cola, Disney, Nike, and McDonald's, which take their cues from huge multinational corporations, hip-hop in Japan draws attention to an improvisatory working out of a cultural movement in the language and among peer-groups of a particular generation of youth.

The on-going experimentation with what works for a Japanese audience (from fans, to writers, to record company execs) is what distinguishes the *genba* of a hip-hop nightclub from something like Wal-Mart, Disney or McDonald's. It may be a matter of degree, but I would argue the distinction is worth making. Several scholars have made important contributions to our understanding of cultural globalization by showing how Disney and McDonald's in Asia take on particular local features, and therefore do not constitute a straightforward "Westernization" (Watson 1997; Brannen 1992; Raz 1999). Nevertheless, I would argue that the kind of circular interaction among the participants in a club, especially between artists and fans, offers a more fluid space for producing a collaborative movement. Wal-Mart, McDonald's, Disneyland have a more formalized range of experiences that generate feedback loops primarily through consumption. One could argue that each of these is a *genba*, but I would say they are less influential as *genba* because the performative and social networking features are less pronounced and because the character of the experience is more rigidly defined by the producer. Personally, I'm less interested in defining what is and is not a *genba*; rather, I suggest that *genba* offer a window on some cultural processes better than others. In performative and media contexts, I believe *genba* is very useful for broadening our understanding of the mutual construction of cultural forms (like hip-hop) beyond "producers vs. consumers" to include other actors (artists, record companies, media, fans, etc.) in dynamic feedback loops.

Another aspect of hip-hop's movement from underground niche pursuit to mainstream presence deserves clarification. Although the appearance of two million-selling Japanese rap groups in the mid-nineties prompted articles in music magazines declaring J-Rap's "citizenship" (*shiminken*), criticisms of the music's inappropriateness to Japan did not cease. Rather, the skepticism was transposed from the formerly dominant discourse of hip-hop's association with African-Americans and the English language (in contrast to Japan's ethnic and linguistic setting) to a new discourse challenging Japanese hip-hop's authenticity on the grounds that it was "simply commercialized (*komasharu*) pop music." But as I discuss in more detail in chapter 3, it is important to understand the fluidity between "commercial" and "underground."[9] Many commercial pop artists spent years honing their styles in underground clubs, and underground artists often aim for wider recognition and more lucrative contracts. I picture the link between commercial and underground in terms of a pyramid structure, with the amateur artists, underground performers and independent label musicians working in the base. The fewer but more visible artists working for major record labels, and the rare mega-hit stars taper off in numbers toward the top. The artists in the upper echelons receive far more attention, and often come to stand for hip-hop today even though they represent a small fraction of the overall number of artists, fans and promoters in the overall scene. The point of clarification, then, is that hip-hop did not go from an underground era to a commercial era, but that the pyramid expanded with those at the top breaking into mainstream media coverage, while the base of the pyramid expanded as well, though largely unnoticed by people removed from the scene. Moreover, this aspect of hip-hop suggests ways of pushing forward several intellectual debates about the relationship between Japaneseness and global popular culture.

Toward a More Complex "Japaneseness" Amid the Global Popular

An emcee who calls himself Kohei Japan illustrates how rappers not only playfully rework hip-hop but also play with notions of what Japan means as well. In one song, he remixes food, rap, and Japaneseness in a particularly interesting way. Kohei lived with his parents in Yokohama into his twenties, and while pursuing a music career with a rap group named Mellow Yellow, he has been working as a chef. As his stage name suggests, he does not shy away from imagery of traditional Japan. On the cover of his debut solo CD (see figure 3), he is portrayed as if he were a kabuki character in a woodblock print.

This image of a kimono-clad emcee could be taken as representing Japan, but a closer look reveals a more contradictory message. His fingers make the gesture of the so-called funk sign (a reference to one of the songs on the album), and the funk sign appears on his kimono as well. The Kangol hat also appears unusual for a kabuki actor. A look at the lyrics of one of the songs on the album shows that while Kohei highlights his Japaneseness, he does not expect to be taken seriously.

[I'm] always all-natural, completely Yoga	*tsune ni shizentai maru de yoga*
not bread, but rice; not ramen, but soba	*pan yori raisu ramen yori soba*
not meat, but fish; not cooked, but raw	*niku yori sakana yaku yori nama*
not flowers, but dumplings; my cap is Kangol	*hana yori dango, kyappu yori Kangol*
wearing a hunting cap, it's my time	*hanchin kaburya ore no jikan*
K-O-H-E-I, the Japonica	K-O-H-E-I *za japonika*

—Kohei Japan (2000) "Hungry Strut" *The Adventures of Kohei Japan* (Next Level/File Records, NLCD-037)

3. Kohei Japan (2000) *kabuki* woodblock CD jacket. Next Level /
File Records, Tokyo, Japan (NLCD-037).

As the verse continues, he says his lyrics are "dope" (*dōpu*) and "deeper than
enka" (a more traditional form of popular music). The playfulness operates
on a number of levels. He demonstrates his lyrical skill by rhyming the first
couplet, using internal rhymes for the second couplet, and adding a punch
line by reworking his stage name so that it *does not* rhyme in the last line.[10] He
plays on stereotypical representations of Japan and the West in food (e.g., raw
fish not meat). He makes a pun out of the brand name for his hat (Kangol)
and an old proverb "*hana yori dango*" (literally, "I'll take a rice dumpling to eat
rather than a flower to look at"; or, "sustenance before beauty"). If anything,
rather than representing Japan, Kohei parodies theories of Japaneseness that
define national identity in contrast to Western modes of behavior. In other
words, Kohei's rap implicitly critiques a simplistic Japanese essentialism, asking in effect, "Is eating rice really what it means to be Japanese?" Calling
this a hybrid cultural form may be accurate, but it also raises the question:
Why this particular form of hybridity? In naming his album *The Adventures
of Kohei Japan*, Kohei suggests that what we are hearing is not so much hybridity as the outcome of his life's paths. He draws on his personal history as
a chef, shows his talent for song-writing, and also humorously presents Japaneseness in a way that undermines stereotypes. These cross-cutting valences
operate on numerous levels, thus bringing attention to the particulars of how

identity, language, and intersecting histories are implicated in the cultural connections we call globalization.

Intellectual Contexts and Major Findings

Taken together, the circulatory character of nightclubs, the battling between styles at B-Boy Park, and the playfulness of Kohei Japan's rendering of national identity speak to the major intellectual debates that underpin this book, particularly in regard to the study of Japanese culture and globalization. In the postwar period, the anthropology of Japan has increasingly dealt with media, popular culture, leisure activities and global flows as a way of deepening our understanding the ways cultural identities are produced. In contrast to research on officially legitimated realms of activities—school, work, organized religion, high culture, etc.—David Plath (1969) argued for the importance of studying the "after hours," that is, leisure activities, as an entry point into Japan's changing lifeways, an approach that continues to yield important insights (see e.g., Linhart and Fruhstuck 1998; Mathews 2000; Spielvogel 2003). At the same time, the significance of free time activities is often related deeply to real world concerns. Anne Allison's (1994) ethnography of a Tokyo hostess club shows how the mutual interpenetration of "work" and "play" in after hours socializing affects participants' understandings of gender roles and corporate hierarchies. Similarly, in nightclubs, hip-hop musicians operate in a world where work and play merge in the combination of performing, socializing, and networking that makes up their clubland activities. In this we can see how popular culture is created through social activities that at times reproduce, at times subvert long-standing patterns of social relations undergirding daily life. This is the lesson of Jennifer Robertson's (1998) fascinating historical and ethnographic study of the all-female Takarazuka Revue. She illustrates how popular culture's main impact can be, in many ways, fundamentally ambivalent, for example, when the stars of the revue who play male roles offer inspiration for adoring fans to follow their dreams, while the public discourse surrounding actors' scandals often reinforces traditional gender roles. This reminds us that the urge to see hip-hop as consistently a forum for the expression of protest on the part of under-represented social groups should be tempered by a recognition of the limitations imposed on such voices, particularly as artists gain increasing corporate support. *Hip-Hop Japan* builds on these important works by drawing attention to leisure realms where competition among artists produces a dynamic and contradictory (or ambivalent) realm of debate about what it means to be Japanese.

Hip-Hop Japan also aims to extend our understanding of the interrelationship between the global and Japan in the realm of popular culture. The study of Japan's pop world has expanded dramatically in recent years, as scholars' convey the importance of what is sometimes dismissed as "merely pop" (trivial, commercial, ephemeral) music, TV, film, writing, comics, etc. by illustrating their connection to enduring patterns of Japanese culture and history (Treat 1996; Martinez 1998, Craig 2000; Kelly 2004). I would argue, however, that we must be cautious of enclosing the meaning of popular culture within a Japanese setting.[11] When the analytical frame is "Japan," then we have a more difficult time grasping the articulation between Japanese artists and their foreign sources of inspiration. For example, Joseph Tobin (1992) argues that the "domestication" of foreign cultural styles subverts the too-simple stereotype that the Japanese are "imitators not innovators." But in highlighting the process of remaking the foreign into something Japanese there is a risk of blurring together the very debates about Japaneseness that are often at the core of using foreign styles. In other words, in the effort to show that something like hip-hop in Japan "really is Japanese" in some sense, we risk underplaying the mutual construction of the global and the local. The methodology this book adopts involves developing theory from the particulars of ethnographic description, and to use fieldwork incites a cultural production as a way of grounding global flows in particular spaces and among specific people (artists, fans, promoters, etc.). Rather than focusing on the hybridity of hip-hop in Japan, which suggests an original Japan and hip-hop elsewhere in the past, my goal is to show the unfolding of the cultural movement over time. The performative contexts have changed as hip-hop has evolved over the years, and mapping those changes provides the key to understanding.

In some ways, an anthropology of globalization raises an opposite set of challenges compared to identifying the Japaneseness of popular culture. By this I mean that the study of transnational cultural flows tends to emphasize the movement of people, objects, and ideas across boundaries, while blurring their locatedness when embodied in different places. In contrast, I draw inspiration for performance theory which locates meaning not only in texts, but in the ways they are performed, consumed, and recirculated as a means of approaching global flows. Globalization refers to an "intensification of global connectedness" and, more deeply, to "a basic reorganization of time and space" (Inda and Rosaldo 2002b: 5). The explanatory value of the concept does not lie in its vision of an endpoint at which the world finally becomes one, "a single society and culture occupying the planet" (Waters

1995: 3). Rather, globalization draws attention to connections across boundaries, transcending borders between nation-states and encouraging analysis across disciplines of economics, politics and culture, as electronic media, migration, and modern transport bring all corners of the world into a more tightly woven web. Arjun Appadurai's (1990) formulation of transnational cultural flows in terms "-scapes" is one of the most influential ways of thinking about these dynamics. He identified five spaces of exchange—ethnoscapes, mediascapes, ideoscapes, financescapes, and technoscapes—to show that these flows do not run simply from more powerful to less powerful regions, and that these flows are "non-isomorphic" (i.e., flows of one do not necessarily entail flows of others, as for example in the way Japan accepts foreign ideas more readily than foreigners themselves). But as more and more terrains of flow can be identified (religion-scapes, sport-scapes, food-scapes, hip-hop-scapes), we clearly need a way to think more generally about how people, media, ideas, finance, and technology can be analytically brought together to assess their mutual interaction rather than dividing them up. In *Hip-Hop Japan*, the answer I propose is that we view "flows" in terms of performative potentials in specific locations. In this, I draw on the work of Louisa Schein (1999), who shows that modernity is not simply a context or a discourse, but rather something that is negotiated and contested through performance and, in this sense, actualized. By analogy, I am interested in hip-hop performance as the actualization of a global Japan. As in performance studies, I integrate what happens on stage with a sense of how the response of the audience (including fans, critics, record execs, club owners, etc.) is part of dynamic that evolves over time. The idea of *genba* is to identify nodes where collective activities have performative effects, in terms of artists moving the crowd, convincing gatekeepers in record companies and clubs to give them a chance, and the performance of a CD in terms of sales. The *genba* provides immediate access to these interested actors and intersecting lines of cultural influence. My focus on *genba* also relates to broader initiatives within anthropology to move away from seeing fieldwork as situated in bounded, geographical locales (Gupta and Ferguson 1997). As such my focus is not on "culture of a people" nor "culture of a place" so much as "culture as it is performed." This offers a way of analyzing the complex linkages of global and local that operate in different artists' work.

What, then, are the major findings this *genba* methodology produces? First, the development of hip-hop in Japan shows that localization and global connectedness can proceed simultaneously. One of the central debates about cultural globalization revolves around the question of whether transnational flows are leading to a more homogeneous world culture, or whether processes of localization ultimately transform borrowed styles into distinctive domestic versions. In the case of hip-hop in Japan, I found that neither global homogenization nor localization accurately captured the ways the musical style has changed. Instead, we see a deepening and quickening connection between hip-hop scenes worldwide, at the same time that a wider diversity of styles appears in Japan and globally. In other words, the opposition between globalizing and localizing turns out to be a false dichotomy. What we require is a different conceptualization of how cultural settings and flows interact. A focus on spaces of cultural production provides a means to accomplish that.

The second major finding focuses on the power of media industries. Although hip-hop in Japan was largely dismissed by elites in major media companies from the mid-eighties until the mid-nineties, young people nevertheless developed the scene in clubs (rap and deejaying) and in public parks (breakdancing and graffiti). This illustrates the importance of gathering places, networks of peers, and underground paths of cultural flow in the early days, and which set the stage for hip-hop's later expansion into the mainstream. Once some Japanese rappers attained commercial success in 1994–95, major record labels became increasingly involved in promoting some styles of Japanese hip-hop over others. Major labels tended to focus on playful, light-hearted party rap while those artists who took a more oppositional, socially conscious stance toward underground hip-hop performed primarily in small clubs and recorded on independent labels. As Japanese hip-hop entered the new millennium, the music of the best-selling artists became increasingly commercialized, but the underground scene expanded and diversified as well. I argue that we can come to a deeper understanding of the relationship between commercial and underground media worlds by viewing the development of the scene as a kind of pyramid, with top artists reaching greater heights at the same time a wider base of would-be artists emerged away from the public spotlight. In this sense, the power of media industries is clearly limited, and commercialization captures only part of the scene's dynamics. Thus, I argue that the analytical divide between the power of culture industries on one hand, and the organic creativity of underground artists and active fans on the other, should not be viewed as oppositional, but rather in terms of their networked interaction. Record companies, artists, fans and media each bring a particular kind of power in developing this cultural world, but the power of each is contingent on the actions of the others.

My hope is that showing how a methodological focus on *genba* offers a way of grounding our understanding of media power as contingent, networked, and evolving may be useful in other studies of transnational media.

Mapping the Book

In the chapters that follow, I describe Japanese hip-hop by moving through a series of analytical discourses: race, battling, performance, fans, language, gender, and the market. Each chapter's theme provides a frame for understanding different aspects of hip-hop in Japan. Taken together, the chapters provide a portrait of how the paths of cultural globalization go through *genba*, where a myriad of committed players interact. In this, I attempt to move the analysis away from a variety of common analytical binaries—global/local, authentic/imitation, commercial/creative—in favor of considering the ways diverse groups produce what I call "hip-hop Japan." The ethnographic material is drawn from an array of sites and performances in which hip-hop is enacted, debated, practiced, negotiated, commodified, and consumed.

In chapter 1, I discuss the racialized meanings at work in Japanese hip-hop. Analyzing the debates surrounding the appropriation of so-called black style—from tanned skin to dread hair to ideologies of personal expression—I show how Japanese hip-hoppers debate the significance of racial differences and transracial alliances. Borrowing from Cornel West (1990), I argue that Japanese rappers are engaged in a "new cultural politics of affiliation," that draws inspiration from African American struggles while generating distinctive approaches to race and protest in Japan. Race forms a part of Japanese hip-hop, but it operates in the context of an identity politics different from that in the United States. When Japanese artists proclaim that they are yellow b-boys, they are not asserting a pan-Asian identity, but rather drawing attention to their specific location in a differently configured racial matrix. In this, they suggest the possibilities for a transnational cultural politics of race that improvises on their understandings of hip-hop's core values.

Chapter 2 describes the history of hip-hop in Japan. I use the metaphor of "battling samurai" to emphasize the competitive dynamic that has helped shape the evolving scene. I argue that the contexts in which these battles unfolded have shifted over time and reflect the changing circumstances of three eras of Japanese hip-hop. In the first era (1984–94), Japanese hip-hoppers struggled to clarify for a Japanese audience what hip-hop is. After the breakthrough hit singles of 1994–95, the second period was characterized by competing ideas concerning a different question, "What makes hip-hop *Japa-*

nese?" Here, party rap versus underground hip-hop formed one of the pivotal lines of debate. After 1999, a third era of increasing diversity without a center illustrates that amid the widening array of regional and stylistic approaches to hip-hop in Japan, we see the disappearance of the idea of any single scene. This sets up the argument for the rest of the book by suggesting that the effects of cultural globalization are necessarily paradoxical, that is, working in several directions at once.

In chapter 3, I zero in on what I call *genba* globalization by showing how the location of hip-hop performances in nightclubs gives us a way of thinking about both cultural flows and media power. In particular, I consider the underground group MSC and its political songs in contrast to major label performers Dabo and Rip Slyme. By developing a model of the hip-hop scene in terms of committed actors with different roles, I argue that the debate over whether producers or consumers have more power sets up dichotomies that reveal only part of the picture. Instead, I propose thinking of *genba* in terms of how networking and feedback loops among participants operate to produce a diversifying music scene, a scene that can be usefully conceived of in terms of a pyramid structure. In the ways Japanese artists compete for legitimacy and their own artistic visions, we can see how power is dispersed, spread, and recentered in a dynamic, interlocking network. This vision of *genba* globalization, whereby the variety of global forces is refracted through performances, offers an alternative model to common analytical binaries, such as the Frankfurt School's visions of an opposition between circumstances of production and creative forces. It also helps us understand the contrasts between the underground and pop realms in producing differential outcomes with respect to fans, language, gender, and markets. This chapter extends the idea of *genba* and clarifies the book's conjoining theme — performativity — for evaluating cultural influence.

In chapter 4, I discuss hip-hop fandom in the context of consumerism in Japan. A transformation in the 1990s shifted attention from the flashy *shinjinrui* (new breed) trendsetters to the *otaku* (isolated and obsessed fans) as symbols of Japan's popular culture. Drawing on sociologist Miyadai Shinji's (1994) notion of *otaku* as inhabiting disconnected "islands in space," I analyze the ways this concept teaches us something about the specific character of specialization that accompanies information superfluity. Hip-hop fandom provides a way of evaluating the effects of an "*otaku*-ization" of popular culture.

Chapter 5 discusses the Japanese language and the ways it is implicated in contests over the meaning of hip-hop and Japaneseness. The Japanese language was viewed by some as an impossible wall that would prevent rap music from expanding in Japan. I compare the discourses surrounding rap and the Japanese language with debates about English-language and Japanese rock in the late 1960s. Japanese rappers also implicitly critique *Nihonjinron* (theories of Japanese people) notions of homogeneity, often premised on assertions of the uniqueness of the Japanese language. Japanese rap thus offers insights into the fluid relationship between language and identity. I retain the Japanese term *genba* untranslated in this book in part to remind us that such actual sites are deeply conditioned by the linguistic setting.

Chapter 6 looks at women emcees and their important, if underrepresented, role in Japanese hip-hop. In particular, I discuss the ways women rappers have managed to move away from the hegemony of cute (*kawaii*), a kind of pressure analogous to male machismo that might be called "cutismo" for female music artists. This chapter allows us to take the analysis of language and identity to another level by exploring questions of women's language and popular music as well, particularly through comparisons between hip-hop artists Ai, Hime, and Miss Monday and pop R&B artists such as Utada Hikaru.

Chapter 7 examines the market of hip-hop in Japan, building on scholarship in cultural economy. In part, I respond to a critique that could be aimed at the idea of *genba* globalization, namely, the question, "Isn't it all just about the money?" Regardless of Japanese hip-hoppers' political and artistic commitments, some might argue that corporate maneuvering is really what determines the character of globalizing cultural practices. In placing the money chapter at the end, however, I aim to underscore my argument that corporate entities tend to arrive late to the scene, cherry-picking artists who have honed their skills for years, rather than nurturing the conditions for creative production. Contrary to the common argument that we should "follow the money" to explain the movement of popular culture, hip-hop in Japan illustrates that the money tended to follow the artists. I also show how the power of big media arises not from control of aesthetic decisions, but rather from its control of gatekeeping, consumer surveillance, and access to promotion. We also gain a more nuanced understanding of the limits of corporate control by looking at business negotiations in which ideas of hip-hop culture prove central to the development of markets. As an example, I discuss the ways an artist-entrepreneur managed to stay in the business for over a decade through creativity in both music and self-marketing.

In the conclusion, I return to the paths of cultural globalization and discuss the lessons we can draw from Japanese hip-hop for understanding how culture is changing in today's world. I discuss some of the ways the *genba* concept may be extended to help us understand other locations and other cultural phenomena. I also discuss two Japanese rap songs that deal with 9/11. In these examples, we can witness the seemingly contradictory effects of cultural globalization whereby hip-hop in Japan is used to critique America's anti-terrorism efforts. In this we are reminded that expanding cultural networks—*genba* to *genba*—are still widening, spreading more sparks, raising questions of when and where the fires of future movements will develop.

My name is Yellow B-Boy   *Ore no namae wa kiiroi* B-Boy
I'm all that, and number one   *hanpa naku*, number one

— Rhymester, "B-Boyism"

CHAPTER 1

YELLOW B-BOYS, BLACK CULTURE, AND THE ELVIS EFFECT

In a 1998 single, when the rapper Mummy-D of the group Rhymester calls himself "Yellow B-Boy" and "number one," he draws attention to the complicated racial matrix at the heart of hip-hop's worldwide diffusion.[1] What does it mean to be a yellow b-boy in Japan? What is hip-hop doing in a supposedly homogeneous society like Japan's in the first place? Questions of race and hip-hop are a good place to begin thinking about the music's cultural politics in part because racially charged imagery constitutes such a conspicuous feature of rap's presence in Japan. Indeed, the racial underpinnings of hip-hop are also at the center of vibrant debate among Japanese artists and fans. A Japanese rapper who calls himself Banana Ice released a song in 1995 called (in Japanese) "Mane + Mane = Mane" ("Imitation + Imitation = Imitation") in which he ridicules young hip-hop fans who darken their skin as a sign of respect toward African American musicians. "Your parents, your grandparents are Japanese," he raps; "you can never be the black person you want to be."

Although the percentage of Japanese rappers, break-dancers, and hip-hop fans who tan their skin or wear dreadlocks is quite small, such body practices symbolize a dubious two-sidedness to the uses of hip-hop in Japan. Kreva of the group Kick the Can Crew put it succinctly in a personal communication with me when he explained the dreads he wore in the mid-1990s: "First, it's meant as a sign of respect toward black culture, but second, I want to stand out [*medachitai*]." Banana Ice, rapping more generally about skin-darkened hip-hop fans, sees above all the mark of conspicuous, mercurial consumption:

in summer, black at the beach	*natsu wa umi de kuroku*
in winter, black on the ski slopes	*fuyu wa yama de kuroku*
with free time, going to tan salons	*hima arya hiyake saron itte*
skin always black	*itsu mo hada wa kuroku*
take a half day to get dreadlocks	*hannichi kakatte kamigata doreddo*
then give it up to be a skinhead	*yamete yoshite sukinheddo*

—Shitamachi Kyôdai (1995) *Mane + Mane = Mane* maxi-single (Pony Canyon, Japan, PCCA-0084).

The spectacle of young Japanese spending lavishly on dread hair and tanning salons is perhaps the most striking expression of hip-hop devotion in Japan, and for critics both in the United States and Japan it symbolizes a misappropriation and misunderstanding of black music, culture, and style. Hip-hop comes to Japan above all as black music rather than American music, that is, with racial connotations emphasized more than national origins. Over time, this blackness has been interpreted and used in a wide variety of ways (e.g., hair styles, skin tanning, rapping, body language, ideas of self-expression, clothing, musical taste, etc.). This chapter focuses attention on the ways race is debated, commodified, performed, and contested, arguing that race indeed constitutes a critical component of hip-hop, even in Japan. Nevertheless, I would argue that it should not be the only lens through which to view the music. One aim of this chapter is to shift attention away from questions of how American understandings of race are interpreted in Japan to focus instead on how Japanese conceptualize and embody ideas of hip-hop and race. As we will see, there is no single answer, but rather a contradictory range of discourses linking music, race, and Japaneseness.

Within the diversity of hip-hop's racialized meanings, I discuss three interrelated themes. First, I ask, what do the criticisms of Japanese rappers tell us about assumptions linking music and race? Interestingly, critics who complain that rap in Japan is primarily superficial imitation or misguided appropriation can be found in both the United States and Japan, and both rely on similar logics. Thus debates about hip-hop overseas encourage us to think about cultural politics of race across national boundaries, not only in terms of criticisms but also of alliances. This leads to my second theme, which, drawing on Cornel West, aims to map what might be called a new cultural politics of affiliation, that is, ways in which Japanese hip-hoppers draw inspiration from African American art forms and struggles. This analytical thread draws together different rappers' approaches to using hip-hop and race in their lyrics. I also briefly consider the diversity of black music forms in Japan (e.g., jazz, doo-wop, reggae) for comparison. Third, I examine the ways Japanese ideas of race arise from different conceptualizations (e.g., based on "blood," rather than appearance) and a different history (e.g., World War II in Asia). If we know that race is constructed, the question becomes how can we learn from different patterns of construction in different places, serving different ends? In the end, I argue, moving beyond global-versus-local (or black-versus-Japanese) debates allows us to explore a more pressing question related to globalization, namely, "What can transnational cultural politics accomplish, and how?"

Race and Keeping It Real

One place to begin considering race and hip-hop is with the idea of "keeping it real." The rhetoric of realness in American hip-hop encompasses a wide range of concerns, including debates over whether the negative images in gangsta rap actually just reflect reality,—thus distinguishing pop, commercial rap from real, underground hip-hop—and over whether a white rapper such as Eminem can be "real" because he comes from a working-class background. Of course, being African American does not in itself confer realness.[2] Claims of realness, or lack thereof, become weapons in debates about who is black enough among African American rappers as well. But what would it mean to *know* hip-hop, and what would be required to *participate* in the production of hip-hop, in a language other than English and for people with little (if any) historical connection to the largely African American communities that gave birth to the style? How can a Japanese artist "keep it real"?

Consider the artwork for two albums released in 2002 (see figures 4 and 5) and ask yourself which one could be considered more real? For many Americans, Dabo's body language, clothes, and accessories are likely to reinforce the idea that Japanese hip-hop is merely imitation, superficially copying the styles seen on MTV and in music magazines, missing the deeper significance of hip-hop and reinforcing stereotypes about African Americans. Does not Dabo's cover suggest that what Japanese youth learn from hip-hop is that black Americans, if they are successful, are most likely gun-toting gangstas, microphone-wielding emcees, or professional athletes? On the other

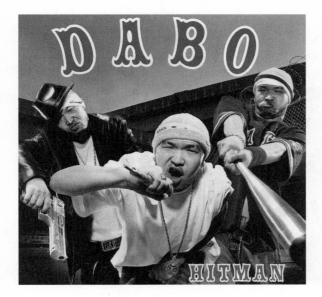

4. Dabo (2002) "Hitman" (Def Jam Japan / Universal,
UIC-1005). Def Jam Japan/Universal Music, Tokyo, Japan.

hand, when Japanese rappers like Uzi incorporate conspicuously Japanese elements, are they not ignoring—or, worse, disrespecting—the origins of hip-hop culture?

Note the double bind that tends to shadow all foreign emcees. Japanese rappers are expected to respect the African American roots of the music while also producing something uniquely authentic and original. Their success in achieving this balance thus depends very much on the eye (or ear) of the beholder. Uzi represents a model of local creativity by relying on recognizably exotic markers of Japanese ethnicity—namely, samurai imagery—and, in fact, he claims descent from a samurai family. He also prints the title of his album in the kanji characters for *kotodama*, an archaic concept roughly meaning "the spirit of words." In contrast, Dabo uses a gun, do-rags, platinum chains, and prison walls topped with concertina wire as signifying elements, thus relying on supposedly globally recognizable markers of hip-hop style.

But if you ask the average Japanese hip-hop fan to choose between Dabo and Uzi and to identify the more authentic (*honmono*) or "real" (*riaru*) artist, most would choose Dabo. Why? Because he performs with a more skillful flow, better musical production, more provocative lyrics, and a stage presence that commands the crowd. Dabo's performance skills in a club thus pro-

5. Uzi (2002) *Kotodama* (Pony Canyon, Japan, PCCA-01825).
Pony Canyon, Tokyo, Japan.

vide a measure of authenticity despite not having a particular racial heritage. Rather than seeing his style as imitative, Dabo's supporters are more likely to see him as competing directly with the best (i.e., American) hip-hop performers in the world. At one level, Dabo can be seen as trying to participate as an equal in a shared world of hip-hop iconography, a more respectable stance, he would likely say, than relying on clichéd images of Japaneseness. Indeed, from a Japanese perspective, samurai have become overdetermined by media representations on par with those of US gangstas. Moreover, Dabo's uses of Americanized imagery constitutes only one side of a kind of mutual borrowing and remixing that happens in American uses of Asian imagery, as when the Staten Island–based hip-hop crew Wu-Tang Clan uses kung fu imagery and sound samples in their videos and songs or produces Wu Wear shirts with gibberish Japanese writing. Dismissing such gestures as orientalist or racist implicitly invokes notions of cultural authenticity that may prove ill-suited to such transnationally oriented productions. If anything, a transnational cultural politics should encourage the perspective of locating the meaning of gangsta or samurai or kung fu rappers in broader contexts, not simply in terms of the visuals of album covers. How then can we understand the politics of these cultural gestures?

A New Cultural Politics of Affiliation

I would argue that the projects of Japanese hip-hoppers can be usefully viewed in terms of what Cornel West (1990) calls a "new cultural politics of difference." West illuminates the advantages of conceiving of racial politics in nonessentialist terms. West's new cultural politics of difference contrasts with artistic projects that represent positive images of a singular black community, representations, he notes, that can be biased toward heterosexist, patriarchal, middle-class norms. Instead, he applauds critical interventions of African American writers and artists who draw attention to the diversity of black lives and struggles. This new cultural politics aims to inspire alliances without essentializing, by, in his words, "projecting alternative visions, analyses and actions that proceed from particularities and arrive at moral and political connectedness" (35). West's perspective emerges from a different context, but the lessons for a study of black culture in Japan are profound. In particular, the application of his ideas exposes the limitations of searching for *the* local or *the* Japanese in overseas hip-hop. Indeed, although I use the term *black culture*, we should bear in mind that the term is shorthand for a complex range of practices, ideas, and discourses, never meaning any one single thing. Similarly, highlighting the local features of hip-hop in Japan risks reproducing images of *the* Japanese people while underplaying the ways in which Japanese emcees are engaged in critiquing mainstream standards of what it means to be Japanese, among other artistic and political goals. As we will see, some Japanese rappers address racism in their own society by drawing inspiration from the racial underpinnings of hip-hop, as when Mummy-D calls himself a yellow b-boy. In this, I would argue, Japanese rappers, by allying themselves with African American rap, engage in what might be called a new cultural politics of affiliation. By this I mean that the gestures toward alliances across racial boundaries demand analysis in terms of their multiple frames of reference. I would argue that many uses of hip-hop in Japan attempt to produce a kind of political affiliation, but that the politics must be situated in the spaces and contexts in which they are performed. This reorients our attention away from questions of whether the Japanese "get it" or "don't get it" when it comes to race and hip-hop, and instead draws us toward questions of what Japanese hip-hoppers are doing with the music in their own worlds.

I would add a caveat. While there exists great positive potential for hip-hop in Japan, both as a space for articulating alternative visions of Japanese identity and for providing a comparative context for thinking about hip-hop's border crossings in the United States and elsewhere, it would be misleading to suggest that the hip-hop reaching mainstream Japan is only, or even primarily, a vehicle for progressive change. Generally in Japan, corporate support has flowed more quickly either to those who accommodate the marketing world's fetishization of blackness as hip, sensual, and rebellious or to those who deemphasize blackness in favor of aligning themselves with Japan's traditionally lighthearted and inoffensive pop music realm. If one's exposure to Japanese rap music comes from television, radio, or the mainstream music press, one is likely to see the edginess of hip-hop promoted through racially coded imagery, often combining an outlaw stance with conspicuous, brand-name consumption. Hip-hop is not only "cool" (*kakkoii*) but also "bad" (*yabai*, meaning of course "good"). It surely is a sign of globalization that in addition to McDonald's, Disneyland, and Starbucks, Japan now boasts its own self-styled thug (*saagu*) rappers, complete with gold teeth, "ice" (diamonds), and platinum chains. Alternatively, J-pop versions of hip-hop that appear on the charts tend to be stripped of any racial nuance.

Because my research focuses on *genba*, that is, key sites of cultural production (mainly nightclubs and recording studios), I witnessed a wider range of musical expressions and in general more politicized messaging than is commonly found in major record labels' offerings. Examples of superficial, imitative, and frankly racist uses of hip-hop abound in Japan, but a balanced look at Japanese hip-hop can nevertheless help us understand the stakes and the promise of the music's cultural politics. The blackness of hip-hop in Japan is central to its cultural meaning, and yet it is a blackness that operates somewhat differently outside of mainstream US culture where white, patriarchal modes of dominance remain a standard for judging oppositional stances. Some of the debate about race and hip-hop from US hip-hop studies provides an important context.

Hip-Hop Studies, Blackness, and Border Crossing

In the United States, the discussion about the social and political significance of hip-hop rarely mentions foreign artists, revolving instead around American hip-hop's contributions, positive and negative, to problems facing African American communities and around what hip-hop says about race in America (Baker 1993; Boyd 2002; George 1998). Tricia Rose, in her influential study of hip-hop in the United States, defines hip-hop in terms of its black roots and its social location: "Hip hop is an Afro-diasporic cultural form which attempts to negotiate the experiences of marginalization, brutally truncated opportunity and oppression within the cultural imperatives of African American and Caribbean history, identity, and community. It is the tension between the cultural fractures produced by postindustrial oppression and the binding ties of Black cultural expressivity that sets the critical frame for the development of hip hop" (1994, 21). Here, rap music and black culture become entwined and mutually construct each other, at least partly in the laudable effort to valorize the historically maligned identity of black Americans. Over the years, other axes of analysis have emerged as well in the growing scholarly literature on hip-hop. The publication of a hip-hop studies reader speaks to the value of hip-hop as a teaching tool, providing insights not only into racial dynamics in the United States but also into media power, music and technology, fan cultures, gender oppression, and a wide range of poetics, politics and performance practices (Forman 2002; Forman and Neal 2004; Neal 2003). Moreover, recent critical work deepens our understanding of the links between blackness and hip-hop. Imani Perry (2004), for example, argues that the aesthetics of hip-hop arise essentially from New World black culture rather than from a diasporic culture of the Black Atlantic. Raquel Rivera (2003) explores the complicated relationships between Latino identity and blackness among the "New York Ricans" who contribute to hip-hop culture.

But as hip-hop's production and consumption outgrow the critical frame that Rose identified, the challenges to interpretation become increasingly complex. Does wider acceptance of hip-hop in mainstream America constitute a gain for African Americans? Leon Wynter, a columnist for the *Wall Street Journal*, argues that the ubiquity of black artists in US popular culture means the "end of white America" in the sense that mainstream America "is now equally defined by the preferences, presence and perspectives of people of color" (2002, 5). Although he acknowledges that the success of black popular culture is often viewed skeptically because it lacks a measure of redress for a long history of racial discrimination, he still voices optimism: "The triumph of African Americans in a self-sustaining transracial commercial popular culture will one day be seen as the final catalyst to the wholeness of identity embodied in the phrase 'One race, human, one culture, American'" (281). Personally, I remain skeptical that achieving a wholeness of identity through American culture will prove the solution to racism.

The problem with imagining a transracial utopia through popular culture is that media connectedness does not by itself guarantee action for greater equality. Greg Tate (2003) asks rhetorically, What do white people take from black people? His answer: Everything but the burden. If a sense of responsibility, of a shared burden, extends little further than buying a hip-hop CD or going to the occasional show, it is easy to understand skepticism regarding any political potential of hip-hop. In this context, the work of scholars and critics who describe hip-hop in terms of the deep and enduring connections between African American struggles and aesthetics is political in the sense that it disrupts the too-easy assumption of many privileged white fans that by listening to hip-hop they are getting close to black people.

In addition, a promising avenue for progress in moving from hip-hop representations to engaged politics can be seen in Bakari Kitwana's critical and practical efforts to transform hip-hop from a "cultural movement to a political power" (2002, 195). For example, in the summer of 2004, he helped organize the National Hip Hop Political Convention (NHHPC), which attempted to mobilize young Americans during that year's presidential election by drawing attention to the problems of urban poverty, the prison industrial complex, incarceration rates, and the nation's failed military policies. Yvonne Bynoe (2004), the founder of Urban Think Tank, a resource center for African American youth, argues persuasively that the hip-hop generation should not depend on celebrities to lead but must rather develop leaders among themselves who can motivate people across class and race divisions. This represents an important goal for addressing the limitations of hip-hop's political potential.

In terms of analyzing hip-hop overseas, however, we may get a very limited view of the political potential of the music if we judge foreign artists primarily in terms of their contribution to African American struggles. I support Bynoe's important efforts in the United States, but I worry about her contention that "getting real about global hip-hop" means acknowledging that foreigners do not, and cannot, really get it when it comes to understanding hip-hop culture. She says "technical aspects" of rap music can be learned by foreigners, but "the central part of hip-hop culture is the storytelling and the information that it imparts about a specific group of people," namely, "black people in America" (2002, 77–78). She levels particularly harsh criticism at Japanese youth. For them, she says, " 'Blackness' became a fad to be consumed, without the obligation of learning about or understanding Black people" (2002, 83). The impetus behind such criticism is understandable. Japanese youth who express an interest in another culture should take the time to try to understand where others are coming from, just as white fans must consider the appropriateness of their own uses of hip-hop slang and racial epithets, even when intended as signs of inclusivity. Where Bynoe stumbles, however, is in committing the same offense that she pins on the Japanese; namely, she stops short of understanding the links between history, identity, and expression that draw Japanese youth to hip-hop. It is valid to ask what kind of obligation there exists to learn about other people's cultures in consuming their styles, but need everyone read a book about Japan or live in that country before eating sushi or watching an anime movie? It makes no sense to say we must pass some cultural entrance exam before we can try out the styles of other people, whether it is hip-hop, manga comic books or ukiyo-e woodblock prints. That said, what defines the difference between wrongheaded appropriation and respectful borrowing?

The Elvis Effect

The unease that many Americans, and perhaps especially African American musicians, feel toward Japanese mimicking not only musical styles but also clothes, jewelry, and even gestures associated with black culture is at least partly related to a long history of appropriation of black music by others without acknowledgment or recompense. The August 2002 cover of *Vibe* magazine featured the following headline: "Wanna-Bes: The Weird World of Japanese Dancehall Fanatics." The article's author discusses the popularity of both reggae and hip-hop in Japan but questions their legitimacy: "Any black-music fan knows about the 'Elvis effect'. . . black folk make music, and whites remake it and make big bucks. . . . Where is the line between cross-cultural influence and cross-cultural theft?" (Dreisinger 2002, 134). The author acknowledges that some Japanese hip-hoppers pay homage to the originators, but asks, "what if their teenybopper fans, the ones who met hip-hop through Zeebra instead of Dre, never do their homework?" (138). Here we see another element of the debate about appropriation: African American artists will not get paid. The charge of theft is striking, but the fears, I believe, are misplaced: the spread of Japanese hip-hop is also leading to a deepening appreciation of American hip-hop, and it seems likely that one will not replace the other, but that both will grow in popularity together. The larger question seems more poignant: are Japanese fans doing "their homework"?

Many Japanese artists and fans of hip-hop do in fact make an effort to learn about hip-hop history and its relationship to black Americans through books, films, and Japanese magazine articles. Frequently songs by Japanese emcees outline histories of hip-hop in the United States and describe the Jamaican connections of DJs like Kool Herc and some other key pioneers such as Afrika Bambaataa and Grandmaster Flash. Yet this introduces another conundrum. The more an outsider learns of the links between black history and hip-hop, the more removed he or she may feel. In a column he wrote for a Japanese hip-hop magazine in the mid-1990s, Zeebra, one of the leading Japanese rappers, quotes a fan letter expressing this anxiety about Japanese hip-hop: "No matter how much one likes Black music and culture, both were born from the situations Blacks faced, and the burden of their history and fate. In some ways, it was a brutal process (resistance against whites, the need to be proud of their own identity, their unique labor in the midst of poverty, etc.). If you consider this, I can't help but question the shallow, superficial imitation [*mane*] of us Japanese" (1996a, 94). Strikingly, this Japanese fan describes concerns quite similar to the criticisms made by Bynoe and the author of the *Vibe* magazine article, suggesting that the interpretations of authenticity speak less to an American-versus-Japanese difference than to different understandings about how histories of race and musical creativity are related. Interestingly, the criticisms of Japanese appropriations of blackness reinforce essentialized notions of blackness and Japaneseness.

I would suggest an alternative way of interpreting the never-ending charges of imitation as related to hip-hop musicians. First, it is important to recognize that in one sense Japanese hip-hop is, in fact, imitation. All of it is. If the question is whether the Japanese are trying to create something completely new or completely new within hip-hop, then it is the latter that most hip-hoppers seek (by definition). Even for those musicians who express a distaste for placing themselves in genres—which is, after all, the business of music journalists, not of artists—we can still observe differences in the ways in which musicians work (sampling or live musicians, rapping or singing lyrics, self-identification as hip-hopper, etc.) that suggest genre alliances, while acknowledging numerous exceptions. But if we define imitation as working within a genre of music, in the case of hip-hop perhaps characterized as sampled and programmed tracks over which emcees rap rhythmically nuanced rhymes ("two turntables and a microphone"), then all contemporary hip-hop—in Japan and *anywhere else*, for that matter—is imitation.

Second, the idea that a certain background is necessary to make an authentic rapper obscures the fact that assertions of authenticity almost always come after musicians have proven their musical skill by standards other than their ethnic or racial background. Skill as an artist seems to define the tipping point *after which* questions of authenticity begin. If our definition of hip-hop is, as Bynoe argues, a form of storytelling about black Americans, then there is no place for Japanese, French, or even black South African rappers. Yet these emcees exist, and they form part of an emerging global movement taking up issues of economic oppression, government injustices, diverse forms of racism, and other important political battles alongside, it must be added, more playful and innocuous productions. Whether they are considered authentic or not is an arbitrary identification, but one that helps us understand conventions of inclusion and exclusion.

Race in Japan

ECD, a pioneer of Japanese hip-hop who remains active today, was one of the early artists who addressed race issues in his songs. His working-class background and radical take on Japanese society are relevant to grasping the political messaging of some of his songs about the failures of education and the healing powers of popular culture. In an interview with me in 1996, he described how his initial physical feeling (*nikutaiteki*) for the music of Grandmaster Flash and Afrika Bambaataa was gradually replaced by a more nuanced understanding of hip-hop and black culture. He dropped out of high school at age seventeen, got involved with a motorcycle gang, but says he "graduated" (*sotsugyō*) when he turned twenty. He worked in temporary jobs like construction and moving, all the while pursuing his musical career. His first, self-titled, release in 1992 on the independent File Records label included songs that detailed the forefathers of US hip-hop, his own transition from an interest in punk music to reggae and hip-hop, as well as a paean to the Japanese world of manga comics. He also included a song called "Blue-Eyed Asian," in which he rapped about the Japanese fascination with other races, questioning why "Japanese want to be white people / Japanese want to be black people." Most strikingly, however, he noted that the idea that "the Japanese are simply Japanese" misconstrues history. In lines that were bleeped out of the final version of the CD because the record company viewed them as too inflammatory, he points out that the Ainu were the original people of Japan and that the original emperor came from Korea; the Japanese themselves are interlopers on Japan's soil, or "aliens" as he says in the refrain. While Japanese youth are often represented as being innocent about race, musicians like ECD have, in fact, a rather nuanced understanding of racial identity and are willing to express such ideas in lyrics sensational enough for record companies to feel the need to censor them. ECD also implies that the racial homogeneity of Japan is at least partly a myth.

Japan is often portrayed as a homogeneous society, and in terms of racial differences, this seems an accurate-enough characterization, at least compared to the heterogeneous United States. From an American perspective, the Japanese are clearly "Asian": they have straight black hair (unless dyed or curled), and they share certain other physical characteristics that Westerners associate with "the Asian race," mainly, eye features and skin color. Yet these seemingly obvious differences betray deep cultural conditioning among Western beholders who see these differences as significant. The notorious Western notion that Asians have slanted eyes, one depicted, for example, in the Disney animated film *Mulan* (1998), is foreign to Japan, where eyes are evaluated on the number of folds in the eyelids. This reminds us that race constitutes, scientifically speaking, a meaningless category. Although we can imagine prototypical caucasoids or mongoloids, the boundaries between what many term races are impossible to identify. Taking the analysis to the level of molecular differences does not solve the problem either because there is more genetic variation within so-called races than between them (Marks 1995, 144).

Since Japanese tend to refer to themselves as a "single ethnicity" (*tan'itsu minzoku*), some might conclude that it is a misnomer to speak of a Japanese "race," but the presumed biological signifiers of Japaneseness suggest that the distinction between *jinshu* as "race" and *minzoku* as "ethnicity" is in practice blurred. Yoshino Kosaku describes a strong tendency among Japanese to perceive themselves as a distinct racial group, a notion he traces to a late-nineteenth-century ideology that viewed Japan as a family state (*kazoku kokka*) in which the Japanese are related to one another and to the emperor by "blood" (1997). Such notions persist today; Kosaku has found that Japanese perceive Japanese Americans as likely to have less trouble than Korean Japanese to assimilate to Japanese culture because they have "Japanese blood" (203). Similarly, current immigration laws in Japan put into practice the myth of Japanese blood; foreign migrant labor is generally prohibited except for *Nikkeijin*, descendants of Japanese people (Weiner 199, xiv). Most *Nikkeijin* working in Japan are second- and third-generation descendants of Japanese emigrants who settled in South America after 1899, most of whom worked on sugar and coffee plantations. These new migrant workers are designated "spouse or child of a Japanese national" and given long-term resident visas that allow them to live and work in Japan for three years (Sellek 1997, 187–92). Along with their spouses (who may be of any race), those from South America numbered around 175,000 in 1993 (185). By 2003, Brazilian citizens in Japan totaled 275,000 and Peruvians 53,000 (Ministry of Justice [Japan] 2004, 2). As the anthropologist Joshua Roth (2003) has shown, however, a Brazilian Japanese's legal status, based on shared blood, still does not guarantee societal acceptance.

Demographic differences between Japan and the United States help explain why Japanese hip-hop deals less with racism and more with youth issues, as well as with hierarchies of class and gender. According to the 2000 census, blacks and Latinos each made up a little over 12 percent of the US population, while Asian Americans constituted another 3.6 percent (Grieco and Cassidy 2001). Among Japan's population of roughly 127 million, there are about 1.7 million registered foreigners, or less than 2%. This includes over 600,000 Koreans from both North and South Korea, many of whom were born in Japan. There are also roughly 2 to 3 million *burakumin*, that is, descendants of an outcaste group of butchers, leather tanners, and executioners. Because they are physically indistinguishable from other Japanese, they form a kind of "invisible race," yet they face terrible discrimination in terms of getting jobs and getting married, thanks in part to private investigators who maintain lists of these families (De Vos and Wagatsuma 1966, Neary 1997).

Even so, this internal racism does not go unnoticed. The rapper You the Rock describes his recognition of the plight of *burakumin* as one reason he was deeply moved when he first heard the US groups Boogie Down Productions and Public Enemy (Fujita 1996, 98). He also notes that he was primed to understand the struggles of African Americans that he heard recounted in rap music thanks to school textbooks that included Malcolm X, Martin Luther King Jr., and other civil rights leaders.[3] Recently, Japan has also witnessed the appearance of Jin Back, an artist who raps about living in a *burakumin* neighborhood in Osaka (Uehara 2000), as well as a rap duo called KP who are resident Koreans (*zainichi kankokujin*) and who rap in Japanese, in some cases about relations between North and South Korea.[4]

Yet the presumed homogeneity of Japan has not meant a disinterest in racially coded music. The popular music scholar Shuhei Hosokawa shows, on the contrary, that black music in Japan has enabled artists to highlight racial issues within Japan, though the extent to which this has occurred varies by genre. He describes several contrasting examples of a Japanese adoption of black music and styles from jazz to blues to doo-wop to hip-hop. He notes that in the 1960s, black was "the color of resistance," and, prefiguring later alliances through rap, "the blackness of the blues makes Japanese performers more conscious of their racial status than rock and new American folksongs" (2002, 227). The doo-wop group Chanels (later Rats and Star), whose singers paint their faces minstrel black, prompted sharp debate in 1980, when critics sent letters to national newspapers in Japan condemning the Japanese singers' use of blackface as racism, while the group's defenders excused the practice as a way to "get as close to black people as possible" (227). Hosokawa draws connections between such racially transgressive adaptations and the cross-gendering in all-male kabuki, the all-female Takarazuka Revue, and in the gender ambiguity in *visual-kei* (a kind of glam rock featuring cross-dressing costumes and make-up). He also observes that representing for Japan, that is, making one's Japaneseness a central element in ideological assertions of authenticity, is a hip-hop innovation, especially compared to earlier rock and folk characterizations of authenticity in terms of the feelings and the experience of individual performers, rather than of national identity. Hosokawa's key insight revolves around locating blackness not as some historical core, but as a vehicle for a shifting politics of difference and affiliation.

E. Taylor Atkins (2001), in his fascinating history of jazz in Japan, shows how over the course of the twentieth century a wide variety of strategies have been used by musicians and writers to assert the authenticity of Japanese performers' efforts. He demonstrates that the discourses surrounding authenticity, although varying dramatically depending on the era, are seldom about the quality of the music per se, but instead revolve around shifting assumptions about the relationship between musical genre and the race and nationality of the performers. As local artists develop, and fans become more knowledgeable about foreign scenes, a dynamic relationship between old and new sets in motion new definitions of otherness. The anthropologist Marvin Sterling's study of reggae dancehall culture in Yokohama, Japan, for example, shows how the image of the Jamaican other shifted over time from a "'pure,' 'simple,' 'natural,' Rastaman" of roots reggae toward more "materialistically and sexually savvy 'rude boys' and 'divas' of Jamaican dancehall culture" (2002, vii). In the hip-hop scene as well, we see a dynamic debate about how to treat race.

Blackface Japan

As hip-hop became more readily recognized in Japan in the mid- to late 1990s, advertising and fashion industries rushed to exploit (they might say "celebrate") racialist iconography—the gangsta with guns, the promiscuous club girl, the youth gang members flashing signs and riding tricked-out cars —that were visually shocking because they relied on stereotypes to convey a sense of danger. Understandably, this fashionable trend has upset people like John Russell, an anthropologist teaching at Gifu University in Japan, who has written extensively about images of African Americans in that country. He argues that "constructions of blackness, even those regarded as positive, are based on stereotypes that deprive blacks of their humanity, individuality, and heterogeneity" (1998, 116). Even if hip-hop fans in Japan acknowledge the individuality and heterogeneity of African American rappers through their sensitivity to the stylistic differences between East Coast, West Coast, southern US crunk, and Miami bass, distinguishing between hip-hop styles is hardly the same as recognizing the diversity of black lives. On one hand, we cannot deny that Russell, along with many other African Americans, feels discriminated against by Japanese attitudes. On the other, Japanese rappers are precisely the ones thinking about race and culture in ways more subtle than those of the average Japanese music fan. Where can we go from here?

Perhaps something can be gained by resisting a Western desire to have Japanese choose sides in an American racial conflict. Instructive in this regard is a brilliant essay by Joe Wood, the late African American writer who traveled to Tokyo to see so-called blackfacers, young Japanese who darken their skin and kink their hair. He not only describes their scene but also explores his own ambivalent fascination with them. At one point, he wants to ask a Japanese writer in his twenties whether Japanese people see a colored person when they look in the mirror. Even before Wood gets a response, he realizes something: "I already knew what I wanted him to say: 'We hate black people. We love white people. . . . We see ourselves as white.' Like Russell, I believed that the Japanese see themselves as white, even when they black up" (2000, 324). But as he talks to more people, he comes to understand that black versus white is only one dimension of a differently configured racial context.

The historian Gary Leupp (1995) suggests that the complicated history of images of blacks in Japan shows how Western European racism has shaped Japanese understandings of blacks, but also how Japan developed its own distinctive interpretive models. From the mid-sixteenth century onward, a significant number of black Africans came to Japan as crewmen, servants, or slaves, and because of the way Portuguese traders treated the Africans, those Japanese who came into contact with them generally learned to view blacks as inferior. At the same time, in distinguishing "civilized" from "barbarian" people, skin color played less of a role than national origin. For most of Japan's history, all foreigners were regarded as barbarians (*yabanjin*), regardless of their skin color. Leupp notes that in Japan's early history, from the eighth century onward, whiteness in skin color (of Japanese) was generally associated with high birth, while darker skin tended to be associated with farmers and others who had to toil outside in the sun. Even so, Leupp describes some cases in which the color black had a positive connotation (e.g., an Englishman writing in 1863 noted that blackening the teeth and having the blackest hair was a sign of beauty). Leupp also points out that the Buddha, when not depicted in resplendent gold, was often portrayed with a dark, sometimes even black, skin tone. Nevertheless, from the late 1880s, when Japan began its march toward modernization, imbibing the ideologies of Western imperialists, prejudices toward blacks were imported as well.

Yet as Joe Wood explores the contexts of Japan's blackfacers today, he notes that both whites and blacks are *gaijin* (foreigners) first, and then white or black. Moreover, he finds that the blackfacers in their hairstyles, Michael Jordan jerseys, Nike shoes, and darkened skin are trying to be *something*, but maybe not primarily *black*. Wood acknowledges a visceral reaction to these blackfacers. "I suppose I should be embarrassed to confess that my heart was actually racing when I saw my first one of *them*," a blackface Japanese girl in line at a club, along with her black friend, who Wood surmises is African. Wood reports a short conversation with her. " 'Do people in school think you look good?' I asked her. 'No,' she said, 'But it doesn't matter.' 'Why do you choose to look like me?' I asked. 'You?' she asked. 'Who?' 'Black,' I clarified. . . . 'Because it's cool,' the girl said, shrugging her shoulders" (2000, 314). Although Wood perceives that the woman desires to be black like he, she is, in fact, more concerned with how others perceive her look, or style, in a fashion sense. In some ways, her appearance is meant to be cool even more than it is meant to be black, and a certain context is necessary to make sense of it.

It is also worth noting that not all blackface style is associated with hip-hop. The *ganguro* (literally, "face black") style among teenage girls addicted to tanning salons reached its peak in the late 1990s and was seen as largely separate from hip-hop fandom. Most *ganguro gyaru* (gals) would be expected to go to house or all-genre music clubs, dance in large groups *parapara* style (i.e., waving the hands and shouting in a way that resembles a Japanese *matsuri*, or festival, dance), and to dislike the ways hip-hop b-girls put on airs (*kakko tsukete*). The US visual artist Iona Rozeal Brown blurs these different streams of Japanese popular culture in her art when she calls the subjects of her Japanese woodblock–style paintings *ganguro* who are into hip-hop. She says, "I find the *ganguro* obsession with blackness pretty weird, and a little offensive" (Genocchio 2004). Yet if it is acceptable for a non-Japanese painter to use ukiyo-e woodblock style (I think it is), why should Japanese be admonished for using hip-hop?

The female clubber mentioned by Wood, with her getup and dark skin and black (African) boyfriend, might sometimes get denigrated as a *burapan*, especially by jealous Japanese men. The term relates to an earlier era's word for prostitutes, namely, *panpan* or *pansuke*, especially those who attended to American servicemen during the Allied Occupation after World War II

(Dower 1999, 132). Thus a *burapan* is a woman who prostitutes herself for black men, *bura* being the abbreviation for *burakku* (black). Yet this longing for "forbidden fruit" can also bring liberation.[5]

Nina Cornyetz (1994) has importantly pointed out the interpenetration of black style and a desire for virility on the part of some Japanese hip-hoppers. She notes that for some male hip-hop fans, "blackness is frequently affixed to an antecedent erotic subtext that fetishizes black skin as symbolic of phallic empowerment" (129). While some of these blackfacers may well seek, and may perhaps even gain, a sexual advantage in adopting their appearance, I would caution against reducing the uses of black culture in Japan to a desire to be more sexually attractive. Joe Wood concludes that Japanese hip-hoppers' fascination with and use of black skin and style reveals, at the very least, a conspicuous questioning of the homogeneity of the Japanese people. Where we can go further than Russell, Cornyetz, and Wood, it seems to me, is in examining the fraught debates within Japan over the appropriateness of using dreadlocks and darkened skin. Given the questioning of these practices by Banana Ice and ECD, as well as You the Rock's linkage of hip-hop with *burakumin* discrimination, the larger discourse about race and hip-hop in Japan involves more than fashion styles or images in the media. For our analysis, we must also consider this larger public debate, in lyrics and in public reactions, surrounding rap as part of what brings about a questioning of Japanese homogeneity. Let's turn now to an example from Rhymester that illuminates some of the pivotal lines of this debate.

Rhymester: *Respect* in Opposition to Whitewashed History Texts

In addition to this inward-looking critique of race through hip-hop, other uses of the music and culture in Japan look beyond the country's borders in an effort to improve the racially tinged anger in Korea and China related to the Japanese military's World War II atrocities. Japan's history of military horrors against other "Asian races" may be one reason why a 1999 hip-hop album cover provoked such a harsh reaction in one of Japan's leading daily newspapers. In the United States, slavery stands as the definitive atrocity that sets the stage for the current debate on racism, but in Japan, the imperialist aggression of World War II provides the key historical pivot around which questions of race revolve. As John Dower (1986) argues, World War II was in many ways a race war, not only because of the Nazi Holocaust but because of

6. Rhymester (1999) *Respect* dressed in military uniforms. Next Level / File Records, NLCD-026, Tokyo, Japan.

the ways in which both the Japanese and the Allies conceived of and treated their enemies. Japan's rhetoric of allying itself with other Asians against the white, European colonial oppressors was integral to the notion of building the Greater East Asia Co-prosperity Sphere, a sphere nevertheless premised on the belief that the Japanese were destined to preside over a fixed hierarchy of peoples and races and a policy that involved massacres and forced labor. This helps explain the public reaction to the cover of Rhymester's third album, *Respect*, which featured the three musicians dressed in Meiji era (1868–1912) military uniforms (figure 6).

The European-style uniforms mimic those adopted after the Meiji Restoration in 1868 and include samurai swords or *katana*. The album is titled *Respect*, pronounced as a loanword (*risupekuto*). Using the album cover as a springboard for discussing the popularity of the term among Japanese youth, the author of an *Asahi* newspaper article criticizes youths' lack of understanding. A Japanese sociologist quoted in that article explains that hip-hop in the United States serves as a weapon for transforming the circumstances of black people, and that the word *respect* is meant to remind the current generation of youth about the importance of remembering past struggles. He takes offense at the use of the word in the context of images that seem to promote a militaristic nationalism:

Youth should be expressing the pain in their hearts and bodies, not with some hackneyed phrases, but with their own words. So why, in bars, are they expressing the kind of preachy, empty morals of old folks? Plus, the members of hip-hop groups are mostly men, not women who have felt what it's like to be a minority. Japan's hip-hop groups also come mainly from the upper middle class, and I guess they reflect an era that is calling for the flag and the national anthem. Even in Japan, there are minorities such as Okinawans and Koreans living here, and I think the rappers should imagine their standpoint a little more in their songs. ("Risupekuto" 1999)

Utamaru (seated on the left), one of Rhymester's emcees, responded with anger, and for good reason. In the hip-hop scene, he is one of the more outspoken opponents of the right-wing Liberal Democratic Party that has been in power in Japan virtually throughout the postwar period. According to Utamaru, the cover's image is meant to evoke a time of vibrant cultural ferment in Japan. During the isolationist Tokugawa era (1600–1868), the military government prohibited foreigners from entering and Japanese from leaving Japan. But with the restoration of imperial rule, Western culture washed over Japan.

Around 1868, at the time of the battles surrounding the restoration of the Meiji Emperor, Edo [old Tokyo] culture had matured, and Western culture came rushing in. Those two styles mixed. For example, samurai sporting traditional topknots [*chonmage*] and wearing their swords would also dress in Western clothes, sometimes even wearing the old-style sandals [*zōri*]. As Western culture came in, there was a sense that Japanese things needed to be improved, and in that chaotic mixing, entirely new things were created. We feel a lot of sympathy with that because that's the stance we've taken ourselves. (Kinoshita 1999, 17)

For some, hip-hop likewise challenges young Japanese to think about how they can improve their culture through selective mixing.

We can also see glimpses of a transnational cultural politics of race in a song by Utamaru, a collaboration with DJ Oasis (of King Giddra). In particular, he raises the issue of Japanese government-approved history textbooks that whitewash Japanese atrocities in Asia during World War II. The song is called "Shakai no mado," which translates literally as "society's window" but is a colloquial expression meaning "zipper on one's pants." This is a song about opening the zipper, but this "window" does not open onto just anyone's private parts, as the song's refrain suggests: "When something's rotten, put a lid on it / [but] sometimes it's fun to open it up" (*Kusai mono ni wa futa o shite / tokidoki akete tanoshimu n da*). As the song progresses, it becomes clear that Utamaru views the zipper as hiding the rotting phallus that is the Japanese government. He blasts the Ministry of Education for approving history textbooks that downplay the atrocities of the Japanese military against other Asian peoples during World War II, a perennial source of friction with South Korea and China. Utamaru begins his verse by likening the government to an imperial inner sanctum (*akazu no ma*), closed off, behind a rusted zipper, completely rotten.

If left alone, it's a cancer on the world	*Izure hottokya sekai no gan*
do you want to make such a strong stench?	*tsuyoku akushū sasetai no ka*
I can't understand you, you shitty old men	*ki ga shiren kuso jiisan tachi*
entrusted with the textbooks,	*kyōkasho ni takushita*
you make up a smoldering fantasy	*kina kusai fuantajii*
on the pretext of representing Japan's "pride"	*iwaku repezen okuni no puraido*
huh? I misheard you, you must mean "blind."	*etsu, kikichigai jyan? mushiro*
	buraindo.

—DJ Oasis feat. Utamaru "Shakai no mado" (single) (Sony/Associated Records, 2000, AICT—1274)

It is important to recognize that racism in Japan is also related to attitudes toward Korean and Chinese others. In this sense, Utamaru's song does constitute a kind of transnational cultural politics of race because it thinks about race issues beyond Japan's borders.

It does seem that the politicians who approved the misleading textbooks did so because they wanted them to represent Japan's *puraido* (pride). A member of a Tokyo school board that approved textbooks with pale versions of World War II atrocities explained to the scholar and translator John Nathan why he thinks such texts are essential for the future of Japan: "Our children have been taught they mustn't love our flag, our rising sun. They are taught to think of themselves as the grandchildren of the devil. What good can that do us? And is that an objective account of history?" (2004, 149–50). But Utamaru says that is not pride but, rather, blindness that leads to such historical distortions. For Utamaru, pride in Japan depends on acknowledging Japan's history, including the borrowings from other cultures and acknowledging the enduring anger, especially in China and Korea, regarding Japanese textbooks' portrayal of history. He explicitly aligns himself with Japanese historians who point out the failings of the ministry-approved textbooks. Moreover, at the end of the verse, the emcee makes clear that the misinformation issuing from the government requires the younger generation, his listeners, "to do a pile of homework, or else we are all going to fail," suggesting there may be more to learn from rap than from textbooks. This is the kind of pivot that brings us a new cultural politics of affiliation (inspired by African American struggles against a racist government) and employed in a transnational cultural politics of race by critiquing the enduring racism among right-wing Japanese toward their Asian neighbors.

Although this example from Japanese rap music points to the potential for politically oppositional messages, entertainment companies do censor some kinds of lyrics. In an earlier version of the "Shakai no mado" song recorded for release on one of Sony's imprints, Utamaru takes more direct aim at the late emperor Hirohito who was in power throughout World War II and remained a postwar figurehead until his death in 1989. Utamaru accuses Hirohito of being a sex criminal, a reference to the so-called comfort women from Korea and China, thousands of whom were raped to service Japanese troops during the Second World War. Utamaru explained to me in a personal communication that a few days after he recorded the lyrics, high-ranking management officials at Sony decided the song was too inflammatory. Fearing the lyrics could provoke Japan's right-wing extremists to set up enormous sound trucks (tractor trailers with huge speakers) outside its corporate headquarters, Sony refused to release the song under its label. The rappers managed a small-run, self-produced vinyl pressing. As we saw with ECD, corporate Japan acts as a self-appointed gatekeeper of what is and what is not acceptable to consumers of popular culture. Above all, criticism of the emperor remains off limits.

One could argue that Utamaru's call to "open the zipper" illustrates the emergence of a cosmopolitan identity. John Tomlinson and others see great promise in such cosmopolitan identities as a step toward a transnational politics that can deal with the tragedies associated with globalization (see, for example, Tomlinson 1999). But what I find most promising is not the identity per se, but rather signs of an emerging transnational cultural politics of race, in the sense of promoting action on racial issues that transcend national borders and of doing homework to share the burden of history. What remains uncertain, however, is whether such political messages will be transformed into focused political movements. Vijay Prashad (2001) argues that having a sense of what he calls "polyculturalism" can in itself provide a tool to combat racism, yet we see in the examples here that a transnational cultural politics of race requires thinking not only of the multiple origin points of heritage but a reimagining of the links that can lead to a more promising future.

The Rapper A-Twice: Not Half but Double

The importance of grasping the "trans-" rather than the local in Japanese hip-hop was poignantly brought home to me through the example of Lafura Jackson (aka A-Twice), an African American Japanese rapper and DJ. I saw him perform in June 2000 in a small, underground club called Web in Tokyo. He came on at around 3 a.m., urging the sparse crowd of about twenty people to crowd around him as he rapped in both English and Japanese. After the show, I asked about his stage name, A-Twice, which he explained was a reference to the Japanese term *haafu* (half) to describe people who are half-Japanese, half-something else. "I'm not 'half' anything," he said. He was African American *and* Asian American, and the doubling of As made him "A-Twice." He grew up in both the United States and Japan and attended high school in Tokyo and college first in Massachusetts and then California, before returning to Tokyo to pursue a musical career. What he did not tell me when we met was that he had been diagnosed with cancer the previous fall. A couple of months after his performance, he died in a Tokyo cancer ward at the age of twenty-four. When I met him, I did not think there was a place for him in my study of Japanese hip-hop, in part because I tended to look down on American artists who were rapping (selfishly, I thought) in English. But A-Twice made a mark on the scene, prompting a stunning tribute song, "Candle Chant," by DJ Krush and Tha Blue Herb emcee Ill-Bostino.[6] Neither choosing either-or nor simply representing his Japaneseness, A-Twice helped me see another "both/and" aspect of hip-hop in Japan.[7] This provides insight into the limits of defining authenticity by primarily looking at racial heritage in an attempt to define a core meaning at the risk of underplaying the performative character of activities in the present.

Conclusion

Japanese hip-hop does deal with race issues, but often in ways that contrast with hip-hop in the United States. In both countries, however, hip-hop creates a space for questioning race and power by laying bare the constructedness of racial identity. Japanese hip-hoppers are not engaged solely in transforming hip-hop style into something purely indigenous, but rather in reconfiguring the cultural politics of race such that the issues do not revolve primarily around dichotomies of Japanese versus other. Many emcees use their lyrics to highlight divisions within Japanese society (e.g., between impotent politicians and outward-looking youth). In this they echo Cornel West's call for a new cultural politics of difference. Japanese rappers also contribute to a new cultural politics of affiliation, one that eschews national distinctions in favor of thinking about transnational connectedness among different groups, for example, in the ways Utamaru promotes a politics aimed at easing tensions with Korean and Chinese neighbors while criticizing the Japanese government.

If hip-hop is defined primarily as possessing four elements of artistic expression—rap, deejaying, break dancing, and graffiti—then hip-hop is open to everyone. But like jazz and blues before it, hip-hop is also seen as fundamentally black music, so that a desire to "participate" in hip-hop can also be seen as unjust appropriation. Intriguingly, the presumed agents of misappropriation may be shifting. In Japan, the United States, and in other countries as well, we are witnessing a widening discourse that views hip-hop as a culture and a way of life or a lifestyle. In the United States, a growing number of hip-hop artists, fans, and writers point to a fifth element of hip-hop, namely, knowledge (or "overstanding"), which encompasses not only the aesthetics of music, performance, and art but also a deep recognition of the history and political promise of the style, an orientation that coincides with fans' desires to protect the culture of hip-hop in the face of increasingly intense cycles of commodification (Uno 2004). Perhaps before long the appropriation deemed most worrisome will be less focused on the ethnic identity of the artist and more on the ways that entertainment companies often exploit artists regardless of their background. We see this in Japan as well, where the idea of hip-hop as a culture (*bunka* or *karucha*) indexes a desire on the part of artists and fans to evaluate the music based on skills rather than sales. This suggests that global culture may be best defined not only in terms of shared ideologies ("we are all hip-hop") but also of shared burdens and practices ("what will it take to move hip-hop forward?").

Before such politics can take hold, however, we in the United States may need to rethink a common American ethnocentrism that tends to equate foreign interest in U.S. popular culture with a desire to be American or, by analogy, Japanese interest in black culture with a desire to be black. Not only does this oversimplify the kinds of engagements that diverse people have with popular culture but such dismissals also play into the hands of Japanese critics of local hip-hop culture, who also see youthful uses of rap music as imitative and misguided and who use such critiques to reinforce notions of Japanese homogeneity and essential difference from people of other races and ethnicities. The tendency to defend hip-hop as black culture at times works in Japan as a double-edged sword to reinforce discrimination on the basis of race. The critical articles in the American magazine *Vibe* and the Japanese *Asahi* newspaper I discussed both focus primarily on album covers, clothing, and hair styles, but fail to consider how young Japanese talk about hip-hop and how their uses of the music relate to their own struggles in the midst of what Utamaru calls "shitty old men's" politics. By looking at what Japanese rappers are saying and relating this to Japanese debates about corporate entertainment, politics, and inequalities that bear the traces of racism but are constituted through other social differences as well, we can hope to move the discussion of world hip-hop away from local-versus-global debates to questions of what transnational cultural politics can accomplish and how.

Tricia Rose calls hip-hop "black noise," an abrasive affront to the quiet certainties that support racism, economic inequalities, and other forms of discrimination in the United States. Yet Japanese hip-hop is in no way simply "yellow noise" because it is not so much the binding ties of Japanese (or Asian) cultural expressivity that hold hip-hop together as it is an unfolding history defined by shifting battles and widening battlegrounds. When Mummy-D calls himself a yellow b-boy, he is more interested in reminding new fans that race forms a necessary part of hip-hop consciousness than in asserting a pan-Asian racial identity. The criticisms aimed at Japanese hip-hoppers illustrate that certain kinds of assumptions observers make regarding how to judge the music can work at cross-purposes with the very politics that progressive students of hip-hop hope to support. Seeing beyond these criticisms can lead us to a deeper understanding of the mutual inflection of race, popular culture, and nationality.

Black clouds, rain and lightning   *Kuroi kumo ame ni rakudai*
wandering in wind, today's samurai   *kaze ni sasurai aruku genzai no samurai*
if I grab my rhyme sword, look out!   *in no katana tsukandaraba abunai!*

— King Giddra, "Heisei ishin"

CHAPTER 2

BATTLING HIP-HOP SAMURAI

If Japanese hip-hop cannot be explained in terms of racial dynamics, what are the terms in which emcees compete for authority and fame? In this chapter I consider in more detail the history of hip-hop in Japan to explore why neither the term *global homogenization* nor *localization* accurately describes the scene's evolution. The challenge is to explain a widening diversity within Japan's scene amid a deepening global connectedness. I argue that "battling samurai" offer a metaphor for this dynamic historical process.

Perhaps it should come as no surprise that Japanese emcees often clothe themselves in images of samurai toughness. The idea that hip-hop artists must prove themselves in public battle encourages artists to pose for photos with *katana* (samurai swords) to assert that "the mic is my sword" and to describe a ponytail hairstyle as a *chonmage* (topknot). On their 2002 album, the group King Giddra (Zeebra, K Dub Shine, and DJ Oasis) even uses images of samurai to call for a Heisei restoration (*Heisei ishin*), that is, a present-day version of the Meiji restoration of 1868, when the military shogunate was overthrown to restore the Meiji emperor to power. However, Zeebra's goal of restoration does not involve the emperor, nor even the government, but rather suggests that a youthful generation inspired by hip-hop should lead Japan. What kind of globalization is this?

At first listen, "Heisei Restoration" seems to be evidence that hip-hop samurai are attempting to legitimate their styles by emphasizing their Japaneseness. Yet one of the striking developments in Japan's hip-hop scene in the first years of the twenty-first century has been the increase of this kind of traditionalist imagery of samurai alongside a more pronounced use of the "Americanized" imagery of gangstas, platinum chains, and expensive cars. Although one might expect a somewhat linear process of domestication in Japanese hip-hop over time, we instead see both global standardization and local indigenization becoming more pronounced simultaneously. Standardization is evident in the ways that, in comparison to novice rappers a decade ago, young rappers today show a more subtle understanding of lyrical flow, rhyming, the ideals of self-emphasis (*jibun shuchō*), and the historical origins of hip-hop in African American culture. At the same time, Japanese hip-hop artists in recent years increasingly use traditional instruments (koto, *shamisen* [a three-string, banjo-like instrument], and *taiko* drums) in sampling, adopt vocal styles mimicking traditional voice performers of kabuki or bunraku puppet-play narrators, and promote imagery of samurai, ninja, geisha, and so on. Some songs even liken club performances to town festivals where groups noisily transport portable shrines (*mikoshi*) on their shoulders.[1] Sometimes the same artist can seem to be pulled in two directions at once, as when Uzi, whose samurai album cover I discussed in the past chapter, also posed for a magazine photo spread waving a samurai sword while wearing a Los Angeles Raiders hat and jersey. If neither more global nor more local characterizes the trends in hip-hop, what can we say about the processes that extend global connectedness while also multiplying the diversity of local, individual outcomes?

The idea of battles between groups and families of groups provides a dynamic perspective on the music's unfolding history in Japan. To battle means to work within certain rules of engagement and to acknowledge that not everyone will prevail. The idea of battling hip-hop samurai suggests a way of conceptualizing the somewhat paradoxical features of deepening connectedness and widening plurality. Hip-hop in Japan shows connectedness across national boundaries: rappers around the world grasp the aesthetics of rap flow, of sampling in music production, and of a playfully brash, in-your-face attitude. We see a widening plurality globally in the multitude of languages and settings, diverse intersections with race, and different kinds of integration with commercial, governmental, and social forces.[2] There is no simple flow from more powerful to less powerful elements of society (or vice versa), but rather improvisatory, expanding networks of links, often fueled by competition among groups. We have already seen some contours of this connect-

7. Zeebra street promotion sticker distributed with purchase of "Street Dreams" single (6/05). Future Shock, Tokyo, Japan.

edness and plurality. In chapter 1 we saw how race issues are acknowledged and transposed in Japan, forcing a rethinking of context and the contingency of racial politics. In this chapter, I put the idea of shifting contexts and transformative *genba* into motion by looking at the historical unfolding of Japanese hip-hop dance, rapping, and music production.

How Japanese Are Samurai?

The idea of battling samurai offers a way of thinking about Japaneseness and a transnational imaginary. We might draw some lessons from films. From an American perspective, a recognizable exotic—samurai, geisha, sushi, anime—often comes to stand for a Japanese authenticity. When Tom Cruise (*The Last Samurai*, 2003) and Uma Thurman (*Kill Bill, Vol. 1*, 2003) pick up swords, we see how the samurai—with their skill at handling the *katana*, their commitment to death with honor, and their unwavering loyalty—often stand for a narrow range of Japanese ideals in the Western mind. I would not deny the entertainment value of these films, but as tools for teaching about culture, they err by essentializing samurai ideals while underplaying the conflicts that arose among samurai themselves. Yet what makes these American visions of samurai instructive is not so much what they get wrong, but what they deem essential to get right.

A somewhat similar essentializing conceptual move occurs when the Japanese are characterized as "good at borrowing." Such depictions mistakenly suggest that transnational flows can be explained in terms of the country's national character. Roland Robertson (1992, 177–78), for example, argues that the syncretism of Japanese religion, namely, the importation of Buddhism and its linkage with indigenous Shinto forms, has given the Japanese a privileged role in the current round of globalization because they are well suited to glocalizing foreign cultural elements. Arjun Appadurai (1996, 37) uses Japan as a way of contrasting "ideoscapes" with "ethnoscapes" to show how flows along one dimension (ideas) are not necessarily matched by flows along another (people): "The Japanese are notoriously hospitable to ideas and are stereotyped as inclined to export (all) and import (some) goods, but they are also notoriously closed to immigration." Such portrayals can reinforce the notion that cultural borrowing is a matter of national essence, when it can more accurately be described as fraught processes of learning, adaptation, and transformation, processes that unfold unevenly because they are always caught up in shifting relations of inequality. Indeed, it is the unevenness of American samurai movies—what they portray and what they do not—that provides the most insight into the processes of global flows.

In Japan, while the samurai still offer a model of a courageous Japanese spirit, they also evoke an exceedingly troubled past. The Japanese film *Twilight Samurai* (*Tasogare seibei*, dir. Yamada Yōji, 2002), for example, depicts class differences among and conflicts between samurai themselves.[3] Some samurai were chivalrous noblemen, but others were murderous vagabonds, while yet others were insensitive members of elites, living off the efforts of starving peasants. In Japan, samurai do not stand for a singular image of "us versus the West." Rather, samurai are widely acknowledged to be important, while their actual meaning, a relative concept to begin with, has always been very much contested. Thus battling samurai can be seen as evoking a contest over the meaning of Japaneseness, more than a particular national character. This is analogous, I would argue, to the kind of conceptual move required to understand hip-hop in Japan in that its meaning does not come down to one monolithic form vis-à-vis the US scene, but rather is animated by an unfolding series of debates about what hip-hop means, a debate that attends to hit trends and countermovements in both the United States and Japan. The battles unfolding in Japanese hip-hop offer a way of grasping the relationship between the widening global reach of hip-hop and the increasing diversity of styles in different social and geographic locations.

This chapter is more about battles than samurai per se. But given the way samurai themselves changed dramatically over the course of Japan's history, we can learn from the analogy. Hip-hop in Japan has changed the ways we view youth culture, musical creativity, and the meaning of political engagement through expressive culture. Why do Japan's hip-hoppers battle, and for what do they battle? If today's samurai really are hip-hoppers, what does this suggest about the loyalties of youth in contemporary Japan?

A brief overview of Japanese popular music history gives a sense of the dynamic interaction between imported Western music styles and social changes within Japan during the postwar period. *Genba*, as networked performance spaces and sites of production, provide a way of conceptualizing broader shifts in the practices of media and record companies as the music business developed. I then discuss the history of hip-hop in Japan, which I divide into three eras. The first era, circa 1984 to 1994, might be characterized as the period of discovering the nature of hip-hop. The second era, circa 1994 to 1999, is characterized by an ongoing debate over what makes *Japanese* hip-hop, that is, a concern over whether more commercially successful party-rap (or J-rap) artists were more Japanese, or whether more oppositional and underground styles were better examples of Japanese hip-hop. I will also consider why this middle era differed from the development of hip-hop in the United States in that it offered few examples of songs that drew on famous music samples. A third era, from 2000 to the present, might be characterized in terms of widening diversity without a center. That is, we see a shift toward a wider range of hip-hop styles in terms of region, class, and gender, alongside a growing indifference to other approaches to Japanese hip-hop. That is, in comparison to the previous era, when both party rappers and underground hip-hoppers attended to and criticized each other, the later-era hip-hop artists tended not to care about contrasting approaches to hip-hop style. Dividing Japanese hip-hop into these different eras risks overgeneralizing, but it also gives us some guides for thinking about the ways in which families of rap groups organized around different aesthetic commitments and managed to build excitement around their styles. Over time, as the Japanese hip-hop scene expanded, we can imagine it as a kind of pyramid, featuring more stars reaching higher sales at the top, along with a widening at the base to include a variety of artists throughout Japan and on all rungs of the socioeconomic ladder.

A Brief History of Popular Music in Japan

A brief look at the history of popular music in twentieth-century Japan gives some perspective on what is particular about hip-hop, as well as on the variety of mixing between global and local forms. The tension between borrowed and indigenous is in no way unique to rap music. Depending on the era and the genre, music globalization emerges from processes driven from above and below. Changes in business practices and structures of fandom alter the meanings of the popular. We can see this, for example, in the contrasts between the centralized control and marketing of idol singers and the more grassroots development of singer-songwriters in folk music. A *genba* perspective draws attention to the contexts of performance, the businesses that support them, the audiences that come together, and the media that circulate musical trends.

Western music in Japan is closely associated with the country's modernization. During the Tokugawa period (1600–1868), the military rulers largely closed off Japan to the outside world, prohibiting foreigners from coming to the country and Japanese from leaving. In 1853, US Commodore Matthew Perry brought his "black ships" into Edo (now Tokyo) harbor to forcibly open the country to foreign trade. Shortly thereafter, several feudal clans introduced military marching bands along with European military education. The establishment of the Meiji government in 1868 inaugurated Japan's modern era, and for many Japanese music scholars, this moment marks the beginning of popular music (*popyuraa ongaku*) as well (Hosokawa, Matsumura, and Shiba 1991, 1).[4]

Popular music in early-twentieth-century Japan emerged in diverse ways. Military songs celebrated Japan's wars with China (1894–95) and with Russia (1904–5). Opera in the Asakusa district of Tokyo, with Western costumes and scenery, proved a sensation among fashionable youth until the devastating Kantō earthquake of 1923 drove the opera musicians to other parts of Japan. The first Japanese jazz group got its start when it traveled to San Francisco in 1912 as a ship band and brought back sheet music. Before World War II, the term *jazz* encompassed a wide range of foreign music, including tango, rumba, foxtrot, and Tin Pan Alley jazz (Atkins 2001). In 1929, the song "Tokyo March" ("Tokyo kōshinkyoku") had great success, celebrating the lifestyle of jazz and dance halls in Tokyo's upscale Ginza shopping district, the new center of evening entertainment after Asakusa's decline.

Popular music's meanings shifted with the introduction of broadcasting, publishing, and recording. The 1920s saw Japan's first music copyright law go into effect (1920), the start of radio broadcasts (1925), and the establishment of three of Japan's major record companies (1927). In 1930, French films popularized chanson and imbued this romantic music style with Parisian artiness. Dance promoted the spread of Western music as well, with a tango boom in 1937 (Savigliano 1995). By the late 1930s, the effects of war in China were being felt in the music world. The number of patriotic songs about Manchuria and South China increased, while songs about love were prohibited by the government. In 1940 and throughout the Pacific War, tango and other "degenerate" styles of music were forbidden. As the war went on, the Japanese government took a more active role in censoring popular song and in promoting patriotic compositions (Tonoshita 1993).

According to Shuhei Hosokawa, Hiroshi Matsumura, and Shun'ichi Shiba (1991, 11), after World War II, the history of *kayōkyoku*, a broad term for Japanese popular song, was animated by a battle between native and American elements. While this might be the case in terms of the sound of the music, I would draw attention as well to the ways different contexts, especially different *genba*, provide a way of seeing how these battles also reflected broader changes within Japan. The immediate postwar period was marked by Japan's embrace of a new, peaceful, and democratic national identity (Dower 1999). The soundscape reflected these new borrowings as well. Shuffle rhythms appeared in popular songs, and even traditional instruments like the three-stringed *shamisen* were used to grind out boogie-woogie. Japan's defeat by the Allied forces also led to a wide-ranging adulation of things American, symbolized especially by the growing popularity of jazz brought by and played for the occupying forces. By 1953, jazz was more popular than any other kind of music in Japan (Hosokawa, Matsumura, and Shiba 1991, 13).

In the postwar period, we can see how the associations Americans make between social class and musical genres in the United States can be turned upside down in Japan. The Japanese who formed country-and-western bands were often sons of the aristocracy. This seeming incongruity, however, has a simple explanation: they were the ones with sufficient leisure and education to develop an interest in new foreign music and to understand, if only partially, the language in which it was sung (14). In Japan, hillbilly music, as it was sometimes called, was for the elite.

Jazz and Questions of Japaneseness

Sites of performance and the character of the audience clearly played a role in defining the limits of creativity in popular music. In E. Taylor Atkins's (2001) examination of the history of jazz in Japan, we see how Japanese musicians catering to American troops during the Occupation played in self-consciously American styles, reproducing as accurately as possible the sounds they heard on records. Later, interest in jazz deepened with the visits of Art Blakey (1961) and John Coltrane (1965). Jazz coffee shops (*jazu kissaten*), where patrons could listen to records being played on expensive audio equipment and where talking was prohibited, also appeared on the scene. In the 1960s, more avant-garde approaches to so-called yellow jazz emerged, attempting to define a Japanese jazz distinct from America's. This included efforts to create a hipster culture of renegade Japanese who met regularly to experiment with improvisatory jazz in Ginza performance spaces. Atkins (2001, 226) calls this period the most prodigious flowering of Japanese jazz creativity. Here we can see the centrality of a kind of social, networked *genba* where creative artists could perform, and, perhaps as important, could find knowledgeable and engaged audiences who provided the necessary support and criticism. Atkins notes that the discourse surrounding authenticity in Japanese jazz reflected a desire for exclusivity, for example, in regard to the importance of a unique sense of space, or *ma*, between notes. The artists sought to produce a jazz that only Japanese could play and that foreigners could not imitate. Some other jazz musicians attempted to formulate a linkage with American black nationalist discourse by drawing on *min'yō* (traditional folk songs) to mimic a historically indigenous, vernacular culture that paralleled the blues. Such efforts make sense, however, if we think of jazz not as a single style of music (either universal or particular), but as a diverse collection of competing artists. Interestingly, some of the challenges Japanese jazz artists faced in trying to authenticate their music played out differently than they would with Japanese rap musicians later in the century. Because Japanese rappers wrote Japanese language lyrics, which is something they shared with other Japanese musicians who sang in their native tongue, they had less trouble defending their Japaneseness.

A Musical Generation Gap Develops

After 1955, Japan experienced two decades of dramatic economic growth, and the 1960s saw rapid changes in the music world as well. Although Japan's popular music scene is known more for importing songs and styles than exporting them, Sakamoto Kyū's "Ue o muite arukō" (Walking Along, Looking Up) proved a major exception to that pattern. Sung in Japanese, the light jazz tune reached number one on a 1963 US Billboard chart, an unequalled accomplishment for a Japanese musician. In the United States, the song became known as "Sukiyaki," the word for a sweet beef noodle soup, which is somewhat ironic given that no food is mentioned in the Japanese original. We might also note that Kyū symbolized a certain style of popular music production that relied on in-house musicians and songwriters. The song's longevity is such that Snoop Dogg made a parody of it on his debut album *Doggystyle* (1993).

As the 1960s progressed and the trappings of middle-class lifestyles spread to broader segments of the population, hints of a global youth culture expressed through music and closely allied with urbanization and the rise of consumer culture in Japan emerged. Economic growth also generated income for the recording industry. With the release of more music, generation gaps appeared in the kinds of music that people consumed. A range of upbeat variety groups appeared, such as the Crazy Cats who borrowed the style of Spike Jones. Their management company adopted the epoch-making strategy, also borrowed from American business, of using television to create hit songs. Visiting foreign groups like the Ventures, the Animals (both in 1965), and the Beatles (1966) sparked a wide range of similar bands, collectively categorized as "group sounds" or simply GS. Given that no equivalent category of group sounds exists in the United States or the United Kingdom, one wonders how Western it is. More critical than the Westernness of this new genre was the way it expressed a youthful resistance to older traditions. Before long, electric guitars and long hair had become so popular they were banned in high schools.

The late 1960s also saw a folk (*fuōku*) boom, which refers not to indigenous folk music, but to performers who imitated American groups like the Kingston Trio and Peter, Paul and Mary. In a split that replays itself generation after generation, at first many cover bands appeared, mouthing the English words of imported hits (college folk). Later, people who sang serious protest songs in Japanese (underground folk) came to the fore. Some of these latter folk singers performed in the outdoor *genba* of the Shinjuku train station's west gate, drawing the ire of police who tried to break up these self-identified folk guerillas. The folk-music ethic of self-made, self-performed songs was somewhat new to the music business in Japan, which, prior to this, had relied almost exclusively on in-house producers and lyricists (Asō 1997). After the folk boom, a Japanese style of folk rock came to be known as "new music." One of its main characteristics was its emphasis on the singer-songwriter expressing self-written lyrics.

Coincidentally, the mid-1960s were also a time of Japan's asserting its return to the international scene as a powerful country. In 1964, Tokyo hosted the summer Olympics. In 1968, Japan's GNP was second only to that of the

United States, and a year later Japan became the world's leading manufacturer of television sets (Allinson 1997, xii). The nation's recording industry was maturing as well. From 1945 onward, Western music had consistently dominated sales in Japan, but in 1967, sales of Japanese music (*hōban*) overtook sales of Western music (*yōban*) for the first time in the postwar era (Kawabata 1991, 335).[5] In addition, the volume of music sales grew tenfold during the 1960s.

At the same time as locally produced music was coming to dominate the market, there was a growing debate among Japanese rock bands about whether one should sing lyrics in English or in Japanese (Uchida et al. 1990, 84–85). The debate hinged on two factors. Should artists aim for a global (i.e., American) audience or cultivate the local scene? Is the Japanese language suitable to the rock rhythm, or is English better? In chapter 5, I will examine this dispute with particular attention to language issues. For now, it is worth noting that this debate emerged in the context of Japan's growing economic power, an expanding national market, and the appearance of a new style of music journalism. According to the music scholar Shuhei Hosokawa, music-magazine reporting on GS-type bands tended to focus on trivia like the lead singer's blood type and favorite color. But in the late 1960s, he told me in a personal communication, *New Music Magazine* introduced the tone of a critic (*hyōronka*), so that questions of authenticity in music, social background, and so on became common topics for reporting. In each case, we witness a kind of feedback loop among the networks of artists, *genba*, record companies, fans, and media that reinforces particular aesthetic and business approaches, both of which shift depending on the era and the genre of music.

The 1970s witnessed a growing generation gap in musical tastes among the Japanese. *Enka* offers a key example. With its wavering melodies and melancholy themes, the music echoes earlier *min'yō*, or indigenous folk music. Although sometimes likened to country and western because of its association with rural Japan and blue-collar audiences and themes, *enka* differs in that it generally appeals to an older generation. The anthropologist Christine Yano (2002) presents a compelling story of the ways *enka* stood for a disappearing past and thus the "soul of the Japanese" (*nihonjin no kokoro*). It depicted—through songs of love and loss, harbors and tears, and above all sake—a rural, harborside Japan upstaged by a young, urban, postwar generation. Yano shows how the emotionality of *enka* provided a sentimental way to imagine an enduring nation in the midst of such rapid change. *Enka* also heralded a new era in which popular culture would become increasingly segregated along generational lines.

Rock, folk, new music, and Japanese pop all appealed to a younger generation of listeners. These genres brought new ways of looking at youth, not as the bearers of an older tradition, but as the people imagining a new social order under the collective banner of the new middle-class Japan. As a result, the "kind of song that was sung by both young and old became extremely rare" (Hosokawa, Matsumura, and Shiba 1991, 11–12). This phenomenon highlights one outgrowth of diversifying media industries as well. Although *enka* remains largely absent from prime-time television (except for public TV) and FM, it endures, firmly rooted in karaoke, AM, and wire broadcasting. Although today *enka* is viewed as a more traditional style of music, certainly when compared to J-pop, it is worth recognizing that *enka* was viewed as pop music, not traditional music, in its early days. The use of Western instruments, especially the violin, created a newfangled music that only later was seen to represent a traditional past. In this, *enka* parallels the performance genres discussed by Marilyn Ivy (1995), who examines discourses of vanishing cultural forms in the face of modernity.

Idol Singers Drive Television Hits, YMO Starts Sampling

In the late 1970s, good-looking teenage singers of Japanese pops (*poppusu*), as it is called, appeared in rapid succession and ushered in the age of idols (*aidoru*). These performers sang pop songs with guitars, bass, drums, and keyboards. They closely mimicked Western styles, but in many ways there was also an equally noticeable localization of idol music, despite the performers' imitative qualities. Idol singers gained their authenticity from reaching out to an ever widening crowd, localizing the music through its wide consumption. Idols were linked very strongly with advertising and the public-relations industry. Talent counted for much less than the ability to appeal as a cult object on TV and radio. Music magazines, too, proliferated and diversified, becoming an increasingly important medium to promote artists (Skov and Moeran 1995). The burgeoning teenage consumer culture can be credited for the popularity of these idols (Hosokawa, Matsumura, and Shiba 1991, 19). The slick packaging of singers with a notable lack of musicality continues unabated and has even been taken to a further extreme recently (Aoyagi 2000). In 1995, the idol style entered the Internet era with the debut of three female virtual idols, whose computer-generated images appeared on magazine covers. They released CDs as well, with the identity of the actual singers kept secret. It appears to have been a short-lived (and failed) experiment.

In the 1980s, Japanese pop music grew by using the marketing insights of idols, but it kept diversifying in terms of performance spaces. Large venues like the Budōkan (literally, Martial Arts Hall) featured leading pop stars from Japan and from the United States. Small clubs and discos supported a solid underground scene that followed Western trends in punk, new wave, and by the mid-1980s, rap music as well. One group worth noting is YMO (Yellow Magic Orchestra), which included the composer Sakamoto Ryūichi. The group's synthesizer-based music was a precursor to the style of constructing music (i.e., not playing instruments) by cutting fragments of sounds and looping them using computer technology.

Even in this brief sketch of popular music history in Japan, we can see how genres more or less borrowed from the West gained their meaning not only from their points of origin also but from the context of Japan's shifting popular music scene amid broad social and economic changes. While the sounds of different music styles could be distinguished by a conflict between indigenous and foreign elements, it was more generally the changes in Japanese society that gave meaning to the contrasts between Japanese and Western. During the postwar period, Japan witnessed large internal migration from rural areas to cities, as well as a shift in employment from agriculture to manufacturing and, later, to service-industry jobs. Economic growth also encouraged the rise of a consumer culture that became not only more widely shared but more finely tuned to distinctions of taste and status in various social groups and age cohorts. Social classes and generations came to be distinguished by their consumption patterns. To reduce the logic of popular music in Japan to localization would give the wrong impression if we concluded that there was some inherent aptitude for syncretism on the part of all Japanese people, or simply a linear trend toward domestication.

During the 1980s, when the bubble economy was booming, the new breed (shinjinrui) of twenty-something consumers flocking to expensive restaurants and then dancing at glitzy discos provided the dominant image of nightlife. In the music business, the success of idols reflected the marketing prowess of record companies, but for many Japanese it was symbolic of a consumerism devoid of value or deeper meaning. For those youth seeking more of an edge, rock music was getting old, and even punk was losing its radical chic. By the mid-1980s, some young people — and even somewhat established musicians — found inspiration in their first encounters with hip-hop.

Given Japan's continuous importation and adaptation of Western music styles, it is hardly surprising that hip-hop came too. Indeed, the more intriguing question is why the flow of foreign music styles to the United States is so limited compared to the abundant flows of Euro-American musical styles to Asia.[6] For now, let us consider how the distinctiveness of hip-hop in Japan emerged less from an interplay between foreign hip-hop and Japanese culture than from the shifting character of hip-hop battles as they unfolded.

The Early Era: What Is Hip-Hop?

Japanese hip-hop offers an intriguing example of cultural globalization in part because it expanded despite skepticism on the part of record companies and major media outlets. In addition, the history of hip-hop in Japan shows that certain kinds of cultural exchange begin not from complete understanding, but rather from some interaction that can incite a desire to learn more, to participate, and to contribute something of one's own. From the mid-1980s to the early 1990s, hip-hop in Japan was rather informal, smaller scale, experimental, and often, truth be told, not very good, at least by today's standards. It was a time during which performers asked, "What is hip-hop?" Given the relative lack of information, in some ways they had to make up the answers themselves. The early days of hip-hop in Japan are also notable because neither economic forces nor powerful national leaders can explain the emergence of this cultural form in Japan.[7] Instead, we must examine the particular youth drawn to the style, as well as their own efforts to participate in a globalizing process that had little to offer in terms of economic incentives. In this regard, breakdancing offers an example of globalization through body movement that can hardly be explained by the imposition of some outside force.

On the other hand, the early days provide some clues regarding the character of crossovers and the motivations that keep cultural movements alive. What provided the first sparks? What resonances provoked some people to take up hip-hop? Early hip-hop was clearly not led by corporate interests; indeed, it was largely ignored by large record companies and performance venues. This was partly because, in Japan, breakdancing was one of the leading edges of hip-hop, and one would be a fool to get into that art form for the money.

Crazy-A and the First Sparks from Breakdancing

Although the American rap records of Grandmaster Flash and the Sugar Hill Gang could be heard in Tokyo discos earlier, an important spark for hip-hop in Japan came in 1983, not through music alone, but when breakdancing appeared in Tokyo through film and live performances. While break-dancers may have become less visible in the United States in recent years, in Japan the movement continues more than two decades after its initial appearances in film. World breakdancing festivals exist, and multitudes of small groups practice and perform to this day, not only in Japan but around the world. How did breakdancing develop in Japan? What explains its persistence in spite of what some observers dismiss as its faddish and ephemeral character? It is easier to imagine how ballet becomes a globally recognizable form, supported by elite communities, institutionally secure performance venues, and a network of schools enrolling hopefuls at the youngest ages. But that breakdancing became a worldwide phenomenon shows that paths of globalization do not flow only from the most powerful segments of society. Robert Farris Thompson (1996) describes the diverse cultural mixtures of the Bronx that gave rise to hip-hop, a history that reaches back to African rhythms and resistance to slavery, passing through Congo Square in New Orleans and moving a language of the body across centuries and national boundaries. From original New York break-dance groups, such as Rock Steady Crew (RSC), the phenomenon spread around the world through informal channels, honed on the cardboard ground of public battle.

Films and traveling performers prompted the initial crossover. Crazy-A, one of the forefathers of Japanese hip-hop, was nineteen years old and on a blind date when he went to see the movie *Flashdance* in July 1983. As he told me in an interview in December 1996, the scene featuring Rock Steady Crew so mesmerized him that when he got home, he tried to moonwalk and spin on his back. Yet at first he was skeptical about the idea of dancing. "I always thought dance is something that only women do," he said. Although he occasionally went to discos, "I only went to drink and to get into fights" (Krush et al. 1998, 10). In October 1983, *Wild Style* (dir. Charlie Ahearn, 1982), a low-budget film featuring the first generation of American rappers, deejays, and break-dancers was shown in Tokyo theaters.[8] At the time, many of the performers also came to Tokyo to promote the film, performing in an Ikebukuro department store and also in a couple of clubs (Pitekan Toroposu and Tsubaki House). The hip-hop writer Egaitsu Hiroshi (aka Egaluzee) describes the events of the era: "Of course, in 1983, it was huge that the cast and crew came to Japan to promote the classic hip-hop film *Wild Style*. Futura, Cold Crush Brothers, Fab Five Freddie, all the important old school players came to Japan. It was a complete shock, but maybe one that only those people who actually saw it can fully understand" (Egaitsu 2002). What did this shock convey? Takagi Kan, another of the first generation of emcees, says, "I couldn't tell what was what with the rap and the deejaying . . . but with the breakdancing and graffiti art, you could understand it visually. Or rather, it wasn't understanding so much as, 'Whoa, that's cool' [*kakkoii*]. With rap and deejaying, I couldn't imagine what could be cool about it" (Goto 1997, 27).

When breakdancing appeared in Japan, the people initially influenced did not fully understand the movement's roots in New York City and African American culture, but they were nonetheless attracted by its newness. For breakdancing, the body was a medium of globalization, but it was also carried importantly through film. Interestingly, it seems that breakdancing in New York City owes a debt to movies from East Asia. According to Crazy Legs, a leader of RSC, "The only place I'd say we learned moves from, which was universal for a lot of dancers, was karate flicks on Forty-Second street, 'cause those movies are filmed the best, you could see the movement of the whole body" (Fernando 1994, 18). Dance, movement of the body, and the visual language of graffiti can move easily across linguistic and cultural boundaries. Movies and videos were clearly an important channel for this exchange. It is also clear, however, that a flow begins not from complete understanding, but rather from some interaction that can incite curiosity and a desire to participate.

What were some of the early resonances? Dilapidated urban backdrops and the idea of battle proved key. When Crazy-A saw *Wild Style*, he could relate to the bombed-out look of inner-city New York, with the trains rolling by overhead and people hanging around on street corners. It reminded him of where he grew up near the San'ya section of Tokyo, a place where many of the people who have fallen through the cracks in society come to pick up day-laborer jobs (Fowler 1996). Crazy-A even produced a dance-centered music video that, although set in Tokyo, mirrors the *Wild Style* setting. The video highlights train tracks, empty lots, and unemployed men as Crazy-A's brother Naoya, wearing Japanese construction-worker clothes, break-dances among the down-and-out.

Crazy-A described himself as a gangster boy (*gyangusutaa shonen*) and offers oblique references in his songs to fighting in back alleys. Yet breakdancing, he found, offered a more satisfying focus for his energies. As he explained in a December 1996 interview with me,

Hip-hop after all is battle. So, instead of fighting, I quit the violence and started doing hip-hop. You can fight and get stronger, but—how can I put it—in the end, nothing of substance remains [*katachi ga nokoranai*]. It's not as if there are brawling tournaments or anything, so nothing lasts. But with dance, there are competitions and a sense of form stays with you. You can say, I'm number one, and appeal to an audience. That gives you something that lasts.

Although not all of the early participants in Japanese hip-hop had a *furyō* (bad boy) background, some did. Intriguingly, the ones who allegedly had the most experience with gangs were, at least in the early days, the ones least likely to talk about it, especially in their music. This may have something to do with the somewhat different connotations of gang membership in Japan and the United States. In Japan, the Yakuza are notoriously hierarchical, and the hazing of subordinates is a finely tuned art of humiliation (Hill 2003). Being young and in the Yakuza is not particularly cool.

DJ Krush tells of working for the Yakuza when he was young (Krush and Sekiguchi 1995). In one case, he ran an errand to pick up a package, delivered it to one of the bosses, and then saw that what he had been carrying held a severed finger (a self-inflicted sign of loyalty). Krush credits the film *Wild Style* with saving him from a life in a gang. He says that the day after he saw the film, he went to buy turntables and turned his attention away from crime and toward deejaying, a career that would allow him to support a family. MC Bell also acknowledges a gang background, but in his lyrics with B-Fresh he always tended toward lighter visions of youth culture. Bell also says that the hip-hop dance forms he learned from American servicemen at discos in Yokohama gave him a way to stand out. The stories of these early encounters with hip-hop emphasize the genre's newness and the ways it provided alternative paths to status and pleasure for its adopters.

Hokoten as an Outdoor Genba

Sites of performance where groups and individuals could compete and others could watch nurtured early hip-hop. Yoyogi Park, located between the youth shopping districts of Shibuya and Harajuku in Tokyo, has for decades served as a gathering point for all manner of youthful fans and performers (Stanlaw 1990). Every Sunday until the late nineties, traffic was stopped and diverse bands and dancers would gather to perform outdoors along the street, which became known as "Hokoten," short for *hokōsha tengoku*, "pedestrian paradise."[9] Not long after the film *Wild Style* was shown in Tokyo, Crazy-A heard that breakers were gathering in Yoyogi Park on Sundays. When he went to see the action, however, "there was only this older guy who had a big Disco Robo [boom box] playing rap music," he said in the December 1996 interview. Crazy-A described the scene where he and other late-teen enthusiasts hung out:

But as time went on, people like me gradually gathered there to listen to the music. Once there were about three or four of us, we gradually started to adopt the posture [*soburi*], and move to the rhythm. More people would come by, and I'd ask if anyone knew where there was dancing going on, but no one was doing it. Then I suggested that maybe we start. From the next week on, four of us started dancing. At first, with a radio cassette and cardboard laid out on the ground. Sometimes we had turntables and a PA system. It was like a block party, a natural phenomenon [*shizen genshō*]. And then people like B-Fresh started to show up too.

With that practice and exposure, by 1984 Crazy-A was dancing on a television show (*Dance kōshien*). He also toured Japan as a backup dancer for the teen idol Kazami Shingō. Meanwhile, other US films (*Breakdance, Breakin' 2*) were shown in Tokyo in 1984. Other groups of Japanese break-dancers came to perform in Harajuku as well (Krush et al. 1998, 20). There was a kind of feedback loop between practice, performance, media spotlights, and widening influence that initiated a break-dancing boom. Groups met, competed, and split up, drawing audiences and honing their skills. DJ Krush, MC Bell, and Cake-K (of B-Fresh), Crazy-A, and others were all there and helped define this early movement.

Crazy-A says it was an American woman working as a model in Tokyo who told them during one of their Sunday performances that "in New York they would call you 'b-boys.'" That was when Crazy-A started calling his group the Tokyo B-Boys. This collective later was tapped by Crazy Legs of the New York City–based Rock Steady Crew to join their world network of groups, and thus was born Rock Steady Crew Japan.

Breakdancing illustrates that *genba* need not be built around business interests but can develop from a kind of performative sociability that draws people into a universe of shared interests. From the beginning, breakdancing was clearly more than just a new kind of dance. The dance involves the appropriation of public space, not unlike graffiti. Sidewalks, public parks, and underground shopping mall hallways are transformed into a public stage, sometimes marked by cardboard or linoleum being rolled out, but often simply created by the dancers themselves. We also see in these youths' fancy footwork, gymnastic spins, and coordinated steps a reminder of the fact that the body is not only an empty hanger on which to display one's consumer choices but an active site of performative identity. Thus the body and the street take on meanings outside the realm of consumerism and give some concrete meaning to the ideal of street culture. A different notion of street fashion is widely circulated through teen fashion magazines, with roving photographers capturing the fractured styles of hip Tokyo youth with impromptu street snaps. Thus youth wandering the trendy districts of Shibuya,

Takeshita Street in Harajuku, or the back alleys of Ura-Harajuku perform in a parade of fashion to see and be seen. Unlike school uniforms or the salaryman's blue suit, street fashion speaks to more flexible institutions of status and power. Meanwhile, break-dancers' street battles take competition in a different direction, relying on physical prowess and style within certain rules of engagement. Breakdancing is a public assertion of the central place of performance in social life.

Yet if breakdancing highlights certain ideals, it also goes through changes. What attracts young break-dancers to hip-hop, and the contexts in which they can perform, has shifted. In 1996, when I first interviewed Crazy-A, he was thirty-two years old and could no longer compete as he had before. The younger members of Rock Steady Crew Japan were between twenty-two and twenty-five years of age; they clearly represented a different generation drawn to b-boying. Hyaku, one of the dancers, recalled being attracted to hip-hop after seeing Crazy-A on television. Gori, another dancer and a former soccer player, appreciated the physical challenge of b-boy dancing. In a December 1996 interview, Katsu said, "When I first saw it, I thought it was awful. But I started because I wanted to pick up women. Then I saw Crazy-A and others doing it seriously, so I took it more seriously. It was when they said, 'It's not that kind of thing,' that I began learning about hip-hop and really wanted to do it." In 1996, several of the members of RSC Japan came from Sōka Daigaku, a Buddhist university that boasts one of the largest and most successful breakdancing teams in Japan, D-Crew. In 1996, D-Crew had over one hundred members, quite a contrast to Crazy-A going to Yoyogi Park with a few friends.

We can see hints of a generation gap appearing when one of New York City's pioneers judged a break-dancing contest in Tokyo. Starting in 1999, Crazy-A began organizing an annual hip-hop festival in Yoyogi Park called B-Boy Park, a four-day event that included contests in freestyle rapping, deejaying, and breakdancing. At B-Boy Park 2001, Crazy Legs, one of the New York City break-dancers seen by Crazy-A during his fateful viewing of *Flashdance*, served as a judge of the breakdancing contest in a performance space called Liquid Room. The dark room on the tenth floor of a Shinjuku building was packed on a Thursday afternoon with upward of a thousand people. A boxing ring–style stage was set up in the middle, and dancers competed head to head in single elimination rounds. Interestingly, there was no separate women's category; the women competed directly against male groups (and lost). Crazy Legs judged and performed with the dance group Tribal during a break in the competition, while his four-year-old son fidgeted. At the end of the day's events, Crazy Legs offered a critical response to the battles through an interpreter. He was not completely happy with what he had seen. Crazy Legs thought there had been too many "power moves" and not enough attention to footwork: "People have to remember, it's a dance." He sounded a little like an old-timer complaining that the kids were doing it all wrong because it was also clear that if you wanted to win a competition in front of a thousand people, you would need big power moves to wow the crowd, not subtle, fancy footwork. The audience gave its most enthusiastic response to gymnastic tricks, wildly gyrating legs, flips, and handstands. Here, respecting the pioneers was trumped by what it takes to win in the *genba*. A history of breakdancing around the world deserves its own book, but at least we can note that distinctions between generations are appearing in the global scene. This suggests that the key dynamic may not be a rivalry between foreign and local hip-hop but between factions and generations across international lines.

Rap Starts in Classy Clubs

There was another and somewhat separate stream out of which hip-hop in Japan emerged, and it flowed from those who performed in the discos and clubs. Key artists included Itō Seikō and Tinnie Punx, whose hip, irreverent, and oppositional stance becomes evident on one of their album covers, *Kensetsuteki (Constructive [Criticism])*, which features three musicians looking upward and giving the finger (reissued in 1991, Pony Canyon, PCCA-00807). This early era of experimental rap is documented by Gotō Akio (1997), who provides a series of interviews with some of the forerunners of the Japanese hip-hop scene in a collection describing "the birth of hip-hop culture" in Japan. Itō Seikō tells of introducing rap as a kind of "standing talk" in a club called Pitekan Tropos in Harajuku. A number of musicians reported struggling to educate audiences who could not understand why there was no band, and why the "singer" was not singing. And what was that scratching noise coming from the records? Takagi Kan points out that although *Wild Style* was important, the hip-hop scene took years to develop (44–47). He started as a punk-rock musician before becoming entranced by the music of Afrika Bambaataa, who performed in Japan in 1985. Chikada Haruo took the name President BPM and rapped with the band Vibrastone. He says he felt a connection with the South Bronx, the outsider style, and the emphasis on direct communication (36–37). Tinnie Punx (pronounced "tiny punks") included Takagi Kan and Fujihara Hiroshi. Their playfully critical stance on Tokyo society and government planted the seeds of an oppositional perspective through rap.

MC Bell (of B-Fresh) felt a closer kinship to street dancing and calls this club stream the classy (*oshare*) style (Bell and Cake-K 1998, 112). The idea of *oshare*, which means "stylish," "trendy," and "hip," suggests alternative measures of value. *Oshare* can be distinguished not only by these groups' interest in musical performance (rather than the street) but by the kind of audience they could draw. The image of clubs as classy locales also refers to the new breed of conspicuous consumers known as the *shinjinrui*, twenty-something urbanites enamored of brand-name items. They were the see-and-be-seen type of consumers who contrasted with a darker, more isolated version of fan communities called the *otaku*. Early Japanese rap aimed to provide audiences of late-night clubs with a certain urbane hipness. In the following chapter, I will consider in greater detail the ways evolving fan bases shaped the broader scene. For now, I would like to focus on the competition among performers as a way of grasping the evolution of the scene. These early days had only a few artists recording at the independent level, and yet these artists are the ones that others defined themselves against.

Ironically, the early *oshare* rap performers never mention the break-dancing scene in Yoyogi Park, but the break-dancers did come to check out the club rappers. The book *Japanese Hip-Hop History* (Krush 1998) includes the stories of some of the Yoyogi Park performers including B-Fresh, Crazy-A, and DJ Krush. They all acknowledge their awakening to the greater attention being paid to the rappers. One show in particular loomed large.

In December 1986, Run-DMC, riding a wave of attention accompanying their hit remake of the Aerosmith song "Walk This Way," performed two shows at NHK Hall in Shibuya. Itō Seikō, Tinnie Punx, and President BPM performed as the opening acts. When MC Bell, Cake-K, Crazy-A, and other Hokoten performers discuss this event, they offer two conclusions: while rap drew a larger, more excited crowd than breakdancing, the Japanese acts lacked style. In the words of Rhymester's Utamaru, "When I first saw Japanese rappers opening for an American group, I thought to myself, 'It wouldn't take much to be the best rapper in Japan'" (Rhymester 1999). This is an interesting moment because it shows that witnessing a lackluster performance in a favored genre can ignite the desire to become an artist as much as can a virtuosic performance. In other words, a driving force in hip-hop appears to come not so much from a feeling of admiration as from one of self-confidence. This internal battling dynamic has proven central to the style. Succeeding generations of Japanese rappers, some of whom cut their teeth with performances in Yoyogi Park, worked to define their contributions to the genre often in terms of a deeper lyrical engagement with hip-hop core ideals. The battles centered around quality and skill. Even though there was plenty of disagreement about what counted as skill, I was always struck by how well rappers knew other rappers' lyrics, by how carefully and critically they measured their own sound against the sound of others. The fact of artists attending to artists marks another important dimension of the battles surrounding the early scene.

Many streams broke off, dried up, or joined tributaries to build the scene in Japan. From 1988 to 1992, the scene picked up energy in part from a growing number of club events that featured contests for rappers, DJs, and break-dancers. Some were sponsored by companies selling DJ equipment (e.g., Vestax). The DJ Underground Contest, begun in 1988, featured many of the prominent artists of the mid-1990s. ECD started the Check Your Mic contest in 1989, which continued off and on for five years, even producing a live album. Many of the second generation of performers such as Scha Dara Parr, You the Rock, B-Fresh, and others competed in these events. Years later, these groups would rarely appear together, but back in the early days, the different families competed directly, face to face.

The first club devoted to the genre, aptly and succinctly called Hip-Hop, opened in Shibuya in 1986. A regular there, DJ Yutaka is now a member of Zulu Nation (Bambaataa's organization) and splits his time between Tokyo and Los Angeles. Zeebra says he, too, started as a DJ at that club when he was still under the legal drinking age of twenty. From the mid- to late-1980s, rap gained more airplay on the radio as well. A Yokohama radio station began airing the "scratch mix" of the hip-hop DJ collective MID (Egaitsu 1997b). In 1987, a TV comedy show featured rappers giving the weather report. Specialty magazines began covering hip-hop in greater detail, and this meant that there was also a deepening compartmentalization of the hip-hop scene as more and more media options became available. Major Force, a hip-hop and dance-music label founded by Takagi Kan and others, began producing albums in 1988.

In 1989, a flood of American artists traveled to Japan to perform, including the Jungle Brothers, the 45 King, and De La Soul. After Public Enemy's show, which featured armed security pretending to spray the audience with machine-gun fire, Japanese rap groups began to include motionless, silent, brooding "security" in their onstage shows, a practice laughed about today. A second breakdancing boom appeared in 1990, after Bobby Brown visited Japan. On the whole, however, the rap scene was rather small compared to the larger world of Japanese pop music. Record companies, mainstream music magazines, radio, and television largely ignored this burgeoning group of hip-hop musicians. The period up to 1994 is generally regarded as a winter (*fuyu*) or ice age when few record labels, including indies, were willing to release hip-hop.

The Second Era: What Is *Japanese* Hip-Hop?

Things changed in 1994, when the rap trio Scha Dara Parr teamed up with the guitarist-songwriter Ozawa Kenji to produce the first million-selling rap hit. The mellow funk song called "Kon'ya wa būgi bakku" ("Boogie Back Tonight") was an anthem to hanging out with friends and flirting with women in clubs.[10] Music magazines heralded the song's success as evidence of the arrival of a Japanese rap scene because it was now capable of producing hits. Some reported that rap had finally earned its citizenship (*shiminken*). Then, in the summer of 1995, two songs by the group East End X Yuri climbed the charts, eventually selling around a million copies each. The songs "Da.Yo.Ne." and "Maicca" both capitalized on teenage slang to portray a carefree attitude toward everything from school to love affairs.[11] These commercial successes prompted a wave of publicity in music magazines, and the term J-rap was coined to represent the new, up-and-coming genre. Major record labels began to show interest in a variety of hip-hop groups that had been languishing on independent labels, particularly groups that emphasized a more playful approach, generally referred to as party rap (*paateii rappu*).

Not all emcees were enthusiastic about the J-rap boom. In the free paper *Rugged*, Zeebra and others lamented that these "sellouts" could be mistakenly seen as representing hip-hop culture (*Rugged* 1995, 7) In the clubs, groups like Rhymester would talk about respecting hip-hop as a culture (*bunka*), which meant understanding the history, recognizing the four elements, and speaking for oneself. East End, with Gaku and DJ Yoggy (along with producer Rock-Tee, initially), had at least been performing for a few years in the club scene, but Yuri had worked as part of a revolving-door pop group called Tokyo Performance Doll. Unsurprisingly, some viewed Yuri as a poser who ignored hip-hop culture and produced just pop (*tada no kayōkyoku*). The sappy music video produced by Epic/Sony, with corny illustrated backdrops, reinforced this impression.

One response from the underground hip-hop scene can be seen in a song by the group Lamp Eye. In 1995, Lamp Eye (a short-lived unit including Rino, Twigy, and Gama) titled their mini album *Gekokujō*, meaning literally, a samurai retainer overcoming his master. By using a term that referred back to the warring states period of the 1300s, the group explicitly drew attention to the ways that hip-hop offered a space for contesting the hierarchical certainties of the pop world. For them, the master was the mainstream entertainment industry, which they contrasted with their underground scene of lyrical skill. One song that gives a sense of the underground response to the J-rap boom is Lamp Eye's "Shōgen," a title that means "testimonial" or "speaking the truth." The track features other central emcees of the Kaminari family at the time, namely, You the Rock, G. K. Maryan, and Zeebra. Each verse offered a different attack on J-rap and an assertion about what made the underground scene different. For example, You the Rock uses wordplay to ridicule the party-rap group Dassen Trio (literally, "derailed trio") (Zeebra 1996b, 89).

psychotic rules, sucked in by a fad	*kurutta ruuru hamatta buumu hazureta reeru*
running on broken rails, an empty "real"	*no ue hashiru chippoke na kiipu riaru*
get out of our way, you can't cut in	*jama sasen warikomi wa ikemasen*
this is our culture, burning, . . .	*oretachi no bunka chakka . . .*
. . .	. . .
with the strength of words	*kotoba no chikara*
my verbal word spirit spreads power	*ore no kotodama kara minageru pawaa*

—Lamp Eye (1996) Shôgen (Polystar, Japan, PSCR-5547)

These lyrics capture the language of the time, emphasizing a culture of overflowing words, personal expression, the rejection of fads, and scorn for the J-rap boom. A video of "Shōgen" was produced by the graphic designer Ben List, an American living and working in Tokyo who followed the hip-hop scene closely, even producing an online free paper called *Elebugi*. The rough-hewn video is dark, mostly black-and-white, and gives a visual sense of the street image that Lamp Eye and their Kaminari collaborators expressed. Given that the video was edited without a digital time code, matching the visuals to the song also expressed a do-it-yourself ethic. The discourse of toughness was echoed by Zeebra and K Dub Shine in an April 1996 interview with me after the release of the debut King Giddra album the same year. They cited Public Enemy, Rakim, and Big Daddy Kane as gauges of realness, and they talked about the oppositionality at the core of the style arising out of the experiences of African Americans. If lyrics offered no opposition to mainstream society's injustices, they argued, there could be no realness.

From the perspective of some of the so-called party rappers, the street-toughness stance of underground groups is simply an adopted pose. In November 1995, I interviewed Dassen Trio, who use comedy and the regional Kansai dialect in their raps. The trio of rappers hails from Osaka and includes Robo-chu, MC Boo, and King 3K. They argued that lighthearted rap was more appropriate to Japanese teens than the preachy, self-important boasting of underground groups. MC Boo and King 3K expressed doubts about the suitability of the keep-it-real slogan in Japan.

MC Boo: If "keep it real" means "good things should be fun," I think that's OK. Being "real" is fine if you are real (laughs). But we don't want to say things like that.
King 3K: If we said, "keep it real," we'd have no idea which direction to head in to make an album. And to say, "keep it real" in Japan, well—
MC Boo: I think we don't have the kind of personality to do things that way.
King 3K: When overseas rappers say "keep it real," I think I know what they mean. But to say that this is the god of hip-hop, well, it may be cool sometimes, but we can't really say that. To tell the truth, I get a little embarrassed when Japanese rappers say, "Reality!"

They would argue that the measure of being real is whether the lyrics speak to one's audience; therefore, the larger the audience, the more real the music.

It is too simple, of course, to suggest that hip-hop in Japan can be explained by two competing camps, party rap versus underground hip-hop. Factions (*habatsu*) existed within each camp, and all camps followed closely, and shared a musical inspiration from, the latest US underground and commercially successful hip-hop. Nevertheless, the party rap/underground hip-hop dichotomy does serve to highlight alternative orientations in some of the different styles. More lighthearted groups like Dassen Trio, Scha Dara Parr, EDU, and East End X Yuri tended to draw audiences with a greater proportion of young women fans. They were more likely to have major-label contracts and to appear on radio and television. In 1995, East End X Yuri even performed in NHK's year-end musical extravaganza Kōhaku Gassen (Battle of Red vs. White). Meanwhile, the underground hip-hop collective Kaminari held to a tougher, more abrasive ethic. They performed to packed clubs, for example, in an event called Anettai Urin (Tropical Rain Forest). When I attended one of these events at club Yellow in Nishiazabu, the sweat-soaked air, virtually all-male audience, and screaming emcees all moved in a zone of abrasive energy. Interestingly, at this time, there were not clear age or class distinctions that determined whether artists tended toward the party or underground ends of the spectrum.

Magazines are also notable for their role in developing the distinctions that came to guide Japanese hip-hop categories. In my discussions with artists, I found they tended to react with distaste to questions of their own style, but for magazine writers, making such distinctions constituted a full-time job. In particular, the hip-hop magazine *Front*, later renamed *Blast*, helped nurture the underground scene. The magazine usually opens with reports from live shows (again, the *genba*) that are then followed by long interviews with American artists, sometimes translated from American interviews (the magazine has a relationship with the US hip-hop and R & B magazine *Vibe*), more often done directly by their staff. In contrast to US hip-hop magazines, *Blast* gives relatively equal coverage to both commercial, mainstream American artists and lesser-known underground US artists. A US hip-hop magazine like the *Source* is more heavily weighted toward commercially successful groups. One of the striking characteristics of hip-hop fans in Japan is their knowledge and understanding of the US underground scene. Groups like Jurassic 5 or emcees 7L and Esoteric toured in Japan, drawing crowds that might not be smaller, at least in Jurassic 5's early days, than the ones they would attract in the United States. Japan's music magazines cover the US underground scene more than some of the leading American hip-hop magazines (the *Source* and *Vibe* especially). This speaks to differences in advertising revenue as well, because the specialty record shops in Tokyo that advertise in *Blast* carry selections from underground artists regularly.

As part of my fieldwork, I attended monthly editorial meetings in Tokyo for *Remix*, a "street and club sounds magazine," from 1996 to 1997. The magazine was published monthly and covered a variety of genres, including hip-hop, techno, house, dance jazz, and rock. The most contentious debates among the editors revolved around which artist or genre to represent on the magazine's cover. Each editor could make a pitch for a particular cover, and in 1996, Japanese rap struggled to make an appearance. DJ Krush, a crossover artist bridging hip-hop and electronica, was a favorite, that is, he was featured on covers when releasing new albums, but rappers themselves seldom appeared. Although questions of who would be advertising in the issue could play a role, the editors and writers felt responsible for vetting the quality of the music with their own ears first. Nevertheless, the group featured on the front cover was, more often than not, also featured in a paid-for advertisement, and few of the rap artists in this middle era received support for expensive magazine ads.

The artists selected for coverage inside the magazine were those with new releases (singles, albums, remixes, etc.) and those performing live that month. In this way, we can see how magazines focus their attention on clubs and the output of recording studios as well. In other words, *genba* are important because they produce something (a show, a CD) and because this production sets in motion media and fan responses to the performance. The networks themselves are performative, that is, they emerge around hit songs, hit albums, and big stars—just as well as they emerge in the realms of mini-media, word of mouth, underground club events, and amateur contests. Once hip-hop went more pop in Japan, the underground did not disappear. If anything, more groups emerged, and some members of the younger generation emerge with a style more deeply trained in the widening range of hip-hop's history and present.

Families Define Artistic Stakes through Moriagaru

In the midst of the competition between individual groups, so-called families (*famirii*) of rap groups emerged as well, providing a social organization to the scene that helped define evolving artistic stakes. For example, over the years, the Funky Grammar Unit has included Rhymester, East End, Kick the Can Crew (and their precursor groups By Phar the Dopest/Radical Freaks), Mellow Yellow, Inosence, DJ Kiyo, and others. Little Bird Nation includes Scha Dara Parr, Dassen Trio, Tokyo #1 Soul Set, Kaseki Cider, and others. Zeebra broke off from King Giddra in late 1996 to form Future Shock and led UBG (Urbarian Gym), which included Uzi, Tak the Rhymehead, and later Soul Scream. K Dub Shine began Atomic Bomb Productions, including the talented emcee Dohji-T. The large crews provided support and helped define aesthetic approaches generally shared within families and contrasting with other families' approaches. Occasionally, families collaborated on recordings or live shows, but otherwise, the group affiliations remain somewhat fluid. In general, being in a family means that one supports the others' projects when possible. Families also tend to draw at least some regulars who follow the particular family's events over a period of time. From October 1995 through February 1997, I attended the Kitchens family's events almost every week, first Thursday nights at Grass in Harajuku, then Saturday nights at Rowdy in Roppongi. Kitchens was led by Umedy of EDU and also included Now (later Now Now, a three-woman group), Cake-K, Moon Trap, DJ Etsu, DJ Cool-K, and Climax. In the fall of 1995, Co-Key used to attend the nights at Grass to participate in freestyle sessions, but then he moved on to work with other families. Groups with similar aesthetic tastes tended to gravitate toward each other. In so doing, families would gather energy for their particular aesthetic approaches by attracting a fan base, staying active enough to keep in the news, and working toward recording projects, and, ideally, ever larger recording contracts and performance venues.

If families were battling for attention, how can we understand what it takes to win? A key word for understanding how families build energy in the scene through club events is the term _moriagaru._ When the audience gets hyped, excited, energized, that's _moriagaru._ The term suggests a piling on (_mori_) and rising up (_agaru_) of energy and emotion. It describes the energy in the audience when a show is going well. When families hold successful events, the experience of _moriagaru_ can make a lasting impression on audience members. Contrary to the idea that musical taste is all subjective, when a club act falls flat, everyone in the audience and onstage can feel it. Even if you do not appreciate a particular genre of music, or even if you do not understand the language of the performers, I would argue that you would be able to recognize, literally feel on your skin, whether a show is going well or falling flat. In this sense, the battles between groups and between families are waged in the _genba_ with _moriagaru_ as the prize. This _genba_ realization echoes a recent manifesto from several key cultural studies scholars who call for more attention to be paid to "culture that sticks to your skin" (Jenkins, McPherson, and Shattuc 2002). Their vision of the political recognizes that "any viable politics must begin in the spaces people already inhabit" (22). In this they encourage a study of hip-hop in Japan, not as recorded texts but in terms of sweat, pulsating beats through giant speakers, and the pendulum swing between fan adoration and fan skepticism.

Thus families in effect organize groups of fans as well, hardening people's notion of what they do and do not like in hip-hop music. In the late 1980s, many second-generation groups—Rhymester, Scha Dara Parr, You the Rock —would compete against one another in late-night contests. By 1997, each of these groups had developed its own fan following, its own family of like-minded groups. Groups seldom performed with different families, but rather held their own regular or semiregular events. In a sense, each family was working to define a certain approach to answering the questions, "What is _Japanese_ hip-hop? How can we make this our thing?" The underground-party divide seemed at the time a potent struggle for the soul of hip-hop in Japan. Would it go the commercial J-pop route? Or would audiences in Japan awaken to the street-battle ideologies of underground hip-hop, even if it was less suitable to television and karaoke?

Rhymester's "B-Boyism" as a Watershed

One of the elements in the debate over making hip-hop Japanese involved developing a new language that would express both a Japanese and a hip-hop sensibility. (In chapter 5, I will consider in more detail the contrasts between English and Japanese, as well as other ways that rappers used language as a site and constituent part of their hip-hop aesthetics.) If we look at Rhymester's efforts of the mid- to late 1990s to develop Japanese catch-phrases, we can see a notable example of the shifts in aesthetics. In songs like "Mimi o kasu beki" ("You Better Listen Up"), released in 1996, one can hear Rhymester's knack for hooks that encapsulate a generation's yearnings. The rapper Mummy-D focuses on the importance of practice—"washing dishes" for little money, that is, practicing as a DJ (because "plates" is a pun on "vinyl records")—in order to hone one's skills. The group's other emcee, Utamaru, challenges young people to find something they believe in or risk becoming losers in life's game. Above all, they say the people who should "listen up" are the older generation who blithely comment on youth's shortcomings while failing to understand their aspirations.

In 1998, Rhymester created an anthem to Japanese hip-hop ideals. Released that year as a single (and in 1999 on the album *Respect*), the song took its name, "B-Boyism," from Utamaru's monthly column in *Front* magazine. The column reflected on the connections among old movies, old toys, old games, a traditional storytelling performance called *rakugo* which became materials for meditating on the links between hip-hop ideals and aspects of Japan's popular heritage. In Utamaru's worldview, hip-hop made perfect sense. He did not belabor the stark difference between the reality of the streets in US hip-hop and its supposed absence in Japanese youth culture. Rather, he focused on B movies, underground fads, and forgotten individualists (from Japan) who characterized a b-boy ethic even before the term *b-boy* was known.

Rhymester brought together many of these themes in the song "B-Boyism." To set up the chorus in one part of the song, Utamaru asks his fellow rapper Mummy-D to "define the 'B' in "B-Boy."

I'm not surrendering this aesthetic	*keshite yuzurenai ze kono bigaku*
flattering no one, I improve myself	*nanimono ni mo kobizu onore o migaku*
only the wonderful, useless people	*subarshiki roku de nashi tachi dake ni*
get it, and roar, at the edge of the bass	*todoku todoroku beesu no hate ni*

—Rhymester (1999) "B-Boyism" *Respect* (Next Level/File Records, Japan, NLCD-026)

The lyrics use dense rhyming to emphasize the personal ethic of improving oneself ("onore o migaku") by holding fast to "my aesthetic" ("ore no bigaku"). There is also a double meaning in the *B* of *b-boy* and the identically pronounced *bi* (beauty) of *bigaku* (aesthetics, literally, the "study of beauty"), such that beauty and the *B* of *b-boy* become one and the same in the song's universe. Yet the rootedness of Rhymester's aesthetic lies less in the serendipitous homonyms of Japanese and English than in the group's fans. As Uta-maru explained in a personal communication to me in 2001, Japan's b-boys are "wonderful" (*subarashiki*) and "useless" in the sense of not pursuing so-ciety's arbitrary goals, focusing instead on finding their own way. In one part of the song, Utamaru likens the toughness of Japan's b-boys to Barefoot Gen (Hadashi no Gen). A child character in the comic book by the same name, Gen survives the bombing of Hiroshima, but must struggle to get by emotionally and physically after watching his mother die in the flames of their crushed home. The idea that hip-hop in Japan produces a kind of Americanization fits uneasily with the particulars of many lyrics. Viewing the song "B-Boyism" as a performative event shows how cultural flows are actualized at specific moments in the development of the scene.

Rhymester's "B-Boyism" music video brought Japan's hip-hop scene full circle. Rhymester hired Rock Steady Crew Japan to battle on a linoleum mat set out in front of the stage in Yoyogi Park. The videotaping was advertised as a block party on flyers handed out at club events. A veritable who's who of Japanese hip-hop showed up for their cameos, including Zeebra, K Dub Shine, Kreva, MC U, Gaku, Uzi, and numerous others. Crazy-A himself danced for the video in the park where breakdancing in Japan began a decade and a half before.

Although Rhymester says they never intended the song to become a water-shed in Japan's scene, looking back on the moment brings with it a certain feeling of nostalgia. At that time, groups associated with Kaminari argued that Japan's hip-hop scene should aim for a harder edge. Scha Dara Parr and the groups associated with Little Bird Nation focused on wordplay and more ludic criticisms of Japanese society. Regardless of the particular stance, there was a sense that everyone was focused on "the scene." In contrast to the first era, when people questioned what hip-hop was, the second era was character-ized by a shared debate, though not shared understandings, about the proper basis of the scene.

Before turning to these developments, let us consider a back story of hip-hop with regard to battles among Japanese hip-hoppers, namely, conflicts over sampling and copyright. Given that a key crossover hit in the United States, Run-DMC's "Walk This Way," brought rap to rock audiences by sam-pling a hit Aerosmith song, one wonders why similar big sample (*ōneta*) songs did not appear in Japan. Why did not any Japanese artists sample famous Japa-nese pop songs to try for a crossover? The answer lies in copyright laws and practices, market size, and particular histories in the US and Japanese hip-hop scenes.

Sampling and Copyright in the United States and Japan

In hip-hop, one of the striking features of the ideologies of artistic creativity is the sharp divergence between rappers and DJs. If you are a rapper, the idea is that you must express something about yourself in your own words, with your own rhymes and flow. In contrast, the track-makers generally create the music using samples from other people's recordings. Here, personal expression is not virtuosic performance, but rather programming the mix. Of course, borrowing styles from other artists is nothing new in music history. What is different about the current hip-hop moment is that incorporation is done directly from already recorded material through digital sampling and DJ scratch solos. This entails consequences regarding originality and ownership in music that deserve a brief exploration.

A difference between the United States and Japan in the ways samples are used points to a gray area of intellectual property in digital-age musical production. In the United States, rap songs that sample well-known songs arguably have been very influential in creating crossover hits that eventually helped move hip-hop from underground into the mainstream. Run-DMC used Aerosmith's "Walk This Way," Public Enemy used all sorts of James Brown material, A Tribe Called Quest used Lou Reed's "Walk on the Wild Side," Jay-Z sampled from the Broadway show *Annie* the tune "It's a Hard Knock Life," and so on. Yet sampling practices developed unevenly, as we can see from several key moments in US hip-hop history (Baran 2002). In 1992, the rapper Biz Markie used a Gilbert O'Sullivan sample, "Alone Again (Naturally)." Biz Markie's record company had been unable to clear the sample (i.e., pay for permission to use it), but released the album anyway. The company was sued, lost the court case, and was forced to remove the records from store shelves and then deliver them to O'Sullivan's representatives to be destroyed. This event is often credited with a shift in the United States to more conscientious efforts to clear recognizable musical samples and led to the establishment of clearance warehouses, businesses who manage the payments between record companies. One legal case involving sampling even made it to the US Supreme Court. The raunchy, Miami-based 2 Live Crew sampled without permission Roy Orbison's "Pretty Woman," over which they rapped "Big Fat Hairy Woman." The Supreme Court ruled that because the new version was a parody, the use of the sample was permitted under the copyright law's fair-use provision. An overview of some of these musical copyright wars is available through the online exhibition illegal-art.org, which also makes many of the songs available for download.

More recently, a public debate occurred surrounding DJ Danger Mouse's *Grey Album*, a remix album of 2004 that used the a cappella vocals from Jay-Z's *The Black Album* (2003), remixed with samples from the Beatles' *White Album* (1968). Since the Beatles' copyright holder EMI never permits the sampling of Beatles' songs, Danger Mouse's album became a symbol of how copyright laws were limiting the kind of artistic creativity that new technologies make possible. How much control should original artists (or, more accurately, the companies that manage the downstream monetization of intellectual property) have in determining what kinds of artistic production can and cannot occur? Some might argue that stealing the talent of the Beatles to piggyback on their celebrity cannot be condoned, but what about the (sometimes unknown) African American artists whose songs, such as "Money (That's What I Want)," were covered by the Beatles and formed the basis of some of their early works? Does that not constitute a similar kind of borrowing, drawing on cultural heritage to make something new? Clearly, we are witnessing an evolving interplay between ethics and law that as yet is not fully resolved (Schloss 2004).

In Japan, there are far fewer examples of musicians using famous song samples. Why the difference? In the mid- to late 1990s, gossip about a scandal involving Sony was commonly cited by musicians and record-company representatives as the main reason why Japanese hip-hoppers do not sample famous songs. In one recording studio session I observed, a musician brought a demo tape with some new songs. He asked the record-company director whether they might be included on the compilation that the company was producing. The director said no, giving the example of "Da.Yo.Ne." as a reason. End of discussion. As it turned out, it was because the demo-tape songs were too obvious about the origins of the music sampled. Later, when I asked the musician about the exchange, he was reluctant to talk about it because it was gossip and also made Sony look bad. As he put it, "I'll tell you, but this is from 'Mr. X,' OK?"

The story goes like this. Like most rap songs, East End X Yuri's single "Da.Yo.Ne." included a sample from recorded material, in this case a song by George Benson. As the song began climbing the charts, George Benson happened to be in Tokyo for a show at the Blue Note. Apparently, he was riding in a taxi with his manager when they heard "Da.Yo.Ne." on the radio. Benson turned to his manager, asked if they had some deal going on in Japan, to which the manager replied no. And so one thing lead to another. Epic/Sony, which released the single, allegedly ended up paying Benson around $100,000 (¥1.5 million at exchange rates then). It was even rumored that someone at Sony was fired for the mistake. (Another musician later commented that although the payment was likely ten times higher than the normal fee had the sample been cleared, the song was such a hit that Sony still made plenty of money.) As a result, most record companies became very circumspect about the samples they used, requiring artists to change samples if they were famous or recognizable. This also discouraged the use of Japanese samples because they would be more readily caught.

This event highlights part of the relationship between sampling and popularity. Sampling is OK, if no one, at least no one who might sue, hears it. It is noteworthy too, however, that it is not actual lawsuits or court cases that circulate as defining rumors regarding sampling in Japan. Instead, the standard procedure appears to be negotiation and settlement between record companies. Record companies have little incentive for going after small fish—indie labels, mixtape DJs, and so on—but rather attend to releases of those with deep pockets. While artists at the lowest echelons are safest, and those at the upper echelons can get company support to pay for samples, the greatest risk in using sampling arises for those in the middle.

The magazine writer Innami Atsushi found himself challenged by the rapper ECD, however, for participating in a book that revealed the origins of different samples in a variety of Japanese songs (Murata 1997). Innami said he initially questioned the project, but was incensed when the publisher accused everyone in hip-hop of wanting to hide something. After the book's publication ECD attacked Innami for his naïveté:

We [the musicians] are the one's taking the risk. If word gets out that sampling is going on, it's dangerous. But it's part of hip-hop as an art form. If a sample is found out, and money taken, I'm telling you that's like a train wreck. Given that's the case, I think what you did was like putting a rock on the track. . . . It's not that we've decided to hide something. We're the ones taking the risk, so I wonder how much cowardice is involved when you're talking about a risk someone takes to do business. If some problems arose because of that book, they [the publishers] wouldn't be taking any responsibility. The only people who would lose would be us. . . . Since the substance of hip-hop itself is illegal, I can't think of what you did as anything other than a betrayal. (ECD 1997, 63)

ECD recognized that sampling is technically illegal, but asserted that the style of musical production is also the substance of hip-hop. He is willing to take the risk. Besides, it takes a certain kind of skill and knowledge to recognize obscure musical samples. A published book fed a desire on the part of many hip-hop artists and fans, though perhaps especially of DJs, to see which rare grooves were plundered for the melodies and beats, but such a book also made it easy for music publishers to put pressure on record companies to clear samples.

As the market for Japanese hip-hop has grown, groups and their record companies are clearing samples on a more regular basis. For his song "Lonely Girl," ECD, who above defended the illegality of sampling as part of hip-hop, presumably cleared the prominent sample of Marvin Gaye's "Sexual Healing." When Rhymester recorded the song "Uwasa no shinsō" (Truth behind the rumors), they produced two versions. One track featured synthesized horns playing Cream's "Sunshine of My Life," while a second version used a different track. It was only days before the CD went into production that Rhymester's A & R director Okada Makiko was able to clear the sample through a personal contact who spoke directly to Eric Clapton. Major-label record companies sometimes use live bands to reproduce the sound of the sample to avoid directly sampling and to shield themselves from legal challenge. In one case I learned that an American track-maker hired to make a song for a Japanese hip-hop artist actually used a sample from a Japanese pop artist, Matsuda Seiko. Since the major label had also produced the Matsuda track years before, it was a simple, internal process to clear the sample. What becomes clear is that there is no simple rule of thumb for determining what samples can and cannot be used. Indeed, when I asked a record-company rep about trying to get some Japanese hip-hop sold through the US iTunes Music Store, he answered that the potential increase in sales would not be worth the danger of having sampled songs discovered. He used the phrase *yabuhebi*, basically meaning, "don't wake the snake sleeping in the bush." It turns out that "the more popular, the better" is not true of all music, at least when sampling is involved.

The battles involving sampling and copyright point to a gray area in recording-studio practices. In terms of the law, there is no gray area; every sampled sound should be cleared. In practice, however, the calculus of risk depends on a wide variety of factors, such as the fame of the sample, its ownership, the likelihood of the record company being sued, and so on. Because the market for Japanese hip-hop, with few exceptions, stayed relatively small until the late 1990s, there was not enough income from hip-hop albums to justify the expense and trouble of clearing samples. The common philosophy in the studios was simply, don't ask, don't tell. It may be that an era of mainstream samples will yet appear in Japanese hip-hop, and indeed, we are already beginning to see some examples. But the fact that songs with crossover samples, such as Run-DMC's "Walk This Way," have not become prime movers in the history of hip-hop in Japan serves as a reminder that different legal, business, and cultural settings produce alternative histories of genres and that the American experience is not reproduced in every respect overseas.

The Third Era: Widening Diversity, No Center

Although one cannot point to the song "B-Boyism" as the cause of a shift in Japan's hip-hop scene, at least one can note that the idea of a single hip-hop scene has disappeared in the first years of the twenty-first century. Instead, we see scenes among scenes that the party-underground divide can no longer come close to capturing. We find a broad spectrum including rock rap to hard core to gangsta, spoken word/poetry, to conscious, old school, techno rap, antigovernment, pro-marijuana, heavy metal–sampled rap, and so on. Alongside the widening diversity within the hip-hop scene, we also see the disappearance of any orientation toward a center. In the years that followed the release of the song "B-Boyism," regional scenes became more active in Nagoya, Osaka, Sapporo, and Okinawa. For example, Yokohoma rappers, living only a half hour from Tokyo, became more aggressive in asserting their "045" (area code) style. Diversity without a center became the order of the day. The era in which underground hip-hoppers debated with party rappers has given way to more personal conflicts between rappers. These conflicts gesture toward ideas of what hip-hop should be about, but the question of what makes hip-hop *Japanese* seems but a shining artifact of the past.

Among the key developments was the arrival of more popular rap groups such as M-Flo, who entered the mainstream market without passing through years of performances in clubs. The rock band Dragon Ash started rapping, included a DJ, and sang a song called "I Love Hip-Hop" (1999), but was it hip-hop? Few commentators seemed overly excited about trying to police the boundaries, certainly not in the way that East End X Yuri's songs provoked. Meanwhile, underground rappers such as Zeebra broke into mainstream consciousness in part by teaming up with Japanese R & B singers like Sugar Soul and Utada Hikaru. Such widening heterogeneity did not eliminate the importance of the *genba*, but many rappers reported that the clubs were no longer the only places people could learn about hip-hop. Club imagery was appearing in television dramas, thus mainstreaming the club experience. It also became easier to find Japanese rap in record stores and karaoke establishments. Zeebra and Rhymester began making music videos. As DJ Jin of Rhymester put it during a conversation at Club Web in June 1999, "What's different today is that when I say to old grandma-types [*obaasantachi*] that I'm a DJ, they nod and say, 'Oh yeah, I know what that is.' " Intriguingly, the mainstreaming of hip-hop as a recognizable Japanese style also entailed an increasingly niche orientation, with different families of groups attracting distinct types of fans.

In addition, different regions of Japan are producing their own scenes, some of them led to some extent by dominant groups, but even here the notion of a leader seems out of date. A duo called Tha Blue Herb (MC Boss and DJ Ono) put Sapporo on the hip-hop map, particularly because of Boss's poetic lyrics. He is also notable for his general indifference to making his lines rhyme. Nor does he add stress accents to make his lyrics sound English in their rhythmic flow. But newcomers like Mic Jack Production and Shuren the Fire, also from the capital city of Japan's northernmost island, illustrate that there is no single Sapporo style. In the mid-1990s, it seemed unlikely that Japanese rappers would brag about doing cocaine, but after the turn of the millennium, Nagoya rappers M.O.S.A.D. produced several songs depicting their love of white lines. Tokona-X, the lead emcee with M.O.S.A.D., died at a young age, and many in the scene suspect that drugs were involved. Meanwhile, Ozrosaurus represents for Yokohama, Gagle for Sendai (in northeast Japan), Gaki Ranger for Kumamoto (on the island of Kyushu). Even Tokyo rappers now talk about what area of Tokyo they represent. K Dub Shine sees himself as the "Don of Shibuya," while a female rapper named Hime, whom we will meet in chapter 6, represents for Hachioji. Chiba, a bedroom suburb that is generally looked down on as a second-tier industrial zone, now boasts its own rappers who pride themselves on the "big-hair-smelling-of-shampoo funk" that the group Chiba Craziest Channel provides, a reference to the yankee (i.e., biker bad boy) love of big hair.

At the same time, some rap groups have catapulted into mainstream, pop-music-world success. Ketsumeishi, Kick the Can Crew, Rip Slyme, and M-Flo all count themselves as rap groups, yet their primary competition comes from other pop groups rather than from others within the hip-hop scene. Meanwhile, the underground scene continues to try various approaches to develop its own, competing standards of value. For example, the Tokyo-based group Suika performs with a live band and produces lyrics that cross over with the spoken word/poetry slam scene developing in Tokyo. In this sense, battling hip-hop samurai evoke different reference points to locate themselves and defend their personal aesthetics.

The widening use of samurai imagery with swords on album covers and in music videos proceeds in tandem with the increased use of gangsta imagery with guns. Pop rap, conscious rap, Korean Japanese rap, *burakumin* rap—all slide fluidly past one another rather than combining into a single, overarch-

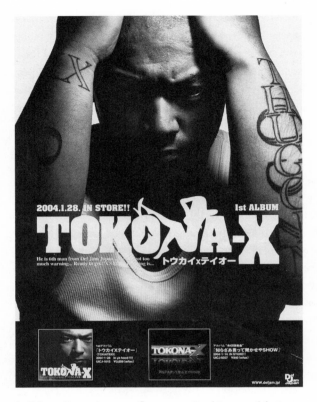

8. Tokona-X, rest in peace, flyer promoting his 2004 debut
solo album with gangsta style.

ing Japanese scene. When the writer Innami Atsushi contributed a monthly
column called "Represent Nippon" to the magazine *Black Music Review,* he
referred to what now seems a distinct era when writers and rappers sought
to lay claim to the Japaneseness of hip-hop for their own ends.

One of the more intriguing recent examples of hip-hop samurai involves
an anime television series called *Samurai Champloo.* The director, Watanabe
Shin'ichirō, also made *Cowboy Bebop,* a TV series (1998) and film (2001) about
futuristic bounty hunters that features jazz and blues artists from Japan.
Samurai Champloo, a twenty-six-episode series, mixes a Tokugawa-era samurai story with hip-hop music by the Japanese artists Nujabes, along with DJ
Tsutchie, Force of Nature, and the American expat artist Fat Jon. In a March
2005 interview, Watanabe pointed to the concept of representing to demonstrate that hip-hop complies perfectly with certain aspects of the samurai war-
rior ethic: "Nowadays, people think of the Japanese as reserved, shy, unable or

9. Suika performing at Flying Books, a bohemian bookstore in Shibuya, 7/05.
Photo by the author.

unwilling to express their individuality, but in the past, samurai understood
the importance of representing who they were. They devoted themselves to
battling through their skills." The weekly, half-hour series, which aired from
the summer of 2004 to March 2005, explored cultural remixing within Japan.
Even the title uses the Okinawan word for stew, *champloo*, to refer to a mixing of everything to see what comes out. Different episodes explored discrimination against Christians, foreigners, Ainu peoples, and so on in ways
that ultimately questioned the oneness of the Japanese people. Again, identity emerges from battling, not from some primordial essence; in this, Watanabe may be onto something. If Japaneseness is not something timeless, or
something encoded in one's genes, then performances that represent Japan
through hip-hop are not paradoxical at all. Rather, performance becomes a
way of understanding identity in its location, among specific audiences, and
occurring at specific historical junctures.

Conclusion

The image of battling hip-hop samurai highlights the processes of competition that drove the development of hip-hop in Japan. Hip-hoppers are samurai in the sense that they draw on histories, language, their own lives, and the
setting of Japan not primarily to make the music local in a way that combats
global homogenization, but rather to make it original, interesting, and note-

worthy—both to their fans and to the record companies seeking new talent. It is struggles between factions, and the ways these factional battles changed over time, that give the clearest sense of how abstract global ideals become enacted in Japan. Yet the history of hip-hop in Japan also shows that the sense of what ideals drive hip-hop also changes over time. The uncertainty about what hip-hop meant in the early days due to a lack of information and understanding has been transformed today into an uncertainty about what hip-hop means because there are so many examples to consider. In this way, widening battles, diversifying scenes, and far-flung regional developments point to processes that suggest a way of thinking beyond localization or domestication.

Part of the challenge of understanding cultural globalization involves recognizing that the global and the local are not so much matched pairs as they are symbolic crystallizations of more fluid, ongoing processes unfolding over time. Does the spread of such popular culture forms ultimately produce cultural homogenization or increasing diversity? Evidence can be amassed to support either claims of global convergence or of local diversity, yet I doubt that we can ever establish, once and for all, a scale of analysis that can legitimately give one interpretation priority over the other. What seems most likely is that we are witnessing both convergence and divergence, albeit in different dimensions and with contradictory effects. The idea of *genba*—actual sites of performance—helps us see how the global is refracted through particular actors and contexts, but what we can also see from the example of the samurai is that the local, too, is refracted through performance. Samurai do not stand for any single Japaneseness, and in this they accurately represent hip-hop and its battles.

Where is the real in hip-hop?   *Hippu-hoppu no doko ga riaru*
In the clubs [genba]   *sore wa genba*
in other words, right here   *tsumari koko ni aru*

—Rhymester, "Kuchi kara demakase," on *Egotopia*

CHAPTER 3

GENBA GLOBALIZATION AND LOCATIONS OF POWER

In this chapter, I focus on the particulars of club events, and their location amid a larger music industry and a changing youth culture in Japan. The mirror balls that provide light in the dark of hip-hop clubs suggest a place to begin. Every nightclub has its mirror balls, turning slowly, painting the smoky haze with light. Mirror balls radiate a semiotics of clubland, illuminating no single star on stage, but rather spotlighting and then passing over all the participants—artists, fans, promoters, writers, industry executives, club owners, bartenders, the regulars, and the first-timers. The dynamic interaction among all these actors is what brings a club scene to life. Mirror balls evoke this multiplicity, splashing attention on each individual for a moment and then moving on, not unlike the furtive glances of desire between clubbers in this zone of intimate anonymity. We are drawn to the circulation of forces rather than to power emanating from a star, drawn to the liminal space between the stage and the audience, drawn to the relationships rather than the identities that animate Japan's hip-hop scene.

In this chapter I examine hip-hop nightclubs to ask: What do these locations of performance tell us about the music's place in Japan's youth culture? Do hip-hop club performances have the potential to influence the broader sections of Japanese society, business, and politics? Like the light radiating from the mirror ball, the particulars of club performances lead outward to larger contexts: the youth's position in Japan's changing economy; the growing importance of so-called content industries—including music—for producing economic growth; and the government's interest in promoting the nation's cultural soft power. Hip-hop music in clubs illuminates certain aspects of Japanese youth culture by drawing attention to the performativity of media power.[1] Put another way, the influence of mediated representations arises from a combination of location and performativity. Artists use club events to show their skill on stage and to convey their particular political and aesthetic perspectives, but their influence depends on whether they move the crowd, something that cannot be determined only in terms of what they say but also by how and where they say it. This is the essence of a *genba* perspective: performativity and location. I would argue that this requires a nuanced understanding of different locations in a music, from the megahit stars to the relative unknowns in the underground, which, taken together, we might conceive of as a pyramid of the music scene. The process of career development, from being one among the mass of amateurs to becoming one of the very few megahit stars, depends on navigating past the gatekeepers, developing connections, and improving one's skills. Of course, rising up in the industry is no guarantee that stardom will be anything but fleeting. An unfolding, historical perspective on key performative locations offers a way of moving beyond conceptions of culture industry power in dichotomous terms. For example, do record companies have more power than artists? Can fans control record companies? Such questions cannot be answered without recognizing the dispersed, networked, and performative character of hip-hop within a larger pop music world and in the midst of a changing Japan. We might call this analytical scheme "*genba* globalization." By viewing club events within the larger pyramid structure of a music scene, we can see more clearly the ways government and business interests focus primarily on the upper echelons of the music world.

I argue that focusing too much on megahit stars leads to a distorted picture of what promotes thriving media economies and a nation's soft power. Japanese hip-hop unfolds amid contradictory discourses surrounding youth culture in Japan. On the one hand, young people are seen as dragging down the economy as *freeter* (temp workers) who value their leisure habits more than commitment to workplaces. On the other hand, content industries depend on youth as discriminating consumers who become, in effect, a national resource through their sensitivity to what is "cool." A look at some of the differences between major-label artists and underground rappers leads to a dis-

cussion of power within the recording industry. Instead of the binary oppositions of artist versus fan, artist versus record company, I suggest a more
dynamic and interactive model of differential power in the cultural production of music. This perspective sets the stage for the further exploration of
other dimensions of Japanese hip-hop's cultural interventions in terms of
fans, language, gender, and markets.

Defining *Genba*

The word *genba* is written with the characters for "to appear" (現 *gen*) and
"place" (場 *ba*). The word evokes a "place where something actually happens,
appears, or is made." *Genba* sometimes refers to a place where something bad
happens, such as a traffic accident or the scene of a crime. The term is also
used for places where something is produced: anime studios, film locations,
a construction site, a recording studio. The use of the term *genba* to refer to
nightclubs where hip-hop is performed draws attention to "the making of
the scene" (*shiin*). Whether as recording studios or as nightclubs, *genba* focus
musicians' energies and provide a particular measure of their skill and success. Rather than asking how accurately Japanese hip-hop represents a kind
of Japaneseness or a legitimate respect for black culture, we can focus instead on how both Japaneseness and blackness are performed by different
groups (underground, pop, etc.) in different locations (in small clubs, in giant
stadiums, etc.).

When rappers emphasize the importance of clubs as *genba*, they stake a
claim to authority based on their onstage performance in front of generally
receptive fans. Clubs can be viewed as a kind of home turf in contrast to other
contexts for determining value. In the mediated world of the market (*shijō*),
value is defined by sales. In the entertainment world (*geinōkai*), value derives
from celebrity renown. In the industry (*gyōkai*), record company executives
make decisions regarding production and promotion budgets by gambling on
what may become valuable based on their understandings of marketability.
In the media (*media*), value depends on attracting audiences important to ad-
vertisers. Each context draws attention to different schemas for evaluating
performance broadly understood. Regardless of the interpretive context, no
single person or group is fully in control of the outcomes.

I use the idea of the *genba* to explore what can be learned through fieldwork
in performative locations.[2] Rather than a place-based analysis, I work from
sites where particular kinds of performative roles emerge through ongoing
negotiation, networking, and debate. I view this as part of broader trends in

anthropology to rethink participant-observation fieldwork (Inda and Rosaldo 2002a; Marcus 1995). An important trend involves the focus on locations viewed not as geographic locales, but rather as sites constructed in fields of unequal relations (Gupta and Ferguson 1997).[3] This reorients our attention away from cultural flows from place to place toward questions of how global culture gains its force from the ways performances energize people in particular locations. Thus genba, I argue, are key paths of cultural globalization because they actualize (genjitsu suru) the global and the local simultaneously. Instead of cosmopolitanism, I use the term genba globalization to highlight the actualization or performativity, rather than subjectivity, of intersections of foreign and indigenous ideas. Unlike aspects of globalization spread by major multinational corporations and powerful governments, hip-hop in Japan is particularly instructive because it represents a kind of globalization that depends on genba for its force. A freestyle session in one of the late-night Tokyo clubs, described below, illustrates this dynamic.

Freestyle as a Metaphor of Genba Globalization

In what ways can a focus on nightclubs as genba help us unravel the question of what drives the globalization of hip-hop? Can we also determine whether hip-hop in Japan is ultimately global or local? I argue that we can gain insight into both questions through the concept of genba globalization, which analyzes the global in terms of how it is refracted through performances in particular genba. Rather than focusing on the cultural form itself, I draw attention instead to performance and the collective energy of the participants. A closer look at a specific club event can clarify what I mean.

With light snow falling on a blustery evening in February 1997, about three hundred people are crowded into a humid, smoky, basement Shibuya nightclub called Family. It is one large, dark room, with a bar along one wall and a mirror ball providing most of the light. Most of the audience members are in their early twenties, with relatively equal numbers of men and women. We have come to see FG Night, a monthly Japanese hip-hop event that has been going since the early 1990s (and continues through 2005). The night's activities begin at around 11 p.m. with a DJ spinning records, but the bulk of us show up after midnight, when the trains stop running for the night. The three live acts—Rip Slyme, Mellow Yellow, and Rhymester—perform from 1:30 a.m. to 3 a.m. The live show winds up with an open-ended freestyle session. Two microphones circulate among the fifteen or so people milling around the low platform that serves as a stage. We in the audience skeptically evaluate the latest new talent. One after another, newcomer rappers grab the mic and shout a minute or two of their rhymes before someone else dives in for a turn. Most of the rappers, in their late teens to midtwenties, are men, but a couple women try out too. It is a free-for-all, ruled by the ability to hold the stage through a clever turn of phrase and a catchy delivery.

Then there is a pause as one of the more well-known rappers takes the mic. The scritch-scratch of the DJ's turntable counts time as Gaku-MC holds the microphone to his lips: "Moriagatten no ka?" (Are you having fun yet?). Gaku tries to move the crowd by screaming "Yo!" but we have been exhorted by the previous fifteen freestyle emcees to yell "Ho-oh!" a few too many times. Gaku has his work cut out for him.

"Do you know what FG stands for?" he yells. "Funky Grammar!" yells the crowd, the name of the hip-hop collective that organized this event. "Eeh?" teases Gaku. The crowd, louder: "Funky Grammar!" Still not satisfied, Gaku demands an even louder response. Then he signals to DJ Yoggy that he is ready, and the opening measures of the Jackson Five's "ABC" start up, looped over and over as the DJ switches back and forth between two records on parallel turntables. Gaku gets his freestyle going (in Japanese), syncopating his rhymes against the catchy track, referring to the club, the heat, and the sweat drenching everyone's clothes. The flow of his lyrics gives us all a bounce, and because it happens to be Valentine's Day, he riffs on dating, saying he is going to "show us his manhood," punning on sweat as a reference to sex, threatening to take off his clothes, then saying, "If you feel like I do, put your voices together and yell!" Now we are all moving, and with an explosive unity, we wave our hands forward and scream. Gaku says, "Yo, peace, I'm out" (in English) and leaves the stage. We in the audience smile and nod to each other. This is what we came for.

As the event continues, break-dancers from Rock Steady Crew Japan battle in a circle on the dance floor. After that, MC U and Kreva, two emcees who years later will top the pop charts in the group Kick the Can Crew, engage in a freestyle battle in which each emcee must rhyme his first line with his opponent's last one. The rhyming is all in Japanese, and the audience is hooked, laughing at the puns and insults flying back and forth. Kreva: "Ha, you're nothing but a laughing stock [owarai]." MC U: "A laughing-stock? I'll never stop!" (Owarai? Owaranai!). Afterwards, the deejays go back to playing their mix of current hip-hop, mostly from the United States, but with some recent Japanese tracks mixed in, along with old funk and soul records. At around

5 a.m., the bartenders usher us to the exit. Outside, dawn is breaking, and the Tokyo trains will soon start running again to take us home.

Beyond Global / Local

What can we learn from this freestyle session to extend our understanding of global and local sources of agency and influence? Does the example of FG Night show us whether hip-hop in Japan is ultimately global or local? Does the event represent cultural homogenization, or does the presence of rappers where there were none before constitute an increasing diversification of Japanese culture? Evidence from FG Night could be marshaled to support either side of the debate.

What we might refer to as homogenization is apparent in that self-described rappers engage in freestyle using English-language poetics (rhyming couplets, accented rhythms). The artists employ hip-hop performance styles including call-and-response, body language, fashion, and DJ scratch techniques. Gaku says in English "Yo, peace, I'm out" as he leaves the stage. Most of the records being played are American hip-hop, and much of the audience knows all the songs, as evidenced by the shouts of approval in the opening measures of the deejays' selections.

But localization is apparent as well. All the emcees rap in Japanese to a Japanese audience about things that are meaningful or cool to them. Few American emcees would have any idea what they were talking about. Moreover, calling this "hybridity" is helpful only to a degree because we would like to know why Gaku's particular mixture of styles differs from those of Kreva or of MC U. The notion of hybrid assumes core sources (whether Japanese or hip-hop), and yet styles in the scene shift over time and depend on whether one is an underground/indie or a major-label star in the pop realm. Depending on what one focuses on, local diversification and global homogenization proceed simultaneously.

Such conundrums recur endlessly in the debate over globalization's effects on culture. Two sociologists whose work emphasizes opposite ends of the heterogeneity-homogeneity spectrum offer touchstones for a much wider range of scholarship. Roland Robertson (1995) focuses more on cultural diversification by local actors. He uses the term *glocalization* to refer to the processes by which the global is transformed by local actors and circumstances. In fact, Japan gets some credit for the concept because, he explains, glocalization is a translation of the Japanese marketing term *dochaku* (to take root), a reference to the process of making global products fit into local markets. For Robertson, glocalization is meant as an improvement over terms like *indigenization* or *domestication* that emphasize the local to the exclusion of the global. Robertson emphasizes their interpenetration.

At the other end of the spectrum, George Ritzer (2004, 73) proposes the term *grobalization* to focus on "the imperialistic ambitions of nations, corporations, organizations . . . to impose themselves on various geographic areas." He emphasizes the ways these institutions aim to "grow" their power, influence, and profits (hence, *grobalization*). He describes such processes in terms of capitalism, Americanization, and McDonaldization, and places them under the overall rubric of what he calls the "globalization of nothing." In this context, *nothing* refers to that which is "centrally conceived and controlled and largely lacking in distinctive substance, while *something* is defined as that which is generally indigenously conceived and controlled and possesses much in the way of distinctive substance" (20; emphasis added). From Ritzer's perspective, a Big Mac is nothing; Culatella ham from Italy is something. Ritzer also identifies credit cards, faceless servicepersons, fast-food chains, and the like as "nothing."

I would argue that both *glocalization* and *grobalization* suffer from an analytical emphasis on the cultural forms themselves rather than on the ways they are put into practice. Capitalism might not be all bad if it promotes the autonomy of underprivileged people, for example, in the ways the Grameen Bank of Bangladesh offers microinvestments to entrepreneurial women. Such capitalism seems somehow different from the kind of capitalism spread via Wal-Mart. Similarly, some global homogeneity can be beneficial if we are talking about the spread of human rights, democracy, environmentalism, clean drinking water, or an end to AIDS. Moreover, depending on the scale of analysis, we can draw different conclusions about effects. Take voting, for example. Voting in a national election constitutes participation in *global* ideas of democratic process; it reinforces a *national* identity by defining rules of citizenship; and it also enacts *individual* choices in contests between *local* candidates. Global standardization, nationalization, and localization all get reinforced simultaneously. Determining whether this is glocalization or grobalization cannot be accomplished, it seems to me, by focusing on the characteristics of the cultural form (voting) itself. Moreover, the global/local debate sets up a contest between abstractions that may not be appropriate to the issues on the ground. Is global/local the appropriate measure for understanding the conflict between global labor standards and global capitalism?

It seems to me that whether something is locally conceived is less important than how it is implemented.

Genba Globalization

In this respect, *genba* offer a way to distinguish between different paths of cultural globalization by focusing on performativity. Now we see why *genba*, as sites of actualization, offer a means to conceptualize the difference between the globalization of Wal-Mart, Disneyland, and McDonald's and the globalization of human rights, democracy, and environmentalism. The latter depend on *genba* for their transnational diffusion. Although Wal-Mart and McDonald's could be conceived of as *genba*, they differ in the sense that actors tend to be more constrained in terms of the patterns of production and transformation. Unlike McDonald's, other global forms that depend more on open-ended *genba* emerge from a collaborative focus of energy and attention, an improvisatory working out of goals and processes, which may be inspired by global and local reference points but which are determined only after the fact in historically contingent positions. In this sense, a freestyle session offers a metaphor for *genba* globalization.

This helps explain the importance of focusing on locations and performativity. By beginning with the *genba*, the actual sites of cultural production, we can see how the global and the local intersect. More important, we can conceive of these intersections in terms of the ways they intervene in ongoing struggles. We might call this process *genba* globalization because it highlights the ways the global, here meaning everything one can draw on (not just "foreign" ideas), is refracted through performative locations and thereby put back into the world. This gives us a model for understanding some of the unevenness of globalization by drawing attention to the terms of competition (or battles) and the conditions required to win. Gaku, performing in the freestyle session after being cut from his major label, underscores his sense that recording again depends at least partly on continuing his performance in clubs. Because these performances generally unfold in the language of the participants, I use the term *genba* in this text rather than an English-language neologism.[4] Hip-hop in Japan is especially instructive of these different paths of cultural globalization (Wal-Mart versus *genba*) because the music is performed at all levels, from highly commercial mass media (e.g., television commercials) to independent, underground club venues.

This discussion raises some key questions. Given that performances gain their force because they speak in a certain way to a certain kind of crowd, how can we contextualize a club event like FG Night in the broader context of Japanese youth culture? Working further outward, how are youth and the music world contextualized by larger business and government interests? After answering these questions, I will return to a consideration of the music scene and the differences between underground club events and commercially successful pop stars.

Youth Culture in a Changing Japan

Japanese youth who came of age around the turn of the twenty-first century face difficult economic times. Although they were children during the boom times of the bubble economy of the 1980s, they entered adulthood after a decade-long recession that started in 1992. As the economy stumbled, businesses retrenched and unemployment rates among young workers rose.

These economic changes have served to undermine a core ideal of Japan's postwar middle-class society, namely, that hard work in school will lead to a good job. The breakdown in the transition from school to work affects the meaning of education and of the working world. I observed firsthand the pressure put on young students to move up the ladder of success through hard work in school when I was employed in a rural Japanese junior high school for a year (1988–89). I was as an assistant English teacher on the JET Program.[5] Each Monday, when the principal addressed the assembled school, he would emphasize the importance of studying in order to pass entrance exams to high school and, later, college exams, which would, in turn, guarantee a good job. By this logic, the status of one's school would influence the status of one's career. This was, in short, the credentials society (*gakureki shakai*).

But if studying hard no longer led to a job, what should one be working for? In 1995, the rapper Zeebra of the group King Giddra commented on this broken chain between school and work.

The "credentials society" crushes even	*Kodomotachi no yume made hakai shite kita*
the dreams of children, that's a good thing?	*gakureki shakai umaku dekita kai?*
. . .	. . .
But things are changing, aren't they?	*Kawatte kiteru n jya nai?*
And aren't you just shutting up	*Tada sore damatte*
and watching it happen?	*mite ru n jya nai?*
This year's survey of college grads	*Kotoshi no daisotsu no koyō chōsa*
says that almost a quarter of them	*kimaranu yatsu no ōsa sō sa*
still have no job. Seriously,	*yonbun no ichi ga mada*

that makes it nothing more	*maji hanahada okashiku tte*
than empty talk.	*hanashi ni naranai n da tada.*

—King Giddra (1995) "Shinjitsu no dangan" (bullet of truth) *Sora kara no chikara* (the power from the sky) (P-Vine/Blues Interactions, Japan, PCD-4768)

As members of an underground group (at the time), King Giddra challenged youth not only to recognize the difficulties faced by Japanese society but also to speak up about them.[6]

The labor researcher Reiko Kosugi (2004) confirms that before the early 1990s, a majority of young people in Japan entered the labor market as full-time workers. After graduation from high school or college, most would get contracts with no fixed term. After the recession, however, many companies hired fewer new grads, and those who were hired typically became part-time employees with fixed-term contracts (53–54). Through the latter half of the 1990s and into the new century, Japan witnessed a dramatic increase in unemployed youth and so-called *freeter,* who are working on an *arubaito* (from the German *Arbeit*), or part-time, basis and who are "free" in the sense that they are not wedded to a single corporation.

About half of the people I spoke to at the hip-hop clubs identified themselves as *freeter* (many of the others said they were students). I was struck by how the *freeters* would acknowledge their status with a bit of pride. They were not beholden to some enormous corporation; they could avoid a salaryman's hours and obligatory after-hours socializing. When I asked exactly what kind of work they did, however, many *freeter* became somewhat embarrassed, not wanting to acknowledge their jobs as waitresses, sewer workers, department store helpers, or convenience store clerks. Yet while they tread water in the working world, they swim against the current when they go out to all-night clubs.

Because the Tokyo club scene is active between midnight and 5 a.m. (with live shows around 2 a.m.), clubbers head out just as many regular office workers are rushing to catch the last trains home. Clubbers are dressed up, leisurely heading out—a literal movement against the mainstream, a rejection of daily work rhythms in favor of leisure and consumer activities. Yet the clubs are not only a space for play, leisure, and the rejection of rigid work lives; they also serve as vehicles for the delivery of some overt political messages in the live shows. So when emcees "move the crowd," it gives us some sense of the crowds they move.

In January 2003, I saw the underground group MSC perform on a Wednesday night at around 3:30 a.m. in Roppongi. MSC's lead rappers Taboo and Kan addressed some of Japan's recent social and economic shifts in a song called "Shinjuku Underground Area."[7] In Shinjuku, an area of downtown Tokyo, one can find government office buildings and gleaming corporate high-rises not far from dilapidated residential areas that have been encroached on to make way for new construction. In the song, Taboo describes the Tokyo governor Ishihara Shintarō as "a pop idol stealing land to make more dollars, francs, yen, marks," and the bankers in the high-rises "plundering for themselves in neckties." Kan views Shinjuku as a microcosm of the hypocrisy of Japan, where expensive new buildings become the sites for government failures, banking scandals, and corruption that differs little from that found among the organized crime syndicates who run the nearby Kabuki-cho red light district. In one line Kan portrays a salaryman, a symbol of Japan's power in the 1980s, now walking dejectedly, looking down and wondering when "restructuring" (*risutora*) will result in his being fired. Kan asks, "Does your life have any purpose?" For the b-boy or *freeter* watching the salaryman, the implicit answer, of course, is "no."

A year and a half later, in July 2004, I saw MSC perform at Milk, a small club in the Ebisu section of Tokyo. They fired up the audience by arguing that it was the fans in attendance who had the power to bring about structural reform (*kōzō kaikaku*) in Japan. They used this bureaucratic language to reinterpret the prime minister Junichiro Koizumi's campaign promise to change Japan's corporate and government inefficiencies (corruption, mismanagement, bad loans, etc.). MSC's song suggests that structural reform could begin in the clubs, with the limitless potential the artists see in their music. The group began with a call-and-response, then broke into the chorus to one of their signature songs.

structural reform! (fans: structural reform!)	*kōzō kaikaku! kōzō kaikaku!*
modern rap moving forward without limits	*shinka suru gendai rappu ni genkai wa naku*
feelings of guilt dying, reform the system	*shinde ku zaiakkan kōzō kaikaku*

The audience nodded in unison and joined in singing the chorus, transforming the slogans of politicians and economic reformers into a language and style appropriate to today's Japanese youth. Kan explained to the audience after the song that the transformation would begin right there in the club.

When rappers promote standards of value different from those of the ruling powers, they also stake a claim to alternative sources of authority. Japanese hip-hop can be seen as a sphere of public debate, oriented toward youth but simultaneously integrated into entertainment-industry structures and, at a remove, government goals for youth in society. MSC's use of the bureaucratic term *kōzō kaikaku*, which refers more commonly to a reorganization of business structures and financial lending arrangements, reminds the group's audiences that Japanese hip-hop functions as part of a public debate questioning mainstream political values. Needless to say, the structural reforms promoted by MSC reflect aims very different from those of Japan's prime minister. We should note that the underground effort of MSC operates within a larger world of commercially successful popular music as well. Interestingly, Japanese government and business interests are increasingly turning their attention to the economic power and soft power of entertainment industries, a development that also contextualizes the location of nightclubs, hip-hop, and youth culture in Japan.

Underground to Pop: Diverse Powers of Popular Music

To develop a more nuanced understanding of power in popular music, we must also consider policy makers who view entertainment businesses as a key to reinvigorating Japan's economy. Like other advanced economies, Japan faces the challenge of responding to the migration of manufacturing jobs to lower-wage countries such as China. One response focuses on strengthening so-called content industries (*kontentsu sangyō*) such as music, film, anime, manga, publishing, and the like. In July 2002, a cabinet-level committee assembled under the auspices of the prime minister's office proposed making Japan an intellectual property–based nation: "Making Japan an intellectual-property-based nation means expressly establishing a national direction which places emphasis on inventions and creation, and in which the production of intangible assets is recognized as the foundation of industry, i.e., the production of 'information of value' including technology, design, brands, and the content of music, movies, and the like. This is a national policy underpinned by the vision of revitalizing the Japanese economy and society."[8] In this vision, music's power is defined in terms of its economic ability to support industry. As a national strategy, the report emphasizes the importance of strengthening copyright, patent, and trademark laws, as well as stepping up enforcement regimes.

A *genba* perspective illustrates a possible shortcoming of such government efforts. Policy proposals such as this tend to provide detailed analyses of how to protect and exploit already-created content, while offering only vague ideas about how to promote the production of creative content in the first place. The strategy report nodded in the direction of revising educational goals to include independent, innovative thinking, but the question of how to get from a credentials society to a society of successful artists, performers, and inventors is left largely unexplored. Part of the problem might lie in the very terminology of *content industry. Content* implies an object that can be packaged, branded, cross-marketed, and sold. Content is valued at the point of sale. But for artists, content emerges from years of practice, repeated performances, and a honing of skills over time. They produce works (*sakuhin*), that is, a kind of art, more than content. Such ideological divergences suggest a disjuncture between the realities of artists' lives and the strategies for exploiting media businesses.

Hamano Yasuki, a professor at Tokyo University, is one of the many economists in Japan who look toward Japanese popular culture not only as means to invigorate the economy but also as a way to strengthen the nation's soft power. The term *soft power* was coined by the political scientist Joseph Nye as part of his effort to urge politicians to think beyond its binary opposite, the so-called hard power of military might and economic sanctions. Soft power refers to a nation's ability to influence other nations through sympathetic responses rather than coercion or payments. Soft power "arises from the attractiveness of a country's culture, political ideals, and policies" (Nye 2004, x). Japan stands well positioned to expand its soft power, thanks to what the journalist Douglas McGray (2002) calls its rising "gross national cool." The overseas spread of Japanese animation, comic books, and video games exemplifies this understanding of Japan as a cultural superpower. Hamano Yasuki (2004) amplifies this theme, arguing that Japan is a child's playground (*kodomo no rakuen*), so that young people's selective consumerism will drive "cool Japan" pop culture industries. These same businesses, in Hamano's view, will also provide satisfying and creative careers. Perversely, Japanese policy makers view youth simultaneously as both unmotivated *freeter* dragging down the economy and world-class consumers whose selective shopping positions the nation as a leader in soft power.

We can also see other contradictory interpretations of youth's proper role in content industries. Are youth expected to be creative producers or primarily specialized consumers? As part of the effort to bolster content industries, there has been increasing pressure to control access to content through technological locks (digital rights management), as well as through legal action against people suspected of sharing media files online (though still a small fraction of the number of lawsuits launched in the United States). Will youth be seen as dangerous, potential pirates, or future producers who need access to a wide range of culture and media to produce the next big thing?

Protecting intellectual property is the more visible policy action for the moment. The irony of this situation does not escape notice. A writer who works in the anime industry (and who shall remain anonymous) reacted to the government's interest in popular culture by noting that protecting intellectual property will benefit entertainment corporations but may offer little of value to those in the *genba*, that is, the illustrators and others who actually produce the works in anime studios. He suspects that copyright protection may generate more income for the production company overall, but is unlikely to trickle down to the animators themselves.

This brings us to questions of how media production operates. How important are hits to the overall music business? How can we conceive of the different levels in an overall music scene? What is the relationship between the underground clubs and mainstream pop vehicles?

One of the challenges in evaluating popular culture forms involves determining how to represent the differences between hit cultural products (hit albums, blockbuster films, best sellers) and the great mass of cultural products that do not sell very well. As one pop music observer noted, too often big hits are viewed as representative of this abstract entity called popular culture, rather than being seen as what they are, albums that happen to have become popular (Ross 2003, 88). This is one reason my study focuses on nightclubs and recording studios, namely, to portray firsthand the kinds of dynamics that determine what moves up into the spotlight and also to provide a wider view of the range of music being produced lower down the scale of popularity. Nevertheless, we must consider the relationship between what reaches the top and what fails to generate large economic returns. This is especially important because the widening interest in entertainment industries' ability to generate economic growth and soft power hinges above all on the major hit products.

The recording industry is remarkable both for its reliance on hit albums and for its general inability to predict what will be a success. Among the record executives I spoke to in Japan, the general expectation was that 90 percent of albums would fail to return a profit. A study of entertainment industries in the United States identifies the same failure rate for new album releases and notes that Hollywood fares only somewhat better, estimating that 60–70 percent of films lose money (Vogel 2001, 35). The reasons for these failure rates are numerous and complex, given that budgets for promotion and marketing can in some cases rival production costs. Moreover, artists complain that some record companies use dubious accounting methods to limit the payment of royalties to the musicians (Love 2000). A key point is that entertainment industries tend to rely on a relatively small number of hits to support the majority of the business.

A look at sales in 2002 Japan provides a window into the range of returns for different albums. Of the 1,274 albums tracked by Oricon during the 2002 calendar year, 5 percent sold over 300,000 copies (hits), 32 percent sold between 30,000 and 299,000 copies (passable, at least in hard times, for the majors), and 41 percent sold fewer than 10,000 albums (low sales). The top-selling album of the year, Utada Hikaru's *Deep River*, sold over 3.5 million copies. This is comparable to the cumulative sales of the bottom five hundred releases for the year. The top ten albums moved around 30 million units total, which is eight times the total of the bottom five hundred releases. If we focus only on albums that could be deemed a success (say, sales above 80,000 units), it would only constitute one-sixth of the releases for 2002.[9] This rate is a little better than the one in ten cited by industry insiders, but given the size of some marketing budgets, situations occur in which 80,000 in sales can seem like a failure. East End X Yuri's 1996 "Ne" single following their million-selling successes is a case in point.

The Pyramid Structure of a Music Scene

I would suggest viewing the structure of a music scene as a pyramid (see figure 10). Rather than focusing primarily on the very narrow slice of performers who have achieved megahit status, we can learn more about the processes involved and the range of participants by considering what it takes to move up to the top of the pyramid. Reading from the bottom upward gives a sense of the historical trajectory of many successful artists, though we must bear in mind that most falter on their way to the top and that movement is not unidirectional.

A few points deserve mention. In thinking about how artists move up the pyramid from newbie fans to amateur performers to paid performers to first recording sessions (often featured on more established groups' songs or on a compilation album), we can see that the steps to getting significant support from a record company depend in part on passing the gates at each level. Depending on their position in the pyramid, artists also face different demands regarding what constitutes success in order to keep a career alive. Selling 20,000 copies at the indie level may represent a huge success, while for a major-label artist such numbers are likely to be seen as a flop. I would emphasize that the arrow on the right of the pictured pyramid indicates relative financial considerations (more outlays and more support), not the general

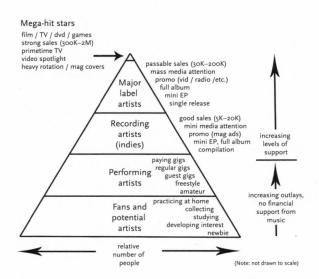

Mega-hit stars

film / TV / dvd / games
strong sales (300K–2M)
primetime TV
video spotlight
heavy rotation / mag covers

Major label artists
    passable sales (30K–200K)
    mass media attention
    promo (vid / radio /etc.)
    full album
    mini EP
    single release

Recording artists (indies)
    good sales (5K–20K)
    mini media attention
    promo (mag ads)
    mini EP, full album
    compilation

increasing levels of support

Performing artists
    paying gigs
    regular gigs
    guest gigs
    freestyle
    amateur

Fans and potential artists
    practicing at home
    collecting
    studying
    developing interest
    newbie

increasing outlays, no financial support from music

relative number of people

(Note: not drawn to scale)

10. Pyramid structure of a music scene. Figure by the author.

movement of artists, who are likely to climb and fall over the course of their careers.

Another key point is that only a fraction of musicians get record deals that can introduce them to huge audiences, and among those, only a fraction become big stars. In other words, top hits may tell us more about what it takes to move through the gates at each level, rather than representing "what most people want." Studies of such gatekeeping by the popular music scholar Keith Negus (1999) show how personal preferences and corporate cultures interact to guide the decisions made about promoting some kinds of artists over others. I consider some of these dynamics in the Japanese hip-hop scene in chapter 7. Notably, even artists who make a living on their music move up and down the pyramid during the course of their careers, depending on whether their sales meet their companies' expectations.

Viewing a music scene in terms of a pyramid provides a more nuanced understanding of how to interpret the significance of different levels and kinds of success. For example, it would be a mistake to use Utada Hikaru's pop success and MSC's relative invisibility as evidence of what the mass of youth want. What reaches the top level of pop-music status reflects competition *among that group* of major-label artists who get visibility in mainstream media outlets, rather than representing the outcome of a level–playing field battle among all the musicians active at any given time (up and down the

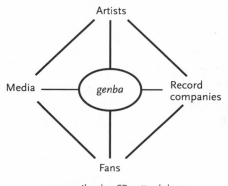

creating styles: songwriting, trackmaking, rap flow
performances: live shows, recording sessions, interviews
networking: collaborations, albums, shows, events

Artists

news: live shows,
new releases,
criticism
promotion:
advertisements,
reviews
entertainment:
interviews, artist
gossip, club
pictures

Media — genba — Record companies

gatekeeping:
choose songs/artists,
schedule releases

positioning power:
place in media
(live, CD, retail,
TV, etc.),
CD distribution

recording studios:
underwrite high tech
production

Fans

consumption: buy CDs, attend shows
fan production: fanzines, web sites, generate buzz

11. *Genba* as intersection of cultural production. Figure by the author.

pyramid). In the diagram of the pyramid, I have tried to highlight how media promotion vehicles shift from minimedia (flyers, free papers, word of mouth) to mass media (magazines, radio, television) depending on the backing of record companies. To some, this structure might suggest that record companies have an overwhelming influence over what music is produced and marketed to the public, but this is only part of the picture. For although record companies have a tremendous amount of power in gatekeeping, they have much less control in determining what will become a hit.

I would propose a second graphic for thinking about power in the recording industry, one that emphasizes the dynamic interaction between the different actors in a music scene (see figure 11). To get a schematic sense of the interacting players, we could begin by focusing on four groups of actors: artists, record companies, media outlets, and fans.[10] Each group maintains a somewhat distinct set of roles in the larger picture. Each has certain types of power, but success depends on all four working in tandem. Artists' success emerges from the buildup of energy and attention among these different players. Each group has power over only some aspects of the process, and only limited influence over the others. In general, artists must network to gain access to live shows and recording opportunities. They are expected to come up with their own musical styles and to perform effectively in clubs and studios. Yet the power of artists (their influence and status) depends on the reactions of record companies, fans, and the media. This model depicts a circular game of rock-paper-scissors that is always unfolding, always in play, and always in the process of becoming. The *genba* is a place where differing orientations and differing roles intersect, and although one site cannot explain all the key factors, the collective focus on the clubs provides a starting point for evaluating the locations of power in popular culture.

Although the *genba* of nightclubs illustrate the different roles and diverse forms of power within a music scene, I do not mean to suggest that everything can be witnessed in these sites of cultural production. As the lines that go around and not through the central hub in the diagram indicate, not all interactions can be viewed through the sites of *genba*. Still, the graphic representation indicates how conceptions of power that focus on binary relationships—such as artist-fan, artist–record company, and so on—tend to underplay the dynamic network effects that generate success.

Now we have an explanation for why politically oriented hip-hop is more likely to be performed in clubs rather than played on the radio. The standards of value for club audiences differ from those of the executives who make programming decisions in the media and in record companies. Groups with powerful oppositional voices can occasionally break into the cultural mainstream if the media and fan support proves sufficient. But if we assume that the absence of political groups in the pop charts indicates a general political disengagement on the part of fans, we ignore the larger picture of media and record company gatekeeping that controls who has access to mainstream marketing muscle. Such gatekeeping is one of the structural reasons why an underground group like MSC may have more potential to bring about change in political structures than their sales alone would suggest. Still, let us consider the more commercially successful major-label artists for points of contrast.

Rip Slyme: The Biggest Hip-Hop Hit of 2002

What is an example of a recent hip-hop hit? After years of performing in small clubs, the five-member Tokyo-based group Rip Slyme finally achieved a big hit. The five band members were born between 1973 and 1979 and released their first album in 1995. Seven years later, they released the album *Tokyo Classic*, which sold over 920,000 copies during 2002. It finished in ninth place among the top-selling albums of the year.[11] Two singles from the album did quite well too. The group's top single, "Rakuen Baby," finished number 31 in the year for sales and number 39 among the most requested karaoke songs. The value of the group's total sales was roughly ¥3.7 billion

($35 million). Although the five-member crew did not sell as much as pop divas Utada Hikaru and Hamasaki Ayumi, or the rock band Mr. Children, that year, Rip Slyme does provide an example of what pop hip-hop achieved in 2002. The album came out in July, and the top single mixed images of beaches, bikinis, suntans, and surfing. Here is the chorus:

endless-summer paradise baby	*tokonatsu no rakuen beibei*
coconuts and sunshine crazy	*kokonattsu to sanshain kureijii*
gonna hold you till the morning	*motte ku asu no asa made*
summer day	summer day

—Rip Slyme (2002) "Rakuen Baby" *Tokyo Classic* (Warner Music Japan, WPC7-10147)

This type of puppy-love imagery and the nonconfrontational, inoffensive lyrics align with the larger J-pop world. The use of English-language lyrics in the chorus, for example, rhyming *"asa made"* (until the morning) with "summer day" (*samaa dei*) is also a common feature of J-pop. The music mixes Spanish guitar and programmed beats in a way that is undeniably catchy— but is it hip-hop? Based on the sound of the group's hit album alone, some rap fans denigrate Rip Slyme as "merely pop" (*tada no kayōkyoku*). Yet Rip (as they are affectionately called) spent many years performing in underground clubs, including participating in the 1997 FG Night event described above. Their passage through the clubs gives Rip a fair amount of legitimacy in the eyes of many hip-hop artists in Japan, even if it is respect tinged with jealousy over the group's phenomenal success.

Dabo: Major-Label Gangsta Fantasies

Not all major record labels promote hip-hop as a subgenre of J-pop. We might consider Dabo, who performs harder-edged, more abrasive tough-guy lyrics. He began with the crew Nitro Microphone Underground and signed a solo deal with Def Jam Japan, whose female head, Riko Sakurai, we will meet in chapter 6. The original Def Jam in New York City was founded by Russell Simmons, and its early, extremely successful artists included Run-DMC, the Beastie Boys, and LL Cool J, to name just a few. In 2001, the original Def Jam launched Def Jam Japan under the umbrella of Universal Music, at the time the largest record company in the world. Dabo was one of Def Jam Japan's early projects.

Dabo's first album *Hitman* was slickly produced, with booming tracks, on-location photo shoots, magazine advertisements, and even music videos (see figure 4 for the album cover). The promotion videos featured Dabo driving expensive cars, waving platinum jewelry, and bragging about being a hit man: gunning down enemies, making hit records, and knocking the ball out of the park. Most striking to me is the imagery in this song featuring Tokona X (of M.O.S.A.D.), which aimed to strike a chord with fans harboring gangsta fantasies.

Yakuza punk, you wanna kill me?	*chinpira, ore o koroseru ki?*
Ha! you're too soft	*Ha! amai wa kochi tora*
I'm a pro, the gunman in the dark . . .	*puro yami no ganman . . .*
Tokarev, rifle, bazooka,	*tokarefu, raifuru, bazuuka,*
machine gun, hand grenade	*mashingan, teryūdan*
you choose how you're gonna die, ha!	*erabe doitsu de shinenda Ha!*

—Dabo (2002) "Murda!!!! (Killa Emcee) feat. Tokona-X" *Hitman* (Def Jam Japan / Universal, UICJ-1005)

For some Japanese fans, hip-hop is attractive because it offers this exciting "realness" of mortal combat. Driving expensive cars, outsmarting other criminals, and outrunning the cops—it beats studying for exams or working at a convenience store. There are, of course, very real differences between rapping about guns in the United States and in Japan. Gun deaths in Japan number fewer than a hundred annually. In the United States, about thirty thousand people die from guns each year (about half of them homicides, half suicides and accidents). African American youth are especially at risk. Thus violence and desire mingle complexly depending on one's location.

So Dabo's fantasy is not real, but is it an imitation of the West? Perhaps not. Japan produces plenty of homegrown gunplay imagery on its own. People get gunned down all the time in the anime series *Cowboy Bebop* or *Ghost in the Shell*, in countless Yakuza films, and in the movie *Battle Royale* (dir. Fukasaku Kinji). One of the more striking examples is manga artist Santa Inoue's series *Tokyo Tribe*. Serialized in *Boon* magazine, the story follows several street gangs from different sections of Tokyo and its environs battling it out with swords and guns in fits of ultraviolence. The youthful gang members listen to hip-hop, eat at Denny's, and mix with various elements of Japan's underworld of drug dealers, prostitutes, and Yakuza. Gangs guard their turf. It could be anywhere, but the comic is set in Tokyo and reflects a domestically produced street-culture toughness. Even calling this "glocalization" suggests a source elsewhere, when in fact the imagery comes from several intersecting streams at once.

I would argue that the central importance of the gun fantasies in Dabo's videos has nothing to do with glocalization or imitation. What Dabo's videos illustrate is that major-label support can buy slick production and promotion styles, yet at the cost of adding to the number of hands contributing to the overall project. The movement away from the artist's onstage performance toward imagery that works in the boardroom helps us understand the links between gangsta and executive. Indeed, the album's title *Hitman* explains it best of all. Using the imagery of guns, expensive cars, and professional sports is less a reflection of stereotypes of African Americans, a theme explored in chapter 1, than the expression of a desire to be associated with commercial success. Whether Dabo came up with the ideas himself or not is unimportant. The key point is that we can see the alliances deemed central to building Def Jam's global brand, as when Dabo shouts out "Def Jam Japan" in songs and in the videos. Dabo is a talented emcee attempting to translate this "stance" (*sutansu*) into the tough language of young people, especially young men, in Japan. At the same time, he promotes an idea of commercial success through gunplay hip-hop that takes performance into the realm of fantasy. Dabo's *Hitman* effort, despite major-label backing, failed to generate a big hit, a reminder that major-label promotion is not sufficient to guarantee success.[12] Moreover, not everyone agrees that Dabo's tough-guy rap is any more hip-hop than Rip Slyme. In fact, one emcee wanted to prove Dabo was not hip-hop at all.

Hip-Hop Proof: The Battle between Dabo and Kan

Hip-hop offers an intriguing case study of popular culture in part because of its ontological questioning of its own ranking of artists, fans, and media networks. The pyramid of the scene does not come ready-made, but evolves through ongoing competition among different groups and families of groups against the backdrop of a changing Japan. A *genba* perspective starts with these performative locations to see how different perspectives highlight alternative values for music. In this regard, clubs are notable for providing a space where the boundaries between the majors and the indies are more fluid and where the battles for legitimacy and significance sometimes occur face to face.

In Tokyo, July 20, 2004, was one of the hottest days on record, never dipping below 40 degrees centigrade (104 degrees Fahrenheit). On the streets, salarymen were wilting, women in light cotton kimonos were dressed for summer *matsuri* (festivals), and hawkers were handing out paper fans advertising the latest cell phones. Although it was a Tuesday afternoon, O-East, a large performance space in the love-hotel area of Shibuya, held a hip-hop and reggae showcase starting at four in the afternoon, clearly hoping to pull in students on summer vacation. The performers ranged from dancehall new-comer Bigga Raiji, veteran emcee Uzi, "the 9 milli," and hip-hop team Haga-kure, whose name echoes the title of an eighteenth-century book of sayings about "the way of the samurai" (Yamamoto 1979). (This gives a small sense of the eclectic references characteristic of artists' group names.) Although the air conditioning cooled the roughly seven hundred fans in the pitch-black space, tempers flared onstage during the final performance. Mōsōzoku, the headline act, opened their set with a video clip showing a fantasy of them as car-jacking toughs, selling high-priced stolen vehicles to Yakuza and then gunning them down when the deal went bad. It was *furyō* (bad boy) style to the fullest. They were clearly competing with the other groups before them — Maguma MCs from Kyoto, Kaminari Kazoku (a Tokyo mainstay), and Romero S.P. from Yokohama — to be the baddest of the bad. Mōsōzoku featured the female reggae sensation Minmi, who led the crowd in a spirited "F.U.C.K." chant. Then one of the group's emcees, Hannya, called Dabo out on stage to join him for a song.

Dabo, trim in a white tank top and low-slung jeans, got the audience mov-ing with his distinctive gravel-voiced style, rapping a song called "Osōshiki" ("Funeral"). In the middle of the song, Kan of MSC jumped on stage, ran up to Dabo, and stood right in his face, staring him down. MSC were not on the bill, but they had performed a song with the previous act Shonan no Kaze. At first, Kan said nothing. He just stared down Dabo as the latter kept rap-ping, trying to back away, clearly wondering what was going on. A few other emcees approached, but Kan would not be pushed away. Then, before Dabo could finish his verse, Kan grabbed the microphone out of his hand, while the DJ stopped the music and a dozen artists and hangers-on ran up and began pushing Kan around. It was a tense moment, clearly one punch away from a full-fledged brawl, and indeed Mōsōzoku had been at the center of a brawl in a major freestyle battle the year before. But before any violence started, Kan challenged Dabo to a freestyle, right then and there. A collective "whoa" rose from the audience. Dabo, looking pained but feigning bemusement, had no choice but to accept the challenge. That Kan could jump on the stage and chal-lenge Dabo in public highlights the openness of this *genba* and the fluidity of boundaries in clubs.

Kan started an a cappella freestyle that drew a contrast between the in-dependent hip-hop scene in Japan, where he and his crew remain, and the majors' scene, where Dabo is respected. Kan said repeatedly that he was showing his "proof of hip-hop" (*hippuhoppu no shōmei*), emphasizing his verbal skill and his choice of themes (i.e., rapping about Japan's poor, not some entertainment-based fantasy world). Dabo then took his turn with an a cappella freestyle, putting down Kan's style and questioning his legitimacy and his motives. Didn't Kan just want to raise his status by challenging a more successful emcee? After the show, I asked Kan about his beef with Dabo. Kan explained, "When I rap, it's not things from a manga or a movie. I'm rapping about real life. The beef isn't about business, even though I only get released on indie labels, and he works with major companies. The issue is that I have higher hopes for hip-hop in Japan. It shouldn't just be for show." (Unlike Kan, Dabo did not come out in the audience after his performance, or I would have asked for his opinion as well.)

In the end, the crowd seemed to respond more positively to Dabo's rap. Based on the bad-boy artists in the day's lineup, it makes sense that the crowd would respond more favorably to Dabo. Although there was no movement by those onstage to determine a winner, Hannya concluded that we all had witnessed "real hip-hop" (*honmono no hippu hoppu*). This speaks to a sense of participation in a global movement that values the connection between lyrics, improvisational skill, and public competition. Such an ideology is not unique to hip-hop, but it does contrast with more mainstream J-pop, where lyrics for the top teen idols are commonly written by others and often speak of generic love or abstract fantasies. Indeed, it was this fantasy side of popular music that Kan was protesting against, something he had also rapped about on MSC's first album, which criticized Dabo (though not by name) for appearing in a video driving an expensive SUV, even though Dabo does not have a driver's license. These tensions between entertainment and politics, business and performance, boil over in today's Japanese hip-hop, thus extending the idea of battling samurai beyond the bounds of hip-hop and out into mainstream Japan. The question is, where will it lead Japanese youth?

Conclusion

The concept of *genba* globalization focuses attention on performative epicenters and outward waves of influence. Clubs in the Japanese hip-hop scene exemplify this kind of epicenter, drawing together the range of participants who actualize the scene by improvising as they go. Indeed, I would suggest freestyle in clubs—as a particular kind of open-ended, improvisatory battle—symbolizes an understanding of globalization that focuses on particular contests for power among diverse social actors. One advantage of this perspective on global culture is that it does not attempt to classify whether certain aspects are local or global, imitative or real. Rather, the global is performed. When it works, history is made. What happens in clubs, of course, is only a small part of people's everyday lives. I also discussed the larger social contexts of Japan's changing society: the rise in the number *freeter* facing an uncertain economic future; the end of the credentials society; and the increasing questioning of middle-class ideals. Meanwhile, corporate interest in content industries and the government's interest in soft power point to a growing centrality of popular culture in the political economy of Japan. Clubs deserve a privileged position in the analysis of hip-hop in Japan because they are the location where the diverse actors converge to evaluate the scene. Clubs focus people's attention and energies. They constitute key spaces for gauging the fuel that keeps hip-hop in Japan burning.

I also argue that the idea of the *genba* offers a way of moving forward with some of the insights concerning new approaches to the study of culture within and beyond anthropology. Gupta and Ferguson's emphasis on location, rather than the local, draws attention to the political consequences of cultural activities. This presents a useful alternative to thinking of cultural styles as primarily defined by a village, community, or, by extension, a national group. This move within anthropology is mirrored by a more folk understanding of hip-hop culture as something that transcends national boundaries while also providing firm ideologies for living and acting in the here and now. By this logic, cultural interventions derive their force not from their origin, but through a collective embodiment in a *genba*. For example, it is there that independent rappers and major-label rappers both get the opportunity to make their case for success.

In this sense, MSC's idea that structural reform can begin in a late-night club, among students and *freeter* questioning their place in a changing adult world, is not so far fetched. To dismiss their ranting because they have not sold millions is to accept entertainment companies' definition of value and the spurious idea that strong sales offer an accurate reflection of democratic desire. In fact, only a small fraction of the artists making music can get the backing needed to produce a hit. As the media increasingly plays a significant role in economies and politics, we need a deeper understanding of these dynamics, and an ethnographic perspective, even from the smoky bowels of underground Tokyo, reveals a wide range of places in which to look for new imaginings of a better future.

CHAPTER 4

RAP FANS AND CONSUMER CULTURE

On July 7, 1996, about four thousand rap fans gathered at an outdoor amphitheater in downtown Tokyo to attend the largest Japanese hip-hop event up
until that time. The showcase, called Thumpin' Camp, featured over thirty
rappers, deejays, and break-dancers from Japan's underground scene. The
heavy rains failed to dampen the spirits of the audience, who cheered and
bounced and waved their arms throughout the three-hour show. The energy
of the crowd had its effect on the performers. At one point, Mummy-D, a rapper with the group Rhymester, paused between songs to acknowledge the
fans. "I've got something to say today, so listen up," he said.

This hip-hop scene was not made only by us. It was not made only by the people on
stage here today. I want you to give it up [*sasage yo*] for all the rappers, deejays, graffiti writers, and dancers in Tokyo! [*cheers from the audience; the* DJ *starts the music for the
next song, but the rapper yells*] Wait, wait. Not yet, there's more. For all the b-boys who
came from outside Tokyo and who are planting the roots of hip-hop in other areas, give
it up! [*cheers*] And last, the people who have come here, you who understand Japanese
hip-hop, for all our supporters (*sapōtaa*), give it up! [*cheers*][1]

With that, the DJ started the backing record. A plaintive bass line droned out
a groove that was gradually met by a pounding backbeat. The rappers started

yelling the title line of their song "Mimi o kasu beki" (You Better Listen Up!), and the audience shouted it back again in response. As the song continued, the rappers encouraged their youthful listeners to "follow the path to their dreams" and to "find the energy to leave something for the next century." A song devoted to youthful vigor and commitment, it was emblematic of these hip-hoppers' stance toward their fans.

This back-and-forth shouting between performer and fan is an apt place to begin a discussion of rap fandom because it highlights that both performers and fans must listen and that both must perform. The circuits of mass culture are given their vitality and meaning at least in part from the style of that communication. Fans and performers together create a scene (*shiin*), but one wonders whether it can be called a community. Will it produce a global hip-hop nation?

For Rhymester, the scene emerges by planting throughout Japan the roots of hip-hop's four elements: rap, deejaying, break-dance, and graffiti. Being in the scene means not only listening to the music but, more actively, taking part in performances and events. Mummy-D calls the fans "those who understand" (*rikaishatachi*), not only because they understand in an intellectual way what hip-hop is all about—from its origins at Bronx block parties in the late 1970s to its global conquest twenty years later—but also because they understand how to feel rap. Rap fans sense the building tension of a song or freestyle session. They anticipate the moments when a rapper will hold out the microphone for the crowd to fill in lyrics. They know when to wave their arms and cheer and when to be quiet. The combination of understanding and action is the essence of being a music fan. But what is it like to be a rap fan in Japan?

In this chapter I examine the relationship between rap fans and Japan's consumer culture. Between the moments of expectant silence and explosive release falls a shadow of doubt about the appropriateness of fans' attachments. The music industry blurs the line between culture and commerce and draws into question the commitments of fans and the claims of performers. One must recognize, for example, that communication between fans and performers remains largely one-way, mediated by marketing teams bent on utilizing communicative technologies for profit. Fans generally have access only to the persona, not the person, of the musicians. Musicians might flicker briefly on a distant stage or on a cathode-ray tube or be immortalized as digital data on a CD or offer their insights in music magazines, but they never drop by for a heart-to-heart talk. The relationship between fan and performer is a social one, but it is a sociality limited by the form of the medium and tinged with a profit-making aspect. How, then, do Japanese fans get down with hip-hop? Do hip-hop fans constitute a symptom of expanding consumerism as a feature of global modernity? The shape of hip-hop fandom—those fans appearing after the trendy consumers known as *shinjinrui* and distinguished from the supposedly asocial and obsessive *otaku* fans—allows us to extend our understanding of the multiple participants who produce the music scene in Japan.

Consumption and Globalization

The mediated sociality of popular music evokes many of the anxieties surrounding consumption and globalization. It raises questions of the power of capitalism and the power of consumers to create their own worlds out of often-standardized, mass-marketed, mass-produced goods. Consumerism shapes capitalism while extending its reach, becoming integrated into notions of national and local identities (Clammer 1997; Miller 1995b). The anthropologist Daniel Miller argues that people's desire to consume creatively is not about a choice, but rather a desire to overcome a "potential state of rupture," that is, an existential uneasiness caused by the recognition that "one is living through objects and images not of one's own creation" (Miller 1995a, 1). Generally, he argues, people admire authenticity through creation: if you make it, it is yours. Defining oneself in terms of consumption internalizes this "sense of rupture" at the core of modernity.

Nevertheless, fans offer a telling example of people overcoming this sense of rupture. In many ways, fans epitomize both the rewards and distortions of consumer culture. For fans, consumption is largely an end in itself. For a magazine writer or a sports gambler, attendance at an event may primarily be a means to some other end—an assigned story or a winning wager. Rap artists who attend shows of other artists are more likely to view their presence as a kind of work. They may come to network, or because they feel obligated to attend a friend's show. Also, as one rapper said, "I can't enjoy the shows because I end up studying [what they're doing]." For the fan, the experience of an event serves as the primary objective. Such an experience will likely become productive in some sense, perhaps circulated as talk with friends or as fan letters or even as a fanzine (Fiske 1992). Nevertheless, being a fan means in part to content oneself with the act of consumption. Fans can be viewed as ideal consumers and thus provide a means of critically examining consumption in everyday life.

The consumption of cultural products constitutes an active process of identity formation, as many have shown (e.g., McRobbie 1993; Radway 1991), but the tensions inherent in this process are not resolved simply through the assertion of identity. Part of being a fan is preserving some distance between oneself and the artist, such that one can discriminate, for example, between excellent and lackluster performances. The anthropologist William Kelly notes that fandom entails instabilities on at least two axes: fans care more and know more than average consumers or audiences, but this intersection of knowledge and passion is always shifting. A second axis of instability is fans' involvement in the intense play between identification and skeptical distancing in enacting fandom. Fandom is a gesture of intimacy toward commodified culture, but intimacy is not identity (Kelly 2004, 7)

These notions of rupture and instability point to the contradictions inherent in being a consumer and a fan. I would argue that we should recognize an additional source of instability, namely, the vague but ubiquitous condition of information overload. One feature of media-saturated, late-capitalist societies is the constant overflow of available information—part commodity, part resource—something that always exceeds the consumer's grasp. This condition helps us extend our exploration of globalization and questions of homogenization versus diversity. Given that there is always too much to choose from, we can observe in selective consumption a source of the unevenness of global flows. In other words, anxieties about the impact of the Westernness of so-called Western-style consumerism may be less important than other distortions caused by particular consumption patterns. Marshall McLuhan (1962) proposed that electronic media would bring the world together as a common global village, but while we may have an increasing awareness of what goes on around the world thanks to the media, I would argue that it is easy to become overwhelmed by the superfluity of information, a condition that can result in heightened feelings of powerlessness in the face of global networks. In this, the sense of rupture has less to do with the fact that we did not create consumer goods (Daniel Miller's concern) than with a sense that we cannot do anything about it.

The language of fandom can give us some clues to the social processes emerging from attempts to deal with these contradictions. How are fans and consumers described? At nightclubs, fans are most often called *okyakusan* (customers/guests), a term that strongly suggests a paying customer for a service. People more committed to a specific group or genre are called *fuan* (fans). Someone obsessed with collecting objects (e.g., records) would likely be termed *maniakku* (maniac). One of the most intriguing designations is *otaku*, which refers to a reclusive consumer of media-generated objects (e.g., video games, comic books, music, animation). *Otaku* are regarded as obsessive fans who exchange the real world for closed-off, media-generated worlds, of which Japanese animated movies stand as the most representative case. The sense in which the *otaku* are closed off from society is something I will explore below. I would suggest that these supposed media geeks are more than the other within mainstream society.[2] Indeed, with the mainstreaming of *otaku* status in digital technology success, the term is already becoming outdated, as "true otaku" are now more likely to be referred to as *ota-kei* (i.e., *ota* type, with *ota*, a shortened version of *otaku*, written in katakana *wo ta*). Nevertheless, there is reason to believe that *otaku* offer a particularly suggestive rhetoric for thinking about contemporary fans. *Otaku* are important not because they (personally) are closed off from society but because one of the consequences of globalization is the marooning of social groups on disconnected islands in space. I would argue that the feeling of being *otaku* is becoming more widespread, and this tells us something about the shape of cultural globalization in an age of information overload.

In particular, I argue that 1990s Japan witnessed a transformation affecting the place of popular culture in society and that this transformation can be observed in the self-organization of hip-hop fans. Put simply, there are two broad trends: one, an increasing massification of popular culture, and two, an increasing diversification of niche markets with intensely specialized fans. With respect to music, for example, there was a dramatic increase in the number of million-selling hit singles in the 1990s compared to previous decades. According to the lyricist and writer Kōtarō Asō (Asō 1997, 12–13), there were two million-selling singles in the 1970s, including a children's song called "Oyoge! Taiyaki-kun" (Swim! Little Fish-Shaped Cake), but none in the 1980s. The Recording Industry Association of Japan (RIAJ) reports that the 1990s witnessed an explosion of million-sellers, peaking in 1999, with thirty different million-selling albums.[3] Since 1999, however, the number of million-selling albums and singles has dropped off sharply, thus pointing to changes in the music business that I will examine in chapter 7. At the same time, specialized scenes in Japanese hip-hop, reggae, and techno, for example, are becoming more established as Japanese artists release more albums and even travel overseas to export their styles.[4] Some sociologists in Japan argue that cultural consumption no longer acts as a broad structuring process in and of society because a growing number of fans come to inhabit relatively autonomous "islands in space" (Miyadai 1994). If this is true (and I will try to show how this phenomenon functions in Japan's pop music world), then we need to reconsider whether cultural consumption retains the structuring power

that Pierre Bourdieu (1984) found in 1960s France. The growing massification and increasing diversification of Japanese popular culture is leading to a
broad restructuring of the meaning of consumption, and this has effects on
social organization as well. One way of understanding this transformation is
through the *otaku* characterization of fans.

To explore these issues, I begin with an ethnographic sketch of two concerts in 1996 that epitomized the distinct kinds of fandom in existence for
party rap and underground hip-hop. Next, I will reexamine the history of
postwar Japanese pop music in terms of music fans, comparing genres and
evolving social attachments of music fans. Then I turn to two trends in the
consumer culture of the 1980s and 1990s, namely, the contrast between *shinjinrui*, a "new breed" of conspicuous consumers, and *otaku*, the reclusive fans.
These two ideal types embody different approaches to media, fandom, and
social relations. Finally, I return to hip-hop fans to consider their process of
self-definition in relation to more widely popular forms of mass culture. I
conclude with a discussion of what these music fans tell us about the intersection of music, media, and fandom in late-capitalist Japan.

Two Worlds of Japanese Rap Fans

As we have observed, the boundaries of Japanese hip-hop are continually
shifting. Like the evolving rap battles discussed in chapter 2, rap fandom can
be viewed in terms of relative competition and relative pleasures, a kind of
creative interaction at the heart of all fan practices, producing more than "personal experience" but rather intimating larger moral economies (see Jenkins
1992, 279–84). Two shows I attended during the summer of 1996 illustrate
key contrasts between two main trends in the rap scene in the mid-1990s,
namely, between underground hip-hop and party rap. The Thumpin' Camp
show provided a defining moment for the underground hip-hop scene, with
its sellout crowd and broad-ranging participants. A week later, in the same
outdoor amphitheater in Hibiya Park, the party rappers convened for their
own sellout showcase. In some ways the dichotomy captures only some aspects of mid-1990s hip-hop. Even in 1996, most rappers objected to the
simplistic dichotomy between underground and party styles for at least a
couple of reasons. Rap groups tend to be organized into loose networks,
often called families (*famirii*), that perform together and collaborate on each
other's albums.[5] These collectives constitute the most appropriate rubrics for
understanding style affinities and differences because they share the most
in their approaches to music, performance, and their audiences. The party-

underground dichotomy overstates the commonalties among the families. Another objection to the party-underground split is that all the artists tend to listen to the same music. Although they are likely to identify different favorites, they all share an appreciation for American hip-hop as a whole. To divide J-rap into two armies is analytically convenient, but according to rappers, it both overstates the similarities within each camp and obscures their shared musical foundation in American hip-hop.

With regard to fans who attend the shows, however, the differences between underground and party rap are undeniable. The most striking difference can be seen in the gender distribution. The audience for Thumpin' Camp was roughly 80 percent male, and this ratio was reversed for the Dai LB Matsuri (Big LB [Little Bird] Festival). In both cases, teenagers ranging from junior high school to college age formed the bulk of the audiences, with a slightly higher average age apparent for the underground show. The baggy b-boy clothing style was more prevalent at Thumpin' Camp, and almost everyone was wearing a hat (floppy Kangol or baseball caps with the visor backwards or short-brim golf hats, etc.). At moments of excitement, the Thumpin' Camp audience would nod their heads to the beat and wave their hands in a fawning motion toward the stage. At the LB Festival, hands were waved side to side (as I have seen at other pop-oriented shows), and a kind of full-body bob with the audience members flexing their knees accompanied the catchier tunes.

It was also striking to note the different approaches to performance and the distinct ideas about what the audience should see and do. At Thumpin' Camp, the kind of propaganda that Mummy-D shouted — "We are all working at making hip-hop in Japan" — was echoed by other artists as well: "So many people are here, clearly a true scene has arrived," and "This is real hip-hop." Fans were encouraged to "spread the word and live hip-hop culture." Almost every group led the audience in a call-and-response ritual of "Say Ho!" All of it was done in the Japanese language. The tone was macho and slightly reckless, as when You the Rock announced, "The show is not over until I stage dive into the audience." The standard greeting of the Kaminari outfit seemed to capture the sought-after emotional response: "How are you? My crazy brothers" (chōshi wa dō dai? Ikareta kyōdai). The performers presented an irate, confrontational stance aimed at unspecified others who threatened the individuality of the rappers and audience (and who threatened their shared commitment to hip-hop culture). One of the few overtly political messages came from K Dub Shine, a rapper with King Giddra, who called on the audience to shout at the Health and Welfare Ministry building visible from the concert area in protest against the HIV-tainted-blood scandal which had dominated headlines in the previous weeks.[6]

At the Big LB Festival, the atmosphere was as different as the weather. A warm, sunny day made the free visors advertising the "LB Nation" a welcome present. The stage had two DJ platforms at the back and an enormous banner that read "Little Bird Nation." On the left part of the stage stood a large bird house. The tone was playful and upbeat. Although there were also several sessions of "Say Ho!" many of the activities between songs were aimed at getting the audience to laugh. A couple of times, for example, a cannon blast went off, clearly startling whoever was on stage, and then a rapper from one of the other groups would come running out of the bird house with a sign reading "b-boy dokkuri" (b-boy surprise!), which elicited much giggling. Most performances had an element of self-ridicule. When Dassen Trio came on stage (the group of Osaka rappers who started out as comedians), two members were wearing white Elvis outfits and sporting huge Elvis wigs. The third member, the self-proclaimed "fatso" (*debu*) MC Boo, was wearing a skin-tight Superman outfit. The show as a whole featured numerous nods to mainstream pop culture, such as a fifteen-minute skit that parodied a popular music information TV show called *Waratte ii to mo* (*It's Good to Laugh*).

In sum, the two events illustrate that style differences are reflected not only in the sound of the music but also in the mode of communication between performers and fans. We see different approaches to framing the program. In Thumpin' Camp, Rhymester gave props to all Japanese hip-hoppers, while K Dub Shine inserted criticism against the government. At the Big LB Matsuri, a festival kind of feeling pervaded, provoking laughs with exploding cannons, outlandish costumes, and comedy sketches. The self-important authenticity of the underground scene contrasted with the self-deprecating parody of the party scene. Before analyzing in greater detail the meaning of these style differences, however, we need to understand a little of the broader context of fandom in Japan's popular music world. How did such fan-performer relationships function in the past?

Historical Perspectives on Postwar Music Fans

As we saw in chapter 2, throughout the postwar period, there has been a dynamic relationship between Western musical imports and Japanese-style transformations. When such forms veer toward the commercial end of the spectrum, they tend to be defined as *kayōkyoku* (Japanese pop). In other cases, such as early Japanese versions of folk, rock, and rap, musicians emphasize their underground (*angura*) status, namely, an oppositional stress on authenticity over commercialism. New genres tend to be defined in contrast to what is popular (commercially successful) at any given time, and rap is no exception. To understand rap fans, we need to get some sense of how they differ from more mainstream pop music consumers. Several studies of postwar pop music give us a look at these developments over time (Asō 1997; Hosokawa, Matsumura, and Shiba 1991; Miyadai, Ishihara, and Otsuka 1993).

In the early years after World War II, jazz rose to prominence as the most popular music genre, experiencing a boom in the early 1950s, but building on the foundation of a prewar fascination with jazz associated with modernism (Atkins 2001; Hosokawa, Matsumura, and Shiba 1991, 13). A counterpoint to this "drunken-craze with American boogie woogie," however, was offered by then child singer Misora Hibari, who restored a "melancholy voice to Japan, at a time of rapid economic growth and generally conservative cultural renaissance" (Tansman 1996, 115). In 1952, at the age of fifteen, Hibari sang "Ringo no uta" (Apple Melody), a sad song about a young girl's longing for her country home, and sold a postwar record of 70,000 albums (122).

Three Japanese sociologists of youth culture have traced the ways the evolution of Japanese popular music set in motion specific types of communication between musicians and fans (Miyadai, Ishihara, and Otsuka 1993). In 1965, there was an "electric guitar boom," started in part by the Japan tour of the Ventures, an American surf music act that maintains a strong following even today. This music was "so strange, it was if the musicians had stepped off a flying saucer," and the music generated for its youthful fans a specific meaning of "us": we youth understand electric guitar music, they (adults) do not (61). In 1966, the Beatles toured Japan and sparked a "group sounds" (GS) boom, prompting many bands styled after the Fab Four and ushering in a new kind of communication between musicians and fans. The "mutual interpenetration" (*sōgō shintō*) of emotion (*kanjōsei*) and experience (*taiken*) became an issue: "The only people who understand this music are us"—the fans (61). It was no longer simply the newness of the sound that made it cool to youth and opaque to adults. It was the specific emotional stake that a music style offered to its fans that became paramount in determining its ability to attract and retain fans.

The question of emotional stake also relates to the media by which the music was experienced. In the early 1960s, singers like Misora Hibari were mostly seen onstage at large concerts or were heard on the radio. In such media, it seems likely that although looks were not irrelevant, they were less valued than a powerful singing voice (Asō 1997, 18–19). As the 1960s progressed, however, a new brand of teenage singers using youth slang and sing-ing about high school life began to appear on television.[7]

In the late 1960s, folk music became popular among college students. The appeal of so-called college folk was its connotation of being metro-politan (*tokai-teki*) as opposed to rural (*inaka-teki*). Mouthing English lyrics and the harmonies of Peter, Paul and Mary became the urban ideal. A hit song by the Folk Crusaders, a group assembled through a magazine talent search, sparked many folk-sounding versions of pop songs. This changed the dynamic in such a way that, afterward, real folk represented anticom-mercialism, while *kayōkyoku* (including its folklike manifestations) was asso-ciated with commercialism (Miyadai, Ishihara, and Otsuka 1993, 64). Hence the new appellation "underground folk" (*angura fōku*) emerged, and the fan base of folk music widened to include working students and young working women. It is striking how the distinction between authentic and commercial appears time and again, often spurred by a noteworthy hit song then decried as "inauthentic." This could be called the paradox of pop, because the fruits of a group's success (popularity) also plant the seeds for a group's demise (criticism of being too commercial). This extends our understanding of the pyramid of the music scene by pointing to the tenuous grasp many musicians have on any particular level of success. It also reminds us that fans' views of their artists "appropriate" level on the pyramid is part of what conditions their attachments. If an artist goes too pop, how can a fan feel special appreciating an artist that millions adore?

Given the important role played by television in the development of Japa-nese pop music, how has it influenced fan attachment? In the 1970s, idol (*aidoru*) singers were largely supported by various so-called best-ten pro-grams. In this world, looks were of paramount importance, and the quality of the singing became less significant than the image conveyed. Numerous best-ten music programs continue to be broadcast, but the social context for viewing them has changed. Earlier there was only one TV in the house, and the head of the household controlled the channels: "So when people watched a music program, it was the whole family together. It was an opportunity for the family to become closer through watching as a household. Nowhere in Japan could you find today's situation of a kid in his own room, talking on the phone with a friend, while watching 'Hey! Hey! Hey!' on his own TV" (Asō 1997, 24). As a result, the big hits of the 1970s came mostly from music programs aimed at the whole family. In fact, a children's TV show song from 1975 called "Oyoge! Taiyaki-kun" (Swim! Little Fish-Shaped Cake) held the record as the biggest hit single in Japanese pop music history (4.5 million copies sold) until 1999, when Utada Hikaru's "Automatic" sold over 9 million copies. The children's song type of prime-time, mass appeal can be contrasted with late-night TV associated with underground folk of the 1960s, which played folk music and presented discussions of problems in love and school aimed solely at teenagers and viewers in their early twenties. Miyadai, Ishihara, and Otsuka argue that this solidified a new type of communication between fan and performer such that the fans could come to feel that "only that person understands us [the fans]" (Miyadai, Ishihara, and Otsuka 1993, 64).

Television can be a unifying force, but depending on the content, it can air images that fracture society as well. In the winter of 1972, the nation sat transfixed, watching a live broadcast of the storming of a Red Army mountain retreat (Mizuki 1994, 22–26). When the revolutionaries were finally apprehended, it came to light that the group had killed twelve of its own in a political purge. According to the anthropologist Patricia Steinhoff (1992), the Red Army murders proved even more shocking in light of an analysis that showed the purge as the result of ordinary social processes. It took little more than cascading events driven by peer pressure to turn people, who otherwise appeared reasonable, into murderers. The repercussions were broad ranging. It became unseemly to use the figure of an enemy to generate individual enthusiasm and group solidarity (wareware), and so began the "reactionless era" (shirake no jidai) characterized by nihilistic disinterest (Miyadai, Ishihara, and Otsuka 1993, 66).

With regard to musical communication, one sign of the change in mood was a declining sense of "we" and a more alienated sense of "I," which can be seen in the rise of the singer-songwriter. Thus an aesthetic of "handmade" (tezukuri) folk emerged in the 1970s, along the lines of James Taylor and Carol King. Music that was made and performed by the same person was contrasted with non-handmade, other-produced kayōkyoku. "New music" (nyū myūjikku) grew out of this folk-song tradition during the second half of the 1970s, and it continues to the present. During the 1970s, professional songwriters and composers would hand over the songs for singers to perform. But the 1980s constituted an era of artists who wrote their own lyrics and played their own music. Musicians poured their energy into making albums rather than hit singles. They did not appear on TV and showed no interest in music-ranking programs, which gradually disappeared. In general, solo artists grew in importance vis-à-vis groups. As Miyadai, Ishihara, and Otsuka put it, the key distinction for fans became "only this person understands me" (i.e., no longer "they understanding us") (1993, 67). At the same time, the aesthetic of "self-made, self-performed" (*jisaku jien*) took on ethical significance, a sensibility echoed by today's underground rappers. The female singer-songwriter Matsutoya Yumi (a.k.a. Yuming) can be seen as a representative new music star.

By the mid-1970s, however, this stress on creating original (*orijinaru*) songs found its counterpoint in the expanding use of parody (*kaigyaku*) by musicians, such as the Crazy Cats, who made a name with their gag songs, and Otaki Ei'ichi, a former rocker who turned to parodies of rumba and meringue. At the height of the new music era, this use of parody presented a reversal of values in musical enjoyment. Pleasure derived not simply from hearing something new and unique but rather from recognizing the musical references (*in'yō*) to older work. In the current hip-hop scene, this intertextual enjoyment proves central, particularly for deejays, for whom identifying the samples (*neta*) that make up a given song is a popular pastime and the subject of articles and even of several books (Murata 1997).[8]

The Diversity of Music Genres Increases

The past fifteen years, however, have witnessed a dramatic transformation in the genres of music commanding young people's loyalty. According to a 1990 survey that asked urban college students to identify "music I like," so-called new music (self-made, self-produced) proved the most popular genre (31.2 percent), followed by rock (21.8 percent), pop (15.4 percent), *kayōkyoku* (7.5 percent), classical (5.2 percent), and black contemporary soul (4.5 percent), with house, jazz, fusion, heavy metal, and folk garnering less than 4 percent each (Miyadai, Ishihara, and Otsuka 1993, 59). Singers who wrote their own lyrics and played their own instruments attracted a majority of these listeners, outperforming pop styles. Rock music is popular as well and parallels new music in the sense that Japanese rockers hold to the same ethic of "self-produced, self-performed." Rockers differ, however, from new music artists in their rejection of the melding of emotions with their fans, and they also reject the parody apparent in pop (76). Instead, they tend to emphasize their underground status as a means of asserting their authenticity. Whether it is the hard edge of X-Japan or the more mellow sound of Southern All-Stars, a few Japanese rock bands have achieved large and devoted followings. Although rock is unlikely to disappear, we also see a rising prominence of black music, with expanding examples of Japanese hip-hop, reggae, and R & B. According to surveys of youth and younger adults (junior high school age to mid-thirties) conducted in 2003 by the trade magazine *Oricon*, hip-hop (17.5 percent) and R & B (14.7 percent) were seen as the styles "most likely to break," that is, explode in popularity ("Nisen sannen bureeku" 2003, 24).

One way to understand the shifts taking place in popular music is to observe how fans are integrated into ever-widening mass markets. We see evidence of greater massification in the emergence of global pop stars like Lauryn Hill and in the movement of Japanese popular culture overseas to other parts of Asia, especially the teen idols from Japan (Aoyagi 2000; Ching 1996). The widening mass appeal of Japanese popular music was also apparent in the spike of million-selling hit singles in the mid-1990s. Asō (1997) argues that the rise in the number of these million-sellers was driven in part by the popularity of the karaoke box, that is, a room rented to a small group of friends for singing along to favorite pop songs. The boxes first appeared in 1986, and by 1988 over ten thousand rooms were in use during the day (29). It was women twenty to twenty-five years old who became the main users of CD-singles (a most user-friendly format), and the songs primarily chosen were those associated with prime-time TV trendy dramas. For the purposes of understanding fans, we should note that for these kinds of hits, communication between artist and listener proves less important than the other associations of the song: "Here, we don't see the stance of consumers [or users, *yūzaa*] who say, 'It's because I like this artist.' They like the sound, the way a song matches the taste of a drama, and that it is easy to sing as karaoke. It may not even matter who sings it. . . . We are in an era of 'song hegemony,' when hits are born with no relation to the artist" (39). Interestingly, although these listeners are not regarded as fans, a theme I reconsider in chapter 7, they are not passive. They take a very active role as consumers of music—they learn melodies, familiarize themselves with the lyrics, and even perform the songs. Still, they probably should not be considered fans. Absent any gesture of intimacy toward the artists, we are left with a kind of consumption that is above all concerned with riding the wave of what is popular and communicating with one's friends via these items.

The Little Bird festival, with its references to mainstream pop culture and the absence of exhortations promoting a separate hip-hop culture, fits more comfortably into this style of consumption. Aiming and sometimes achieving a kind of karaoke box–appropriate *kayōkyoku*, party rap is best considered a subset of popular music. In contrast, the Thumpin' Camp audience is the group better identified as Japanese hip-hop fans. They are the protectors of a niche scene premised on the authenticity of the artists, and they define themselves against the hegemonic model of pop music consumption. This dichotomy can be observed in the broader transformation of Japan's consumer culture.

Changing Tides of Consumer Culture in the 1980s and 1990s

Japanese social scientists, as well as workers in the culture industries, identify a broad shift in consumer culture that occurred between the 1980s and 1990s. The 1980s constituted the height of the bubble economy, a time of rapid economic growth financed on the shaky ground of skyrocketing real-estate prices in Tokyo. The dominant youth culture trend was that of the so-called *shinjinrui*. The word was coined in 1984 as a pun that could be read as *shinjin-rui*, connoting the type of "new faces," or *shin-jinrui*, connoting "new human type" (Chikushi 1986, 229). They were the conspicuous consumers of the mid-1980s, symbolic of the wealth of the bubble economy, as well as a vivid display of its ills: "They are people who link their 'classy,' codelike [*oshare na kigō-teki*] consumer practices with their interpersonal relations. By choosing the right car, the right fashion, the right places to eat, and the right spots to play, they choose their companions [*aite o erabi*] and automatically keep away the kinds of people they'd rather not see. They are also the type who hold a 'brand manual' in both hands and communicate via merchandise language [*shōhin gengo*]" (Miyadai 1994, 153). The emphasis is on a group of youth who unite through their sensitivity to what is trendy and fashionable. The notion of *oshare* (classy) speaks to a kind of elegance that signifies not class in Bourdieu's sense, but rather of being in the know. Tanaka Yasuo's 1980 novel *Nan to naku, kurisutaru* (*Somehow, Crystal*) is emblematic of the era; it not only uses consumer items as a vehicle for the story but also indicates in the endnotes where the items can be bought. The plot and characters are less central to the novel than the atmosphere created by brand-name items, a feature that both delighted readers and incensed critics (Field 1989).

A countervailing cultural trend was the emergence of the so-called *otaku*, who are also defined by their relationship with media and consumption but who can be viewed as opposites of the *shinjinrui*: "*Otaku*. Youth who retreat from the *shinjinrui*-style of codelike interpersonal relationships. Instead, they inhabit distinctive 'worlds' [*sekai*] conveyed by media (anime, science fiction, amateur radio, dial-up message boards, . . .)" (Miyadai 1990, 187). They are defined as fanatics who are extremely conversant within their own field of interest but who tend to be asocial loners, "unbalanced specialists" with extreme manias (187). The word *otaku* is essentially an honorific for *home* and hence means "your home" (because one never uses honorifics in reference to oneself or one's own group) and, by extension, "you." The politeness level conveys respect, but it can also communicate a lack of intimacy between "me" and "you." It may also carry the connotation of someone's closed-up room filled with evidence of mania. The term can be used jokingly or casually as an adjective (*otakii*), but most often the use of the term is a sign of repulsion and scorn.

Otaku acquired a particularly negative connotation after 1989 when a man named Miyazaki Tsutomi was arrested for murdering four elementary school girls. His room was found to be filled with thousands of slasher and child-pornography videos. When people began to question the accused's "ecology" (*seitai*), a public debate was initiated about the dangers of youth who live in worlds conveyed by media as a substitute for reality (Miyadai 1994, 153–54). Over time, the idea of *otaku* as a type of person began to give way to a notion of *otaku* as a kind of cultural orientation.[9]

Miyadai argues that in the 1980s, there still existed a broadly shared sense of hierarchy in consumer culture, such that *shinjinrui* consumption was highly valued, at least among their twenty-something cohort, while *otaku*-type specialists seemed to exude a kind of uncoolness (*kakko warusa*). He notes, for example, that the first disco boom of 1978 emerged from the popularity of *Saturday Night Fever* (dir. John Badham, 1977), while the second disco boom of the mid-1980s was related to a *shinjinrui* snobbishness: those who had never gone to a disco were country bumpkins (*inakamono*) (Miyadai 1994, 153–54). But, he adds, by 1989, things had changed. "Does one go out to a eurobeat spot, or house, or maybe not go to a disco at all? A new problem was that the groove might not be personally appropriate [*nori no chigai no mondai*]." He continues,

It became an era where one didn't feel an inferiority complex [for not going out] nor feel superior [for going out]. In the 1990s, this kind of tendency has become even more extreme in the club boom: hip-hop, reggae, new wave, hard core, jazz; or if it's a disco, "flashy" [*parapara*] style or rave style? Everything is lined up side by side, like dispersed "islands in space" [*shima uchū*]. Among these separate islands in space there is no sense of hierarchy, and moreover, they are mutually opaque [to outsiders]. (244–45)

This idea of mutually exclusive islands in space is one way of understanding how consumer culture has changed in Japan. Japanese hip-hop is characteristic of today's splintering of youth movements into such islands. Within hip-hop, there are clear hierarchies and specific meanings, but it is striking how little these qualities are appreciated by fans of other genres. The debate about authenticity—"real" hip-hop from the street, underground, hard core—may carry deep meaning for Tokyo b-boys, but it is a debate that garners no sympathy and little understanding from those outside the circle.

Miyadai argues that what makes Japan a "high-level information society" is precisely the diversification of consumer culture. It is not that people are consuming more, but that more people are consuming differently (142–43). In the late 1950s, everyone wanted the three s's (washing machine, electric rice cooker, vacuum cleaner).[10] In the late 1960s, it was the three c's (air conditioner, car, color TV). But now the commonplace attitude is to wonder, "Why in the world would anyone want that?" Youth of all stripes are becoming *otaku* (extreme specialists within a media world), and moreover, this *otaku*-ization, if you will, of Japanese youth culture is altering the social meaning of consumption. The sense of superiority of the 1980s that *shinjinrui* felt over those who lacked the consumer skills they had mastered gradually disappeared in the 1990s as it became impossible to make comparisons with the inhabitants of closed-off media worlds.

What does an *otaku*-like world look like? Miyadai offers the following generalizations.

(1) otaku within their own tribe are marked by the same jargon (meaningful words among their friends), the same active space, the same knowledge, and same media; but
(2) they are not warm to each other beyond acknowledging the others as "otaku" (whether they actually call each other otaku is not an issue);
(3) as seen from one otaku tribe's perspective, otaku from other tribes make no impression [*mukanshin*], or are considered to be "weirdoes" [*hen na yatsu*] or "another race" [*ijinshu*]; and
(4) the various "islands in space" of different otaku groups are not hierarchically organized and have no feelings of superiority; rather, they are viewed as equivalent. (245)

These features point to a way of understanding fan attachments within overarching changes in the cosmology of consumer culture. With expanding media networks, it is becoming increasingly difficult to keep track of the wide-ranging possibilities for consumption, and hence more difficult to assess the social significance of different practices.

In Bourdieu's (1984) ethnography of 1960s France, upper-class consumers of culture reproduced their status through highbrow cultural practices. But in 1990s Japan, the compartmentalization of music genres is but one example of a larger trend in which cultural practices are opaque to outsiders and are observed without any sense of superiority or inferiority. People are left unmoved by the attachments of others, at least as long as those others remain confined to their islands in space. This forces a reconsideration of Bourdieu's characterization of cultural consumption and its role in structuring society: "In cultural consumption, the main opposition, by overall capital value, is between the practices designated by their rarity as distinguished, those of the fractions richest in both economic and cultural capital, and the practices socially identified as vulgar because they are both easy and common, those of the fractions poorest in both these respects. In the intermediate position are the practices which are perceived as pretentious, because of the manifest discrepancy between ambition and possibility" (176). These oppositions assume a widely shared understanding of cultural capital that may well be disappearing. Take, for example, the case of luxury goods. With Louis Vuitton bags—both originals and knockoffs—widely available, they can no longer serve as markers of a hierarchy of cultural capital, but, rather, simply as matters of taste. This aristocracy of style has no power to inspire emulation. The notion of *otaku*-like islands in space is useful here. Brand-name fanatics are more likely to be ridiculed as just one island among many.

This subversion of the elite's power to set trends also diminishes the subversive potential of so-called subcultural forms. Dick Hebdige writes of punk's revolutionary appropriation of everyday objects (e.g., the safety pin through the ear) that it is "through style, that the subculture at once reveals its 'secret' identity and communicates its forbidden meanings" (Hebdige 1979, 103). In the islands-in-space scenario, however, these forbidden meanings become opaque; they are no longer a source of shock, but merely cause detached bemusement. As a result, the islands turn inward to build a realm of value predicated on the ideologies consonant with their interests. Yet I would argue that while the notion of islands in space is useful for clarifying the weakening of hierarchies of status in consumption, it does not mean all fans are becoming *otaku*.

Hip-Hop Fans: Islands, But Not Otaku

There is evidence of a shift from eighties- to nineties-style consumerism in the Japanese uses of hip-hop. A Sony Records representative in his thirties in an interview in February 1996 described to me some differences between hip-hop in Japan in the mid-1980s and a decade later. He noted that when Run-DMC became popular in Japan in 1986, the Adidas sweat suits and sneakers associated with rap music first appeared in the punk and new wave scenes.

"In our era, there was everything within the subculture." But in the 1990s, things had changed:

As more and more things came out, it became impossible to say "hip-hop" and stop with Run-DMC. Along with the changing era, each scene [*bunya*] became deeper. You had to say, "Run-DMC is not all there is to hip-hop. There are various styles, various artists." But there were too many things to keep track of. So what happened? This was the beginning of otaku. . . . In other words, now one chooses one genre—reggae, hip-hop, computers, animation—and goes deeply into that.

Two points are worth highlighting. One of the driving forces behind the rise of *otaku* is the abundance of cultural goods, "more and more things came out." The increasing diversity of niche cultures and an erosion of their hierarchical ordering can be partly related to the expansion of consumer options. This expansion is itself an outgrowth of corporate, national, and global economic policies often predicated on an ideal of so-called consumer-led growth, as well as of broad-based shifts from Fordist methods of production to flexible accumulation. A second noteworthy point is that "it became impossible to talk" about hip-hop if you only knew Run-DMC. This reminds us that consumption is not only about securing a personal identity but, perhaps more important, about having things to talk about with one's friends.

The hardening of the hip-hop niche in Japan appears in several ways in the late 1990s. In recent years, rappers I interviewed remarked that what is different about the current generation of up-and-coming rappers is that they are into hip-hop only, whereas the mid-1990s rappers grew up on a wide variety of musical styles. The first generation of Japanese rappers all came from other genres of music, especially rock and punk.

Miyadai's characterization of islands in space notes the use of the same jargon, same active space, same knowledge, and same media. For hip-hop fans, we can see this phenomenon in the use of American hip-hop slang, such as describing one's personal ability as "ill skill" (i.e., able lyricism and delivery) and new albums as *buran nyū shitto* (brand-new shit). Hip-hop media range from specialty music magazines including *Front/Blast* ("for hip-hop and R & B freaks"), *Music Magazine* (all-genre criticism), and *Black Music Review* (generally opposed to Japanese rap in the 1990s) to flyers, free papers, and Web sites. There are also a range of wider-circulation fashion magazines focusing on "street style" (*Fine, Woofin', Dazzle,* and *Boon,* to name just a few).

As I have argued, nightclubs (the active space of *genba*) provide some of the most important clues to understanding the character of these islands in space. As we have seen, clubs are the proving ground for rappers and their lyrical salvos, as well as the places where the knowledge and jargon are most valued. In other words, *genba* produce certain kinds of fans, as well as artists. By attending monthly events sponsored by the various families of rap groups, fans have a chance to meet (and, if they are pushy, to have their picture taken with) the artists. They are also spaces of constant circulation, and open social interactions, where one has a chance to meet many of the other regular club-goers. Indeed, to go to a club and speak only to people you know would be somewhat *otakii*. The interactions observed in clubs would seem to call into question whether Miyadai's concept of islands in space with its assertion that "otaku within the same tribe are not warm to each other, beyond acknowledging that they are mutually otaku" can be completely transferred to the hip-hop scene. Having spent considerable time in clubs with what outsiders are likely to call hip-hop *otaku*, I have found quite a lot of warmth, openness, and cama-raderie among clubbers. Clubs specializing in a single genre of music such as hip-hop are primarily urban phenomena. The people who attend these events from around midnight until the trains start running again at 5 a.m. are per-haps best thought of as "the Mobility" (to borrow a Thomas Pynchon phrase), often linked primarily by their attachment to a kind of music, rather than by ties to a common place. Yet as fans, especially of the groups that regularly per-form at certain events, they can come to see each other repeatedly and often form lasting friendships.

Fans Battle Fans as Well

Rap music clubs, as islands in space, are also sites of contestation about what it means to be a fan. A spectrum of behavior extends from that of the casual consumer to that of the active producer, and each step along the way involves an increasing engagement as a Japanese hip-hop fan. These deci-sions can be read as responses to the sense of rupture Daniel Miller identi-fies in peoples' projects of living through objects produced by others. They are also responses to the problem of how to choose among the plethora of consumer items out there, a rupture that seems to me more daunting for today's Japanese youth. The tensions inherent in fandom appear most clearly in criticisms fans make of each other.[11]

The most common criticism of hip-hop fans is that they only care about fashion. Although hip-hop–inspired clothing is a leading style for teenage boys, only a fraction of all the people sporting the baggy pants are actually con-sumers of the music, at least judging from the sales of Japanese rap. Fashion magazines like *Fine* have been active promoters of hip-hop, but the emphasis is on cool style (*kakkoii*) rather than, as many rappers would prefer, on music. On the other hand, buying music alone is often dismissed as a weak gesture of fandom, dependent on the goal of buying. Itagaki Toshiya, the manager of Manhattan Records (a central hip-hop record store in Shibuya), is skeptical of his customers' intentions. "Only about 20 percent of them care about the music," he said. "Many of them just buy records to fill up their room." It seems, he explained, that having a lot of records impresses potential girlfriends. In a January 1997 interview with me, Itagaki questioned the commitment to hip-hop even of those who bought records and went home and played them: "When I was in high school, it was electric guitar. Now it is a couple of turntables and a mixer that all the guys have. In college, they get a sampler and try making a few songs. But once they get a job, they'll turn to snowboarding. It's just about riding the wave of whatever is popular." Some kids apparently come to the store and ask for the distinctive white-and-blue shopping bags to carry around, even if they do not buy anything. "I don't mind," Itagaki laughed; "after all, it's advertising for me, but it shows how unimportant the music is to them."

"He's Just an Otaku*" and Other Pleasurable Put-Downs*

The discourse surrounding fans in many ways constitutes a criticism of the vagaries of consumer culture. To buy does not make one a fan; rather, one must actively engage with hip-hop culture, and this means finding one's own expressive style. Itagaki, as well as many deejays on the club circuit, note that lots of boys call themselves deejays, but when asked where they play, it turns out they only play in their rooms—hence "they're just *otaku*." To prove one's commitment to hip-hop, one must perform in a club, the scene's *genba*, and to show one's skill through battles and moving the crowd.

This belief that the true fan is also a producer highlights the performative aspects of fandom and the range of possible performances. From simply buying clothes to carrying around an empty record-store bag to buying records to listening and studying the music and artists, there is a progression of increasing engagement as a hip-hop fan. Going to a club, becoming a regular at events, trying out one's own hand at deejaying or writing rhymes or practicing break dancing in the park with friends—these represent a deepening involvement. They also encourage some skeptical distancing, in that decisions about how and where to move deeper into the hip-hop scene become unavoidable. Later, one can perform at a club during freestyle sessions, DJ contests, or impromptu dance battles. At each step deeper into the performative aspects of the genre's fandom, one confronts a tension between embarrassment (the risk of any performance) and seduction (the chance to be noticed and appreciated), which heightens the emotional intensity of the fan experience (Frith 1996, 214–15). It is small wonder, then, that there is criticism of those who fail to take the plunge or who go too far and give the genre a bad name. Thus we can see how the transgressions of fandom, vilified in the accusation "he's just an *otaku*," give us a deeper view of the complex identity issues involved.

Returning to the two concerts described at the beginning, we can see that those at the Thumpin' Camp show best deserve the title of Japanese rap fans. The performances of the rappers on stage emphasized a deliberately closed space ("real Japanese hip-hop") that generates its own cosmology of value—meaningful to fellow b-boys and b-girls, but opaque and unimpressive to those outside the circle of commitment. It is their voiced attachment to hip-hop that identifies the showgoers as fans. In contrast, the show by the Little Bird Nation often veered far from the realm of rap music, including a barbershop quartet, an unusual group composed of a singer, a guitarist and a DJ (Tokyo #1 Soul Set), as well as a variety of rap groups aiming for a more pop-oriented sound. There the audience was not expected to go out and "spread the word of hip-hop" since such ideologies of authenticity and realness remained far removed from the playful associations that reigned at the LB Festival. Little Bird adherents regarded the rantings of self-important Thumpin' Camp emcees as a sign of being *otaku*. In both cases, however, we can see how fans participate in contemporary struggles to find meaning in a media-saturated consumer society in which the mainstream forms of cultural capital (a good education leading to a good job leading to a good marriage) are losing their luster.

Conclusion

This chapter began with the proposition that fans epitomize the ideal consumer because for them consumption is its own reward. Although Daniel Miller identifies an unease associated with consumption, it is worthwhile considering how widespread this discomfort is. In some cases, the ability to consume intelligently, finding the right clothes for a good price, for example, can be an empowering feeling. When Yuka, a dancer with the group Now, discovered that the clothing combination she was wearing was featured in a popular fashion magazine, she showed her friends the photo. "I felt like, 'I did it! [*yatta tte kanji*].'" And, she added, "Each piece I bought only cost ¥1000

[$10]." The job of searching through stores, comparing prices, and perusing magazines for the latest trends to gauge the ins and outs of fashion is viewed by some as a kind of productive work in its own right.

This is particularly true in the case of DJs, where the boundary between consumption and production is difficult to demarcate. Their extensive record collections are the raw material of their late-night performances, which to a large extent involve strategies to get the audience excited (*moriagaru*), for example, by choosing a well-liked track. If, however, a song is overplayed (*dasai*), the effect is dulling. An unknown song can spark interest and even draw a few listeners up to the DJ booth to try to read the name of the artist and title from the spinning disk. But playing too many unknown songs can alienate listeners. As an example of the kind of calculations required, we can take a look at the experience of DJ Etsu, a member of the group EDU. He took great pride in an album he found at an outdoor record sale in the fall of 1996. It had the original version of a song then recently remade by the US rap stars the Fugees. Etsu paid a bargain price ($8) for the LP, then spent the next three hours in a fruitless search, combing through thousands of records in cardboard boxes in hopes of another find. Yuka and Etsu may serve as two examples of how consuming something that someone else has produced may cause less a sense of rupture than some despair at there being too much to choose from and too much uncertainty about what best to choose. Their moments of triumph are the exceptions that prove the rule. It is important to recognize, however, that their triumphs (*kachi*) would only seem so among friends within their own island in space.

The significance of the *otaku* in Japan, both as media geeks and as a description of the compartmentalization of today's popular culture, is that this concept points to a new understanding of the ways consumer culture relates to society in general. On the one hand, concern over *otaku* as unbalanced specialists reveals the enduring anxiety about social relationships based on media-generated objects. Returning to William Kelly's notion of fandom's axes of instability, we see that *otaku* exhibit a perversity of both knowledge and passion; they know too much and their feelings verge on the dangerous, occasionally spilling over into grotesque crimes. As one commentator puts it, "What makes a person an otaku is that no matter what genre he pursues, he never grows tired of it" (Asō 1997, 55). This unending commitment represents the dangers of a social life built on consumer items that can become all-consuming.

On the other hand, *otaku* as a general description of the way consumer culture is becoming more compartmentalized contains an important insight. As worldwide media networks extend their reach, there is every reason to believe that two trends in mass culture will only intensify. In one direction are the increasing opportunities for huge global pop phenomena. But any pronouncements that such examples augur an age of homogenizing global mass culture are decidedly premature because at the same time there is a quieter, but equally deep-seated transformation underway. The growing ease of electronic communication and small-scale production (in music, magazines, blogs, on Web sites, etc.) is spawning an increasing diversity of *otaku* communities. As Internet sites, cable and satellite TV channels, magazines, and so on become increasingly specialized, the assessment of the worker at Sony will likely hold true for more people. One cannot say "rap music" and stop with Run-DMC; rather, one needs to choose one thing and go deeply into it.

The islands in space on which hard-core fans can be themselves and commune with fellow travelers with similar interests deserve closer examination, not only in terms of their internal logic but also in comparison to the uses of more massified mass culture. *Community* may be too expansive a word for what fans create, but even in the case of hip-hop, we can see how fellow fans and performers attempt to define and enforce norms of behavior within the group. We need more research to analyze how such media-based communities differ from locale-based ones, but it is critical that we move beyond the common attitude that they are all merely empty or, alternatively, completely dangerous.

CHAPTER 5

RHYMING IN JAPANESE

In this chapter I explore the intersection of hip-hop and the Japanese language. The seeming mismatch between the Japanese language and hip-hop was one of the reasons record companies and music magazines in the early 1990s were skeptical that *Nihongo rappu*, Japanese rap, would ever take off. Japanese rap demonstrates the contingency of linguistic identity. While some *Nihonjinron* (theory of Japanese people) scholars use metaphors of the language's uniqueness to assert a timeless unity between the people, the land, and the language, the diversity of everyday language practices betrays the limitations of stereotypes. Ineffable, vague, polite—the discourses of Japanese language echo those of society. Meanwhile hip-hop speech is everything Japanese language should not to be: in your face, overly direct, obscene. Part of the cultural globalization of rap depended on the merging of hip-hop and the Japanese language—despite some skepticism early on that it could even be done. Yet as we will see, there was no single solution to the problem. What does this tell us about language and globalization? What does it mean to say the Japanese language is "unsuitable" for rapping? In what ways does rap crack the fissures of language standardization? How do artists learn the art of rhyming? How did battles among different rappers reflect their aesthetic commitments and motivations?

One of the pioneers of Japanese hip-hop, Itō Seikō, offers telling insights into the politics of language and identity on his 1989 album *Mess/Age*. The double entendre of the album's title captures a duality that Itō puts foremost in his work, namely, that a creative reworking of an era ("age") that had become a "mess" could arise through the serendipitous cross-language fertilization in his "message." In one song, he looks back ninety years, calling the end of the century "just a rumor" (*uwasa dake no seikimatsu*) because before the Meiji era (1868–1912), Japan did not use the Western calendar. "It was Japan's first end of the century," he raps, "but no one noticed that." Importantly, Itō views this not as an imposition of Western ways of thinking, but rather as the emergence of a widespread Japanese desire to topple old elitist Japanese ways, a desire spread by word of mouth.

Rumors spread quickly	*uwasa wa sugu ni hirogari dashita*
rumors of whatever kind,	*donna uwasa datte mo*
it didn't matter	*dō datte yokatta*
everyone wanted	*sekai hametsu no imeeji o*
images of the world's ruin.	*dare mo ga hoshikatta.*

—Itō Seikō (1989) "Uwasa dake no seikimatsu" (the end of the century was just a rumor) *Mess/Age* (CD re-release, File Records, Tokyo, 1995, 23FRO31D)

Here, rumors operate separately from official media and government proclamations. In locating the change of consciousness in rumors, Itō draws attention to grassroots globalization that operates concurrently with larger political economic shifts.

There is a lesson here for thinking about issues of hip-hop, language, and Japanese identity politics. It involves resisting a desire to see "the end of the Japanese language" in the presence of rap and to explore instead the particular meanings associated with hip-hop language use. Granted, adding stress accents and tortured phrasing to create rhymes does a certain violence to the language of effete haiku, but beyond the "different sound," how are hip-hop aesthetics and politics interwoven in the language choices artists make? Uses of English can be interpreted as Western domination, and yet some of these uses are aimed at cracking fissures in the hegemonic understanding of the Japanese as one people with one language. Shifting frames of analysis produce new meanings of politics.

A *Genba* Approach to Language, Power, and Identity

What does an emphasis on performative *genba* tell us about language, power, and identity? Like the idea that the Japanese are a single ethnicity (or "race"), the idea that the Japanese share one language reinforces the sense of a homogeneous society. Japan scholars have established that this alleged unity and an ineffable spirit of the language disguises more complicated politics in order to unify a conflicted populace (Befu 2001; Miller 1982). Working from this insight, we can see that the debates about language and rap should be viewed in contexts of English versus Japanese influence, while also considering how such debates are related to conflicts within Japanese society. Rhyme may be a borrowed poetic technique, but this "outside style" was initially spread by informal talk and performance among peers. Quite literally, word of mouth was one driving force that spread the skill to rhyme, dis, freestyle, and rap. Rumors spread rhymes.

A focus on *genba* of performance, both in the clubs and in the recording studios, illustrates the enactment of global culture through everyday interaction. We can see key processes for understanding linguistic dimensions of cross-cultural influence, particularly if we view them in dialogic terms, rather than as imposed from outside.[1] Stuart Hall (1997, 28), for example, argues that global mass culture is centered in the West, driven by the stories and imagery of Western societies. Moreover, he says, it "always speaks English." He notes, however, that this is not the Queen's English, but "a variety of broken forms of English: English as it has been invaded, and as it has hegemonized a variety of other languages without being able to exclude them from it" (28). Hall's insights raise two key questions: How has hip-hop altered the Japanese language? And, does it further the global hegemony of English? In this chapter I aim to problematize the idea of English-language dominance in global popular culture. Rather than beginning with a West-versus-the-rest mode of analysis, I argue for a more multidimensional and historically contingent understanding of language and power.[2] As we will see, Itō Seikō viewed the dominance of commercial Japanese rock music as more worrisome than any dominance of the West. Similarly, he saw Japanese people's desire for world-ending rumors—"it doesn't matter what kind"—as a key engine for adopting a Western calendar.[3]

A second theme to explore involves questioning the hegemony of standard Japanese in Japan, particularly the way in which elite Japanese commentators use the distance of the Japanese language from Western forms as a means to reinforce notions of Japanese homogeneity. The anthropologist Harumi

Befu (2001) accurately calls this the "hegemony of homogeneity." In this context, Japanese rappers using English-inspired poetics and phrases implicitly critique notions of ethnic difference derived from assertions of the timeless character of the Japanese language. From the standpoint of Japanese emcees, language is as malleable as sculptor's clay, which they mold using "proper Japanese," slang, derogatory terms, regional variations, gendered forms, and bilingual puns. They draw inspiration from hip-hop and African American vernacular styles—battling, dissing, freestyling—while also learning from other Japanese rappers and even traditional Japanese vocal performances. Language is always a site and constituent of hybridization, but the consequences of hybridization depend fundamentally on one's location. The idea of a *genba* simply provides a way of clarifying that location not as a national norm, but more flexibly in terms of situated performances and contextualized knowledge.

To unravel the multiple dimensions of language use in Japanese hip-hop, I begin with an ethnographic description of a recording session to show how the concentrated efforts to improve one's rap flow engender a deeper reflection on the characteristics of the Japanese language. Here, ongoing practice and performance mean that being "more hip-hop" involves becoming "more Japanese." Then I move on to consider some broader contexts for thinking about the contrasts between English and Japanese to see how different locations produce different embodiments of language politics, including a look at examples of an American learning Japanese and of *Nihonjinron* commentators, that is, two perspectives that begin with static notions of the Japanese language. Next, I consider the uses of English in Japanese rock in the late 1960s and compare it to rap in the 1990s to evaluate the different historical contexts and varying ideas about authenticity. Then I turn to contrasts within hip-hop, setting playful party rappers (Scha Dara Parr and Now feat. Umedy) against the more hard-core stance of K Dub Shine. Finally, I describe a case of two rap singles that set off a protest due to their lyrics. With these examples, I will apply the model of the dispersed, networked power linking audience, media, and retail outlets (discussed in chapter 3). Although the lyrics were vetted by the record company in the studio, the feedback loop outside the *genba* amplified the objections and forced a redefinition of the limits of acceptable speech.

The Recording Studio as Genba

In the abstract, it seems contradictory to think that becoming more hip-hop means becoming more Japanese (and becoming more oneself), but the experience of musicians as they hone their craft has been precisely that. The intense focus on individual ability to use language in rapping with friends in private, before an audience on stage, or in recording studios with group mates and industry professionals listening helps us understand the *genba* of transnational cultural flows. Although the broader influence of hip-hop includes dismantling the hegemonic view of the Japanese as one people with one language, the actual motivations of individual musicians may be better understood not in terms of large-scale, abstract ideological effects, but in the pressures and motivations that drive their engagement with music as an art form, as business, and as pleasure.

Often what makes hip-hop important in the most immediate sense is the response of one's peers. In nightclubs, it is not uncommon to see a group of friends standing in a circle and rapping new lines over the American hip-hop blaring over the speakers. In general, their inability to understand the lyrics of the American music facilitates rapping among friends in the clubs; the music comes across as constant break beats without the distraction of someone else's lyrics. Driving to shows, I have seen emcees practice such freestyle raps in cars, honing their styles, going for a laugh. It is important that they are doing this in the company of friends as well; a certain kind of verbal exchange—informal, playful, aiming to amuse and surprise—gives a rapper acclaim. As musicians become more professional, these informal moments are then taken to the stage and the recording studio, where the pressures become more intense and the rewards more pronounced.

One of the key spaces for grasping how an engagement with a foreign hip-hop poetics encourages a deeper delving into the specificities of the Japanese language is the recording studio. In a recording studio, the intensity of focus on sound mirrors the physical and emotional intensity of a nightclub. The studio, however, brings the subtleties of the sound itself to the foreground. If you have ever felt uncomfortable at the sound of your own voice on an answering machine, you might imagine what it is like hearing your voice and your lyrics on enormous speakers in front of your group mates, the record company representative, the producer, and the engineer. More important, your job depends on how it sounds. Taking a look at a day in the recording studio as it relates to language will give us some sense of how the routines of being an emcee relate language to hip-hop in Japan.

Between November 1995 and February 1997, I observed about forty recording sessions at Crown Records. Most were one-day sessions. Each day a different group would complete a song to be included in the series *Best of Japanese Hip-Hop*. In the studio, the first step of recording is inputting the sounds from the MPC (the midi processing center, that is, a computer for pro-gramming tracks) onto the two-inch digital tape recorder. At the time, Crown used a forty-eight-track mixing board, and the musical mix normally took up about eighteen to twenty-five tracks. More recently, hard-disk digital record-ing using Pro Tools software has become the norm. Sometimes it could take up to three hours to input the programmed tracks, especially if technical dif-ficulties arose, a common occurrence given the complexity and idiosyncra-sies of each person's equipment and style of work. Then everyone had lunch, delivered to the studio and paid for by the record company, around 4 p.m. While the producer and the engineer input the backing track, Gomi Satoshi, the sole record company representative at the recording session and generally referred to as the A & R (artist and repertoire) rep or the "director" (*direkutaa*), checked for lyrics and samples considered "dangerous" (*yabai*). Each record company uses somewhat different standards for determining what speech is permissible. At Crown, Gomi would generally ask emcees to remove spe-cific references to brand-name products (e.g., a popular pudding) and also discriminatory words (e.g., *kichigai*, meaning "crazy"). Gomi preferred that the lyrics be rewritten on the spot, though sometimes rappers would choose to have the offending word reversed using the recording computer.

Once the tracks had been recorded, usually by 4 or 5 p.m., the recording of the vocals would begin. A rapper would enter the recording booth, which has a glass window or wall so the person in the booth and the producer at the mixing board can see each other. A recording booth can vary in size from a large room with grand piano and big enough to hold twenty musicians to a small (ten by ten feet) room, such as the one at Crown, or even the closet-sized booth in Cake-K's home studio. All recording booths tend to get quite hot because air-conditioning makes too much noise and cannot be run while the recording is underway.

At Crown, the rappers had to close an enormous door handle that locked the soundproof room. They slipped on their headphones and stepped up to a microphone that had a thin mesh screen in front of it to stop puffs of air from making popping sounds. During the recording, the record company repre-sentative generally takes a backseat, while the producer (*purodyusaa*), who controls the mixing board, directs the artists and the engineer who runs the recording tape.[4] In all the sessions I witnessed, the producers were men. For the recording of the *Best of Japanese Hip-Hop*, the main producer was DJ MASA, whose long career as a track-maker, soundboard engineer, and recording-studio producer had garnered him considerable respect among the newcomer musicians. He was also known for playing the music very loud in the studio.

Once the musical tracks had been inputted, MAŞA guided the rappers through the steps in the process. He began by laying down a guide track by having the rappers record a single, rough take of the entire song. With this guide in place on a track, they then decided what to record first.

Let's look in more detail at a recording session by group called DESD.[5] The group has not (yet) become famous, but the scene in the studio proved instructive because the details of honing one's style were made explicit in discussions between the producer and the novice rapper getting his first chance at recording. In all of the recording sessions with rapping that I observed, the emcees worked hard to polish their flow, that is, the rhythmic and tonal (though seldom melodic) nuances of their delivery. While these adjustments occurred in almost every session, the recording session for DESD was a rare case in which different aspects of improving a rapper's style were discussed in detail, out loud, as opposed to the more subtle, even unspoken communication more common between MAŞA and more experienced rappers. Most often, a rapper would record a take and listen to it, at which point a kind of mutual nodding or forehead wrinkling between the rapper and MAŞA would occur before the track was done again. In this case, DESD was getting its first break in recording. The leader of the group, JJay (pronounced "Jay"), was an old friend of MAŞA's, and so the atmosphere was fairly relaxed. For unfamiliar first-time groups, MAŞA could seem distant and aloof. Still, there was clearly some nervousness as the rookie rappers Drunkk and Shima stood in the corner and practiced their lyrics under their breath, waiting for their turn to record.

Let's examine the recording of verse one: At just before 5:30 p.m., MC Drunkk enters the recording booth. The group records a take of verse one as practice. MAŞA: "OK, let's do a take" (*N, torō*). Drunkk raps the first verse with good energy and delivery. He has clearly practiced long and hard: he never trips over words or phrases, nor does he lose the rhythm. This is a good sign for those of us in the mixing-board area of the studio (MAŞA; Kusumoto Jun'ichirō, the engineer; Gomi, the Crown representative; the other group members; and I). A few days before, another group of rappers, who were more established on the scene, had arrived quite unprepared. Their stumbling over their own lyrics offered a frustrating (and embarrassing) display.[6] On hearing Drunkk's forceful delivery—a kind of Run-DMC–like solid shouting of the lyrics—there is a mutual exchange of slight nods and glances, with corners of lips turned down and eyebrows raised, saying in effect, "Not too bad." MAŞA asks simply, "What do you think?" (*Dō?*). Drunkk just gives back a noncommittal and uncertain "Hmm," as if he is not sure what to think, which probably means that he thinks it is pretty good, but, being modest, he does not want to say so.

At this point, MA$A could easily have picked out a couple words or lines to improve, done a couple of more takes and then moved on. But instead, he says, "With your style of singing, everything hits right at the front of the measure [*atamauchi*], don't you think [*jyan*]? It's boring." MA$A suggests opening up a few spaces, letting some words slip behind the beat (*kuzushite*), and coming in a little early on the next line. "For example, when you say 'MC,' move the phrasing back so that the *c*, not the *m*, is at the first beat of the measure."

Drunkk does another take of verse one, but MA$A says it did not change very much: "With 'MC', put the accent on *c*," he repeats. "When you say the line '*kara kuru*,' put a space between the two words and don't say them both with the same tone." Drunkk tries these changes a cappella, but then MA$A calls him out of the booth.

For the next hour, MA$A loops the instrumental track and works with Drunkk to liven up his flow. MA$A makes a chopping motion with his hand and says that with each line cut precisely into the four-beat measure, there is no flow to it (*nagare ga nai*). Instead (now cutting a wave through the air), he says the verse should rise and fall, building and descending to give the rap some style. It is working toward this kind of rhythmic nuance that shows how the paradox of being hip-hop in terms of rap flow, rhyme, and originality leads lyricists to a deeper sensitivity to the potentials of the Japanese language.

MA$A sits next to Drunkk at the mixing board, like a coach scribbling plays on the handwritten lyric sheet: a line between a compound of kanji characters to indicate a break, circled syllables for accents, lines underneath a series of words to link them together, a thick underline to shout out the words. MA$A taps on the mixing board, "Ta ra ra ra, Ta ra ra ra" to show what he means by linking the words together. They work on the line "okusoku kara no shingen-chi" (from the far distant epicenter). MA$A suggests a cut after *okusoku*, then saying *kara no* quickly, and then accenting each syllable of the next word *shin-gen-chi*. In this way, they work through the entire verse by themselves, MA$A saying the phrases, Drunkk mouthing them as they go along. The rest of us sit silently. Cell phone calls are taken outside.

At around 6:30 p.m., Drunkk gets back in the recording booth to try again. The excitement in the studio has built up now, as we all wait to see how well the changes come across. Drunkk tries a couple of takes, but now he is muffing lines and, skipping or mispronouncing words. With each mistake, the engineer, who controls the enormous two-inch tape recording machine by computer, hits rewind and awaits the signal from MA$A or Drunkk to start again. Drunkk tries again, but muffs it again: "Ah, I was too conscious of it again" (*Mata ishiki shite shimatta*). After a couple of more tries, MA$A says, "Just use your body to get with the rhythm." After seven takes, MA$A is encouraging, "It's gotten much better. Now let's try to do it a little more naturally [*shizen ni*]." Eight more takes, and Drunkk and MA$A are more or less satisfied with the first part of the verse, but there is still a timing problem with the line "okusoku kara no shingenchi." The recording technology allows a rapper to punch in at any given point, provided there is at least some space between the words. Drunkk and MA$A use this technique, and after nine more takes, MA$A finds it is better.[7] Now the lines after the difficult one are in good shape, but that one line still needs work. The engineer punches in and out so they can keep working on the tricky phrase. Drunkk practices without the music, where it sounds fine, but with the music running, the "kara no" just will not fall into the right rhythm. Five more takes of just that one line, and then they stop to listen through. Another take; he went too fast. Another take, *okusoku* slipped off the beat. Finally, another eight takes later, the line sounds alright, and Drunkk and MA$A decide to move on. In the end, creating a satisfactory recording of the sixteen measures of verse one required a total of thirty-eight takes: ten takes for the first ten measures, another nine takes for the last six measures, and another eighteen takes to fix the fourteenth measure. Almost two hours after they began recording this first verse, they are ready to move on to the second rapper and verse two. We have already heard the song more than fifty times, and the recording session is likely to go on for at least four more hours. This exercise illustrates the level of detail and type of attention paid to rapping during the recording of a song, in contrast to the process of live performance. The studio is a place of learning through repeated performance and intense scrutiny. After the recording of this verse, Drunkk, almost breathless with excitement, says to JJay, "That was great fun" (*mecha mecha tanoshii*).

Now imagine years of this kind of practice, among hundreds of minor and more or less major groups, performing in a car with friends or in a club onstage, recording in home studios or luxurious labs, working toward the next gig, the next release. With these kinds of routines, the question is not whether Japanese hip-hop will become more diversified, but how far afield the diversities will reach. Yet understanding what language diversity means requires locating language differences in specific contexts. Let's turn to some general considerations of the contrasts between English and Japanese, before attending to the uses of English in Japanese popular music.

Conceptualizing English/Japanese Differences

My own experience learning Japanese illustrates a process of engagement with a foreign language that may offer a metaphor for some of the linguistic aspects of globalization. When I began studying Japanese in college, I was at first struck by core differences between English and Japanese, which I experienced as dichotomies. Over time, however, a second stage of understanding led me to sense an unending complexity in Japanese, not the Japanese in a dictionary or a grammar book, but the language that people used in their daily lives and that depended on a range of mutable status relations—historical, regional, gendered, and so on—to make sense of the meanings. This experience revealed the impossibility of comparing entire languages in terms of binary oppositions. One contribution of this study, I hope, is to suggest some ways to move beyond certain binary oppositions—global/local; English/Japanese— and toward contextualized, performative politics.

As a freshman in college I had to fulfill a one-year foreign language requirement. I chose to study Japanese primarily because it seemed so different, so exotic, when compared to the Spanish I had learned in high school. I could not wait to learn the different writing systems: the two syllabary (kana) scripts, that is, the curvy hiragana (used for verb inflections, particles, and many words) and the blocky katakana (used for foreign names and words, as well as onomatopoeia). Above all, I wanted to learn the kanji, the Chinese characters, of which 1,945 are classified for general use. (There are more if we include people and place names.) For us novices, the characters sometimes evoked a kind of visual poetry, as our teachers showed us (and we showed our friends) how the ideograms for people, eyes, mountains, rivers, and rice fields mimicked iconic representations. Although brute memorization was the rule, at times, kanji displayed a beguiling logic, as when the character for *tree* is doubled to mean *forest* and tripled to mean *woods*. Kanji danced where our pedestrian roman alphabet crawled. When I am with Americans who cannot read kanji, I still experience the magic of understanding what amounts to secret code. Perhaps this is partly what makes kanji cool enough to appear on NBA players' tattoos and on American hip-hop clothing. There is an ingroup pleasure of being privy to an occult meaning, one perhaps not unlike the experience of graffiti writers who can decipher the kind of tortured and stylized writing that remains a mystery to the uninitiated.

Social structure seems embedded in the language as well. My first-year professor, the late Tazuko Monane–sensei, was a tiny, irrepressible Japanese woman who delighted in making connections between the language and styles of thought. She pointed out that in English, when we start speaking a sentence, we must consider who or what will be the subject. In Japanese, one seldom uses the subject of a sentence, and verbs have the same conjugation regardless of whether the subject is I, you, she, we, or they. The common absence of specified pronouns might seem to make Japanese vague or indirect, yet in other ways, the language is much more precise than English, particularly in terms of the close attention paid to the status of the speakers and the social distance between them. For a novice Japanese-language student, there is a dizzying array of options for the proper word forms: honorific or humble, formal or informal? Choosing the correct form depends on knowing one's own status in relation to the interlocutor, the object of the sentence, and in-group/out-group relationships. Even in Japan, a perennial complaint of adults is that youth can no longer speak polite Japanese. The linguistic features surrounding status are sometimes used as evidence that Japan is a vertical society (*tate shakai*), obsessed with hierarchy, but by the same token, complex possibilities for conveying status also provide an opportunity to toy with formality.

In one of the more striking examples of using politeness as a joke, the emcee Kohei Japan begins one song with the most refined Japanese possible, introducing himself exceedingly humbly, like a maître d' in a restaurant where "the revered customer is a noble god" (*okyakusama wa kamisama desu*). Such smooth talk then becomes the voice of a businessman picking up a woman ("Are you a model, or something? With your sense of fashion, accessories, oh, and that perfume!"). Then, shifting politeness register and scenes, he becomes a young man talking to himself, wasting time, about to watch a video and eat a convenience-store lunch, when all of a sudden he gets a call from his girlfriend and says, *Yabee*, a rough, informal exclamation meaning "bad" or "dangerous," but also, in this case, "oh, hell." The presence of honorifics and subtle status markers can be used to reinforce hierarchies, but the language also can be used to undermine them, as Kohei Japan does, by showing how cynically they can be employed. The Japanese language may provide more options than English for expressing status differences, but it also, therefore, presents more opportunities to subtly put down others. Indeed, using Japanese that is too polite provides a way of saying, "we are not close."

This dependence on perspective for grasping English/Japanese contrasts was brought home to me during a year I spent teaching English at a rural Japanese junior high school (1988–89). A Japanese math teacher asked one of the students what she thought about having a gaijin in the school. The girl responded, "*Mezurashii.*" The word, an adjective that can act as a whole sentence, means "unusual, rare" and maybe "a little peculiar." Later I wondered, what exactly was *mezurashii*? Was it me personally, her experience, my teaching, all of the above? Over time, I realized that these questions make sense in English, but are less of an issue in Japanese.

But does this mean that the Japanese think less about individualism because they can avoid the subjects of sentences? There is a beguiling logic to this kind of explanation. On the one hand, it usefully draws attention to the tendencies of different languages to highlight different aspects of human relations. But as Kohei shows, having polite language does not induce acting politely. Similarly, there is a danger of promoting stereotypes of national character if we locate cultural differences in the specifics of the abstract characteristics of language. Yet this is precisely what some Japan commentators do.

Nihonjinron *Views of Language*

Some writers in Japan hold up the particular features of the Japanese language as evidence of the nation's cultural uniqueness. In this they share some analytical common ground with beginning Japanese-language students because both tend to draw conclusions about Japanese society as a whole from Japan-versus-the-West binaries. A body of writing collectively referred to as *Nihonjinron*, or the theory of Japanese people, emphasizes the uniqueness of Japanese—in terms of language, culture, and race (Dale 1986). Language figures prominently in some of these characterizations because a one-to-one correspondence between people, language, and culture makes the uniqueness of Japan appear self-evident. Key concepts, such as *ki* (core energy), *iki* (subdued beauty), *sabi wabi* (rustic refinement), and *mono no aware* (melancholy compassion) are difficult to translate, in part because other languages do not have quite the same words or concepts, but also because they evoke a long history of artistic creations. Yet all languages are unique in this way, and the idea that the language, the people, and the culture are inscrutable to non-natives is in many ways simply the myth of modern Japan (Miller 1982).

To the numerous critiques of *Nihonjinron* discourse, Harumi Befu (2001) has added an important insight by locating some of these writings in the context of the West's criticism of Japan. Befu is no apologist for *Nihonjinron* writers, but he does point out that some of the writings in the 1980s, for example, appeared at a time when the Western world accused Japan of unfair trade practices, closed markets, and excessive regulations that excluded foreign companies. Some in Japan suggested that their characteristic patterns of communication, business relationships, and styles of building trust were misinterpreted as discrimination against foreigners. Of course, this explanation of difference widened the gap between Japan and the rest of the world by asserting the impossibility of mutual understanding. Befu shows the value of locating essentialist arguments in their historical and political-economic contexts.

Assertions of one people with one language, however, are also aimed at disciplining the Japanese. John Lie (2001) analyzes this process by which mono-ethnicity was forged out of what he calls "multiethnic Japan." Like the process of creating a unified national identity, linguistic unification was neither smooth nor swift. Standard Japanese (*hyōjungo*), Lie argues, emerged from the samurai language of Edo (now Tokyo) during the Tokugawa period (1600–1868). The rise of urbanization, a nationwide system of roads, the expansion of state bureaucracy, and a centralized system of schools all contributed to common communication in an increasingly standardized Japanese (187). Even today, however, there are linguistic communities and language schools for Ainu, Korean, Chinese, and English speakers, and therefore, Lie says, Japan is a multilingual society.

Granted, there is more linguistic diversity in Japan than is commonly depicted in television news reports, Japanese language instruction books, and *Nihonjinron* commentary on the ineffable language. Nevertheless, we can acknowledge that Japan is a more monolingual society than many others. The kinds of language choices that take place in Japanese hip-hop are in some ways less drastic than would be the case for emcees of other nationalities. As Jacqueline Urla (2001, 175) has described, in Spain, the Basque group Negu Gorriak made a huge impact when they decided to dissolve their previous band, which performed rock in Spanish, and to reemerge as *euskaldun berriak*, a term for new Basque speakers. In so doing, they brought together language militancy and Basque nationalist pride with the oppositional culture of radical rock and rap, even though this eliminated any chance of commercial radio airplay. In New Zealand, Maori emcees complain of being blacklisted (as in no radio play) if they use the Maori language, but they have nevertheless managed some commercial success in a country where 9 percent of the population is Maori, but only a third of those people speak Maori fluently (Mitchell 2001a, 280–81). In Tanzania, with its history of German and then British colonization, radio stations in the late 1990s focused on promoting English-language rap by Tanzanian artists, rather than on Swahili rap that tended to have lower production values. Now, though, Swahili rap appears on the rise (Perullo and Fenn 2003, 32). Over time, hip-hop in its various settings seems to become embedded in a wider range of language politics and associated with a wider range of social positions, thereby providing new opportunities for emcees to "flip the script" in ways that cannot even be imagined in English.

These examples of contrasting the Japanese language with English point to the importance of locating language differences in specific social contexts. The debate among Japanese rockers about whether they should sing in English or Japanese prefigured, yet also contrasted with, later arguments among Japanese rappers.

English Language in Japanese Popular Music

Depending on the genre of music, the path from Western or popular to something "deeply Japanese" differed, thus illustrating the shifting ground on which musical aesthetics, language, and national identity were performed. This forces us to reconsider Stuart Hall's argument that global popular culture always speaks English because the English spoken, even in Japan's popular music, can vary dramatically. In the 1920s, jazz songs like "My Blue Heaven" and "Song of Araby" were recorded and played on the radio with very free translations of the English lyrics (Hosokawa, Matsumura, and Shiba 1991, 7). Postwar Japanese rockabilly tended to translate the verses and chorus of the song, but leave the bridge intact, which often contained the English title of the song. In the early 1960s, Japanese folk singers would often sing American folk songs by Pete Seeger or Peter, Paul, and Mary verbatim (in English), though over time, more of these songs were translated into Japanese. In contrast, debates surrounding the authenticity of Japanese jazz seldom turned on issues of language choice, but rather on questions of Japanese aesthetics of space (*ma*) or of whether Japan could create a hipster culture as ways of making "yellow jazz" (Atkins 2001). *Enka*, a popular music style that draws on the more traditional folk music vocal styles of *min'yō*, gradually became recognized as the "heart of the Japanese" (*nihonjin no kokoro*) despite the heavy use of Western string instruments (Yano 2002, 4ff).

One of the most striking contrasts with hip-hop, however, is the case of rock. In the late 1960s, Japanese rockers debated whether they should aim for a global (i.e., Western, English-speaking) audience or work to build the local scene. In 1970, a discussion by contemporary Japanese rockers published in a music magazine showed how issues of language and identity could provoke angry divisions over how best to resolve the paradox of being both a rock musician and Japanese (Uchida et al. 1990). The sharpest discussion arose between Uchida Yūya of Flower Traveling Band, a group that tended to use English lyrics, and Otaki Ei'ichi of Happy End, who promoted using Japanese.

Uchida said that his band's aim was to introduce Japanese audiences to the foreign machine (*gaikoku no mashiin*) of rock music, such as Jimi Hendrix and Jefferson Airplane, by writing lyrics in English. Uchida said, "I have tried to sing in Japanese. But in the end, the singing style just didn't work [*noranai*, literally, "didn't ride [the rhythm]")." In addition, Uchida said he was aiming for a worldwide audience.

Maybe my dream is too big, but from the moment I could support myself, I have thought of rock as a way to communicate with the world. I'm aiming to export it. Since we've been invited, we'll be going to the US to perform, but I really don't think it's best to stress that we're some kind of strange "folk Japanese" [*nihon minzoku*]. I don't need to wear a kimono, and besides, I think the world is one, so if you want to wear a kimono, go ahead. Instead of singing in Japanese, I sing in English, and even if the words aren't understood [in Japan], the music can be persuasive if it rides [*notte*]. (Uchida et al. 1990, 84)

In this vision, success means attracting a world (i.e., English-language) audience. Moreover, authentic rock depends on using English to give the lyrics the appropriate rhythmic emphasis.

Otaki of Happy End enunciated other goals and also considered the path to a global audience in much different terms.

My departure point is this: I'm playing rock music in Japan, so shouldn't I take the long view, and try to make it grow here [*dochaku saseru ka*]?[8] Even for myself, I play rock music, but I feel like I'm not facing Japan. That is, even if one starts from a stance of trying to play a worldwide style of rock music, in America or wherever, the best thing is to play rock that speaks to everyday life. Even if you want to do it an all-world style, wouldn't that still be the fastest way? (Uchida et al. 1990, 84)

Here, in the voices of two rockers, we have encapsulated divergent theories of global rock. For Uchida, global popular culture speaks English, but for Otaki the *genba* is the platform for building a global audience. In the end, Otaki was more prescient. Japanese-language rock is far more prevalent in Japan than English-language rock (by Japanese or others). Yet in 1970, it was very unclear who would prevail. Indeed, this debate may seem fairly innocuous to an outside observer, but as the published discussion progresses, the various rockers discard polite language and trade epithets regarding the other's arrogance. The material stakes were quite real because the success of each depended to a large degree on whether fans viewed English or Japanese rock as more authentic.

Japanese Language Politics in Hip-Hop

The contrasts between the early rock era and the early hip-hop era show differences and similarities. Few hip-hop artists imagined appealing to a global market, or at least, the English-speaking market. Both rock and hip-hop musicians complained that Japanese was ill-suited to their respective vocal styles. Early practitioners shared the anxiety that Japanese simply would not ride the rhythm. As popular-music scholar Rei-ichi Kimoto (2002) discusses, one of the key aspects of what he calls Japanese hip-hop localization involved recognizing that not just the English language but also the Japanese language could be cool. Yet when we look at hip-hop in comparison to rock, what appears notable is that English-language hip-hop by Japanese artists remains quite rare. With the exception of some bilingual rappers—Shingo2, A-Twice, Verbal (of M-Flo)—there are very few examples of English-language J-rap. In the early rock era, bands sympathetic to Uchida's viewpoint felt that using English was necessary if one wanted to be an authentic rocker. Their attitude, as the popular music scholar Hosokawa Shūhei told me in a personal communication in July 2001, was, "If you want to sing in Japanese, go do folk or something." Ironically, the rock groups that used mostly English lyrics tended to incorporate many traditional Japanese elements in their sound (bamboo flutes, *taiko* drums, and so on), a kind of sonic kimono wearing. In contrast, Happy End, the group using Japanese lyrics, was free to adopt a more straightforward Western rock-and-roll style (Hosokawa, Matsumura, and Shiba 1991, 16).

In hip-hop, the equation of authenticity as it applied to the use of English took a different course. Why? Japan's status on the world scene is probably one factor. In the late 1960s, Japan was in the midst of rapid economic growth, but still recovering from the devastation of World War II. The music market still remained fairly evenly split between sales of Western and Japanese music, whereas by the late 1980s, Japanese music outsold Western music by a three-to-one ratio. Japan in the late 1980s was at the peak of the bubble economy. It was the "Japan that can say no" to the West (Ishihara 1991). This broader political-economic context and a healthier domestic music industry suggest part of the answer. Still, this explanation goes only so far because other genres of music in the 1980s and 1990s show a different linguistic mix of foreign and Japanese. Orquestra de la Luz records primarily in Spanish, and they tour in Latin America. Japanese reggae tends to have a more balanced mix of Jamaican patois combined with Japanese lyrics, and many groups, including Nahki, Chelsea, and Rankin' Taxi, have performed in Jamaica. A political-economic explanation may show the broader context, but the specific audiences, their pleasures, and politics are what make this context come to life.

Using Rap to Liberate the Japanese Language

In the early days of rap albums in Japan, the innovation of hip-hop was contrasted with other genres and their relationship to the English language. Let's reexamine the text that advertised Itō Seikō's 1989 debut album *Mess/Age*, included as well in the album's 1995 reissue. It presents his manifesto (*sengen*): "There is no rock in Japan because there's no Japanese language in rock. . . . In this era of Japanese rock's golden age, has the language really been freed [*kaihō sareta*]? With release after release, has sound been freed? The answer is no" (Itō 1995, 35). The songs on his album, he said, represented a "great adventure in the Japanese language," both pop and avant-garde, a series of short stories in rap (35). By the late 1980s, a variety of artists were performing in clubs, and American hip-hop acts were performing in Japan, but hip-hop as a culture was as yet little understood. Itō was one of the forerunners for discussing in music magazines the ways that the Japanese language could be transformed by rap.

The idea of rhyming was so strange that Itō even included a "rhyming bible" in the liner notes of his album. In these early days, clearly one of the enchanting aspects of hip-hop was the opportunity to make playful connections between Japanese and English words by making them rhyme. Some of Itō's proposed rhymes, like "don't stop go" rhyming with *jōhōryō* (information level), reflect his playfully critical stance toward Tokyo's frantic, media-saturated lifestyles. A selection from his rhyming bible illustrates the ways rhyming and the heavy use of English-derived words allowed him to make new, often irreverent associations between concepts. Here, from the *a-a* rhymes:

baka	fool
sucker	pronounced *sakkaa* in Japanese
gaka	painter, artist

fucker	pronounced *fakkaa*
kamisama	god
ikisama	way-of-life
konna zama	this plight
ōsama	king

Such a range of mixing English and Japanese words shows that global popular culture "speaks English" in only a limited sense. Indeed, one scholar argues that these supposedly English words are better seen as "English-inspired words" that at times have meanings unfamiliar to English speakers, as in the use of the term *service* (*saabisu*) to mean "free" (Stanlaw 1992, 73–74). The same thing can be said for black English in the sense that it is "English-inspired" but often not understood by those outside a community of speakers. The value of specialized lingo, therefore, depends on the location of verbal performance. Rap slang cleverly used can be influential in a club but problematic in business negotiations, just as academic jargon can seem laughable outside professional circles. The key question, then, is: What processes determine the status of different patterns of language use? Who has the authority to determine "proper" ways of speaking? The world of rap provides a contrast to schools and corporate and government offices where standard Japanese is the norm. But even within the worlds of popular music, language creativity is variously conceived.

Itō suggested that rap's emphasis on vernacular language offered a critical wedge to pry open the submerged diversity hidden by official, mass-mediated, standard Japanese. For him, contemporary Japanese language was artificial, having lost its connection to local lifeways.

Now, the Japanese that everyone is speaking, and what you hear on the news, I would say is an artificial language [*jinkōgo*; literally meaning "man-made language"). In black rap of the South Bronx, for example, if you brought it to the [US] West coast, no one would understand. But that's not true in Japan. Regional culture barely gets wrapped up in language at all. . . . If you sing in this kind of artificial language, no one can understand who you are aiming at. There's no subject to the sentences, no aim, and even if one is facing society [*seken ni mukatte*], the point just drifts away. (Saeki and Itō 1988, 80)

In other words, rap is not just about rhyming and rhythmic nuance, it is about finding a language that can crack the fissures of artificial language, the "standard Japanese," and, in so doing, change society. Itō argues for a revolutionary directness, such that Japanese will say outright, "I love you" (80). This illustrates the importance of locating hip-hop poetics in specific contexts to see how they intervene in Japan's cultural politics.[9]

What Is Rhyming?

In the late 1980s and early 1990s, some Japanese felt compelled to provide explicit answers to the question, "What is rap?" In 1991, the group B-Fresh, which included the rappers Cake-K and MC Bell, produced the first major-label Japanese rap album, *Brown-Eyed Soul*. At the time, in a promotional video to introduce hip-hop to a Japanese audience, MC Bell explains rap and rhyming.

Basically, rap [*rappu*] is not singing. It's talking with rhythm and melody. But talk alone is not rap. For example, the rap you hear on TV commercials is definitely not rap. Rap must have rhyming [*raimingu*], or in Japanese, to rhyme [*in o fumu*]. The first thing you have to understand is that without rhyme, it isn't rap. What is rhyming? In a measure, you need words ending with the same sound. Three rhymes in a measure is called three-link rhyming.[10]

Not only does he have to explain rhyming, Bell also makes a distinction with "what you see on commercials." In this, as in Itō's declaration, we can see how hip-hop poetics are related to discourses of commercialism as well.

These early days of rap music therefore were characterized by explicit explanations of the "nature" of rap. The answers tended to rely on explaining technical features of rhythmic flow and rhyming, and also on making general references to New York City, especially the South Bronx, and suggesting the centrality of black English vernacular speech styles. Black English was also seen as anticommercial.

Much of the early rap lyricists relied heavily on English-inspired loanwords to generate intriguing rhymes. For example, in B-Fresh's song "Mother," the group rhymes *lady* with *taxi* and *bijin* (beauty). The early era also saw more English phrases than the mid-to-late-1990s era.

At last night's disco I met a young lady	*yūbe no disco de atta* young lady
Waiting for a taxi, you are a beauty	*rōjō de takushii matte ru kimi wa bijin*
I say, "Hey you, we are B-Fresh	I say, "Hey you, we are B-Fresh
The rising-star b-boys."	*ninki jōshō-chū no* b-boys."

| Now listen to me, my rhyme story | Now listen to me *ore no* rhyme story |
| this heavy voice is from my parents | *kono* heavy *na* voice *wa oyayuzuri* |

—B-Fresh (1991) "Mother" *Brown-Eyed Soul* (King Records, KICP-228)

As time went on, however, some people tried to get closer to the source of hip-hop slang and to interpret the ideas of New York City hip-hop into the Japanese language. Others viewed this effort to provide a deeper understanding of the language of New York City streets as equivalent to a move away from real hip-hop ideals. We can get a sense of this debate through the example of a *manga* (comic).

In 1995, a serialized comic in a fashion magazine aimed to teach young Japanese interested in hip-hop the "real" language of the New York streets. Ironically, this attempt to get closer to hip-hop's source prompted a sharp debate about how exactly to translate hip-hop into a Japanese setting. Chūsonji Yutsuko, a Japanese woman who lived in New York City and spent some time with African American rappers, used her experience to create the manga story called "Wild Q." It ran in the fashion-oriented *Popeye* magazine from April to December 1995 (Chūsonji 1996). The plot revolves around Dainosuke, a young man from a rural fishing village in Japan who travels to Brooklyn and adopts the street name DNK. Thanks to his proficiency in dissing other people in English, he is eventually accepted into a gang with the warmhearted, welcoming appellation of "yellow, punk ass muddafucka." Chūsonji provides footnotes and katakana transliteration to help with pronunciation. K Dub Shine (of King Giddra) helped write the glossary that accompanied the collected edition, explaining such terms as *word up, represent, dis*, and *da bomb*. Yet according to other Japanese rappers, this effort to learn American street language reeked of a complete misunderstanding of the appropriate way to be hip-hop.

In an essay published along with the collected edition of the comic, the emcee Utamaru (of Rhymester, real name Sasaki Shirō) describes DNK, the lead character in "Wild Q," as an abomination because he misinterprets what it means to be fluent in hip-hop culture: "Unlike singing a song, if someone learns the words and is able to perfectly copy someone else's rap, no one would say that person is 'good at rap.' It's only meaningful if the rapper himself, using his own words, is telling his own story. . . . To the extent that you do not represent [*repurizento*] the things that you are, you will never be able to express yourself within hip-hop" (Sasaki 1996, 146). When I asked, fans often explained their appreciation of hip-hop in terms of its characteristic self-emphasis (*jibun shuchō*). Compared to the rockers of the late 1960s, mid-

1990s emcees had notions of language and aesthetics that revolved around an ideology that one must "represent," that is, expressing who you are and where you are from. Even though this is an English word, the consequence is to direct the focus back on one's individuality within a Japanese context. This means acknowledging one's uniqueness and expressing it in the Japanese language. To "be hip-hop" meant speaking from one's own position, proving oneself in the *genba* of nightclubs, and this produced a range of linguistic experiments aimed at reworking the Japanese language within hip-hop poetics.

Language Differences: Party Rap versus Underground

By the mid-1990s, the debate within the Japanese hip-hop scene had shifted from questions of what rap was to how to make rap in Japanese. In 1995, Microphone Pager rapped that Japanese was "an impossible wall," and using a bilingual rhyme, he argued that it was time to cross that wall: "Got it goin' on, over the wall / go over the impossible wall" (Got it goin' on, *kabe koerō / fukanō na kabe nori koerō*) (Microphone Pager [1995] "Rapperz Are Danger" *Don't Turn Off Your Light* [File Records, 25FRO27D]). A year later, J-rap was in magazines, thanks in part to East End X Yuri's success. But there was also a wider variety of hip-hop music being released, from party rap on major labels to underground hip-hop from the independent labels. The debate was shifting from Itō Seikō's contrasts between rock and rap and between English and Japanese to a debate about party rap versus underground hip-hop. Should one aim to entertain an imagined pop audience or, rather, represent one's own stance, regardless of what the mass of consumers might want? Party rap focused on fun, youth slang, and flirtatious teen situations. The underground stance was oppositional, self-centered, and employed rough masculine slang and often violent situations. Looking at some particular examples can provide a clearer sense of the artistic stakes.

One key aspect of the language of party rap is the engagement with feelings of emotional attachment. In the party-rap category, the three-woman group Now, for example, rapped "Beeper Love" (Sony Music, 1995), an ultracute paean to communicating with friends via numbers on pagers (e.g., 0-8-4 is *o ha yo* is "good morning"). Their song "Conbini monogatari" ("Convenience Store Love Story") depicted a woman reading the latest manga while standing in a store, then falling in love with a boy who walked in but to whom she was too shy to speak.

In one recording session I witnessed, Umedy (of EDU) and Baby Setsu (of Now) performed a duet that exemplified their efforts to express the rollercoaster ride of youthful emotions surrounding mutual attraction. The lyrics used concrete imagery. The girl raps about meeting the boy at a crowded train station, where he greets her by pounding his fists hip-hop style, and, she says, "you were really my type" (*kanari taipu*). He reflects on their dwindling romance, telling her not to return the spare key he gave her and begging for "one mo' night" (*wan mo naito*).[11] Afterwards, in an October 6, 1996 interview with me, Umedy described his effort to create a more pop-music style of rap for a Japanese audience. He argued that he was in fact even more hard core than the tough, underground rappers because he was truer to himself. Rather than puff himself up with false arrogance, he described his particular approach (*ore no sutansu*) as follows: "It's about feelings. In Japanese, we say *kidoairaku* [joy, anger, sorrow, fun—i.e., the gamut of human emotions]. But it's more complicated than that. For example, there is a middle ground between joy and sorrow, between anger and sorrow. Human emotions [*kanjō*] are complicated. My particular stance is to deal with these complicated feelings." He dismissed the all-too-common practice of yelling "I'm great" as an expression of anything but naïveté. Instead, he saw the challenge of self-expression as delving into the problem of how our sense of ourselves is always tied up with our feelings for others. In this, he used the language of emotions to express a sense of youthful longing. Party rappers like him focus on the confusion of first love as a key element of youth culture.

Scha Dara Parr: Transforming Youth Slang

Part of the influence of hip-hop on the Japanese language involves the transformation of youth slang. No one represents rap's playful experimentation with language better than the trio Scha Dara Parr (SDP), with its members MC Bose, Ani, and DJ Shinco. As they say in an early album, their forte is "nonsense rhymes" (*detarame raimu*). Their point of attack is Japanese pop culture. They joke about television prime-time dramas: "Substance, nothing / Everybody watching."[12] They parody the ultimate consumer in the song "Protect Him (from What He Wants)." They take stabs at punk rockers ("beat punk suckers") and offer ridiculous portrayals of uptight adults. Their vision is of maniacal youth expected to conform to what they view as adults' equally absurd notions of appropriateness. For example, their anthem to video games highlights the dissonance between the language and attitudes of young people and those of adult commentators.

I give my all only to video games	*Geemu dake ni ha miseru ganbari*
my way of life is game or die	*boku no ikisama geemu or dai*

old fogey analysts can never understand	*bunsekika oyaji ni surya fukakai*
but they "explain it" anyway,	*rikai dekinai no ni ittokitai*
with just the common put-down.	*kawainai arikitari no kudari.*
[analyst:] "Video games aren't just play	*"Geemu wa sude ni asobi de wa nai*
they've become a separate reality	*mō hitotsu no genjitsu ga sonzai*
kids can't separate reality from fantasy	*kyokō to genjitsu kubetsu dekinai*
and this makes it dangerous for children."	*kono mama jya kodomotachi abunai."*
[youth:] "Shut up!! Get out of my face!"	*"Uruchai! mō hotoite chōdai!"*

— Scha Dara Parr (1993) "Game Boys" *Potent Hits* (Ki/Oon-Sony, 1993, KSC2 93)

This characterization of adults as incapable of understanding youth carries over into SDP's use of language. In one interview, they remark on how entertaining it is to hear adults try their hand at youth slang, but they also credit older folks' dialects with rich possibilities (Koizumi 1995, 62).

Scha Dara Parr, as well as other groups, have become quite adept at creating neologisms out of American rap slang. They take a phrase like *get busy* and add the prefix *geki* (extremely) to make *geki gebbiji*. In a flyer advertising a new album, they promote their *geki yaba shitto* ("extremely bad shit," meaning good, of course). The phrase *brand new shit* has taken on the meaning of "recently released album." Other phrases have entered the Japanese youth lexicon as well and are widely used by rappers. "Yo check it" has been Japanized such that the first word is written with the Chinese character *yō* (as in *hitsuyō*) meaning "necessarily." This produces "You must check it out." Such bilingual puns extend the reach of English while diversifying the uses of Japanese. The same could be said for graffiti art in Japan that transforms kanji characters as aerosol art.

Scha Dara Parr's creative mixing of slang from English and Japanese reminds us that the influence of hip-hop on the Japanese language extends further than simply a choice between the two languages. Their experiments in creating new words and phrases relate to their particular performance style as well, one that mimics a small group of close friends just hanging out and joking with each other. The three-member group is led by MC Bose and the second rapper Ani. (*Ani* literally means "older brother," and he is the older brother of DJ Shinco.) I have seen SDP in concert and while recording a radio show. In those formal performance situations, they exude the warmth and jocular teasing of good friends. Hanging out with them after the late-night live radio show (1–3 a.m.), I was struck by how their onstage antics — joking with each other, playing off the others' dubious habits (e.g., munching on snacks in between songs onstage) — carried into their everyday conversation

12. "Year 2000 Samurai" aerosol art reworks *kanji* as graffiti, Sakuragi-cho.
Photo by the author.

as well. This playfulness indicates another way in which hip-hop and language transformation intersect, namely, not only as resistance against power but also in humor as pleasure and critique. Robin D. G. Kelley has cautioned analysts of hip-hop to beware of reading too much resistance into the music: "Some aspects of black expressive cultures certainly help inner city residents deal with and resist ghetto conditions, [but] few scholars acknowledge that what might also be at stake here are aesthetics, style and pleasure" (Kelley 1997, 17). Similarly, with sdp we see a playfulness that undermines adult-world pretensions and brings to the fore the value of peer-group approval. This echoes the findings of the music scholar Russell Potter who argues that the "spectacular vernaculars" of hip-hop require seeing "the ludic" and "the resistant" working in tandem, rather than operating in separate spheres (Potter 1995, 2).

K Dub Shine: Pride in Oneself as an Alternative Stance of Opposition

K Dub Shine's success in his solo career reflects his ability to write lyrics that continually challenge the limits of what can be said in Japanese hip-hop. More than his distinctive flow, more than his onstage presence, Shine's lyrics make him excellent and provoke thought. A brief look at some of his songs reveals a key player in the underground scene who, by the late 1990s, had built his own record label (Atomic Bomb Productions) and who continues to release albums regularly, now with major-label support. After King Giddra's groundbreaking first album, K Dub Shine released his first solo effort in 1997, *Genzai jikoku* (*The Time Now*), with an eye to message songs. His vision was neither the sentimental party rap of Umedy nor the playful, sideways glance of SDP. He portrayed a darker side of Japan.

The US emcee Chuck D of the group Public Enemy famously called hip-hop "black CNN" because it depicted a side of American life too often ignored by mainstream media outlets. Inspired, among others, by Public Enemy, Shine also portrays aspects of youth culture in more accurate ways than the supposedly objective reporting of journalists. One example is the song "Riyū naki hankō" ("Crime without Motivation") in which he raps about a junior high school boy bullied by his classmates. Day after day, the boy is beaten, kicked, spit on. His teachers know what goes on, but they do nothing about it. Finally, everything "goes white" for the boy, and he stabs the lead bully in the chest. The newspapers report the incident as "a crime without reason," but what Shine shows is that the explanation was always in plain sight, if only parents and teachers had paid attention. Shine uses this theme effectively in many of his songs, pointing to the ways that mass media focus on violence and sex yet never explore the underlying causes and deeper motivations behind the sensational news.

His bleak perspective partly reflects his upbringing. He grew up in Tokyo, but by junior high school, he was ready to flee. "I was the kind of person who was always the target in school," he told me in an interview in April of 1996. "And it wasn't so much the other students as it was the teachers. When I had a chance to go to the States, I jumped at it." In tenth grade, an exchange program transported him to Philadelphia, where he first encountered hip-hop. The style attracted him because emcees were the people speaking out against social problems in the United States. He began college at Temple University, where he studied sociology and black history. He later transferred to a college in Oakland, California, where he started befriending American rappers and working on his own rhymes, at first in English and then later in Japanese.

In Japanese, K Dub Shine has a talent for making striking links through the dense rhyming of kanji compounds, for example in the song "Last Emperor" ("Rasuto emperaa"):

negativity to positivity, a transformation	*negativitii kara pojitivitii henkan*
Space Battleship Yamato	*uchū senkan*

spirit of Japan waking up	*yamato damashii me zamashi*
a programmable drum machine . . .	*puroguramarareru doramu mashin . . .*
[chorus]	
those proud of who they are	*jibun ga jibun de aru koto hokoru*
are the ones who remain in the end	*sō iu yatsu ga saigo ni nokoru*

—K Dub Shine (1997) "Rasuto emperaa" (last emperor) *Genzai jikoku* (the time now)
(Avex/Cutting Edge, CTCR—14094)

His particular style of wordplay appears in the rhyming of "yamato dama-shii" (spirit of Japan) and "waking up" (*mezamashi*) with "a programmable drum machine." The English word *program* is even turned into a Japanese verb, *puroguramarareru*. Certain double meanings stand out as well. The term *Yamato* refers to the original imperial clan and thereby represents the Japa-nese people in the line "the spirit of Japan." But *Yamato* also ends the previous line as the name of the anime show *Space Battleship Yamato*. One could trace this technique of using *kakekotoba* (single words used for two meanings) to eighth-century poems in the *Man'yoshu* (Morris 1986, 578). In any case, this song suggests the density of poetic practices used in some Japanese hip-hop lyrics.

Protest against Offensive Language in Japanese Hip-Hop Lyrics

Shine's songs also stand out for their emphasis on a personal toughness and pride, but can this toughness go too far? Apparently so. In 2002, two singles by King Giddra (K Dub Shine, Zeebra, and DJ Oasis) made Japanese hip-hop history by becoming the first albums to be removed from store shelves by the record company because of disturbing lyrics.[13] In April 2002, King Giddra released two singles "F.F.B." and "Unstoppable." "F.F.B." (short for "fast food bitch") referred to women who took sex lightly. Because the song made refer-ences to AIDS, it was seen as discriminatory against both women and victims of the disease from both sexes. In addition, the record company (Def Star, a subsidiary of Sony Music Entertainment) was forced to take action with re-gard to the song "Drive-By" because it seemed to suggest that the rappers would happily shoot homosexuals (*homo yarō*): "fakers, homos, / with one shot I'll kill you / a drive-by with words" (*nisemon yarō homo yarō / ippatsu de shitomeru / kotoba no doraibu bai*).[14] Three days after the singles were re-leased, Sukotan Kikaku, a private organization aimed at improving the situa-tion for gays in Japan, posted a complaint about King Giddra on its Web site (www.sukotan.com). The head of the organization wrote that he received numerous e-mails from young, gay Japanese saying that they had received threats of violence (Itō 2002). In response to pressure from Sukotan Kikaku, HMV Japan, one of the major CD retailers, decided to stop playing the song on their in-store broadcasts. Two weeks after the initial release, Def Star records removed the remaining copies of the album from store shelves. A rewritten version of "F.F.B." appeared on King Giddra's full album released later. "Drive-By" was cut. According to *Blast* magazine, the members of King Giddra were forbidden to speak about the incident at the time. A couple of years later, Shine said in a published interview, "I don't discriminate against gays, even though that's what has been said. . . . I completely respect gays' contribution to creative works; that's something inside me" (Kobayashi 2004, 31). Shine added that he had wished to speak directly to the offended organization, but that the record company had forbidden it, fearing an escalation of tensions.

An interesting lesson regarding *genba*, retailers, audience, and record companies can be gleaned from this incident. A published discussion between the writers and editors of *Blast* magazine in August 2002 pointed out that this kind of "homo" language was common in the dancehall reggae circles where Zeebra (also of King Giddra) had been performing (*Blast* editors 2002, 116). (The controversies surrounding Eminem's offensive lyrics against gays, as well as those of various dancehall reggae groups from Jamaica, show that gay-bashing is not uniquely Japanese.) This reminds us that *genba* do not necessarily serve progressive purposes and, on the contrary, can be (and at times are) hotbeds of discriminatory attitudes. Whether Shine learned a lesson is anyone's guess. When I caught up with him at a recording studio in 2003, he declined to elaborate on the incident, but he did caution against reading too much social meaning into lyrics. "What you have to realize," he said, "is that rap is basically a tournament to see who can say the most outrageous things [*nan de mo itchatte taikai*]." His dis songs against more pop emcees have earned him anger from many corners of the rap world, but Shine seems to revel in the criticism. If, as Itō Seikō said years earlier, everyone wants images of the world's ruin, Shine is more than willing to provide them.

How Has Language Use Changed?

One of the puzzles of Japanese hip-hop involves how to explain the ways language use has changed in the music and culture over time. Listening to examples from the early years of Japanese rap music, one notes the presence of rhyming and rhythmic flow, but not in a very developed manner. In addition, audience members at the time needed explicit explanations for some of hip-hop's defining features, such as MC Bell's comments on the nature of rhyming. With some J-rap hits in the mid-1990s and a hardening of the underground stance, a somewhat dualistic battle was set in motion in an effort to define *Japanese* hip-hop. This did not mean simply unearthing historical precedents in Japan for hip-hop, but, rather, finding a way to express the attitudes and ideas inherent to hip-hop. Like Rhymester's b-boyism (see chapter 2), K Dub Shine's vision of the "Last Emperor" emphasized a self-defined aesthetic of toughness and language skill that was resolutely Japanese.

Since about 1999, however, the hip-hop scene in Japan has diverged drastically, making it, in actuality, difficult to identify a single scene. Should hip-hop's pop stars be compared with underground hip-hop anymore, or is the appropriate comparison with pop stars of other genres? Even within the category of Japanese hip-hop one may witness the phenomenon of "islands in space." With the increasing diversity of these islands, we find some that hold firmly to the idea that Japanese hip-hop should only be in Japanese. At the same time, the group M-Flo features Verbal, who raps many of his lyrics in English. A Korean Japanese who grew up in Tokyo but graduated from Boston College, Verbal explained in a July 2004 interview that he prefers English "because it rides the rhythm better than Japanese." And so the discourse of the 1960s rockers is kept alive today. Meanwhile, groups from different regions of Japan—including Gagle (Sendai), Infumiai Kumiai (Osaka), and M.O.S.A.D. (Nagoya)—bring their own slang to hip-hop, thereby further diversifying language possibilities within rap.

How might the idea of *genba* help us understand this nonlinear progression? I say nonlinear because there is no simple directional movement toward either localization or toward the meaning of Japaneseness. I considered titling this book *Represent Japan* to convey the autonomy of the Japanese approach to hip-hop. The problem, however, is that in recent years Japanese rappers are less likely to "represent Japan" than to represent a more circumscribed *genba*. It is a characteristic *genba* rather than anything that could be referred to as "the local" because the connections among scenes are not geographically bounded. According to Furukawa Kou, a writer and longtime observer of Japan's hip-hop scene, different regional scenes now inspire like-minded groups in distant locations. There are geographically local scenes. First Tha Blue Herb, then Shuren the Fire and Mic Jack Production—all from Sapporo—resemble each other in their use of more poetic lyrical stylings and less of an emphasis on pronounced rhythmic flow. Furukawa says when these groups tour, they find in different Japanese cities self-consciously "Sapporo-style" rappers as well. This process of differentiation and networking through the connectedness of *genba* makes sense (personal communication, July 2, 2005). It's a progression toward digression, perhaps, because working within a genre means that one must work ever harder to define a particular style. In the recording studio, we saw that process by which repetition, practice, and intense focus on perfecting one's skill drive cultural globalization. As these interactive battles keep developing, one starts to see why predictions of what will happen with hip-hop so often fail. The idea that hip-hop will disappear because one cannot rap in Japanese focuses on abstract features of rap (rhythm, rhyme) and Japanese (the absence thereof), when the motivating factors were (and are) located elsewhere: among those who spread the rumors of rhyme.

Conclusion

What does language use in Japanese hip-hop teach us about the power of English in global popular culture? I think it alerts us to the fact that evaluating the role of English depends on the location—the *genba*—in which the uses of nonstandard Japanese attain their aesthetic, and at times political, force. In the abstract, hip-hop in Japan supports Stuart Hall's assertion that global pop culture "speaks English." In the recording studio, Japanese emcees strive to make accented, rhyming lyrics, thus drawing on English-language poetics. Yet rappers' long-term, ongoing efforts to hone their lyrics generally result in a deeper appreciation of the possibilities of the Japanese language. Being a better rapper requires developing a deeper sense of the ways to sculpt the Japanese language. The competition between emcees to develop a distinctive stance generates diversity within the scene—whether this means rappers like SDP using neologisms, Umedy striving to portray emotional complexity, or K Dub Shine acting tough and depicting the seamy side of Japanese youth culture. As Itō Seikō suggested in identifying rumors as an engine of globalization, language use on the ground may look like Westernization, but it can also be viewed in terms of trying to change old, elitist ways. At the end of the nineteenth century, this may have meant shedding the traditions of Edo-era Japan, but at the end of the twentieth century, Japanese rappers were more likely to criticize the elite media for their distortions of youth culture.

The power of language in Japanese hip-hop, therefore, operates on several levels. We cannot evaluate the influence of the English language on Japanese unless we specify the position of those using the language. I suggested some different perspectives on the collision between English and Japanese by looking at it from the viewpoints of novice Japanese-language learners, *Nihonjinron* commentators, and rappers who see rhyming rap as a way to liberate artificial Japanese. In the end, there is no single location from which to evaluate all the uses of English, but by thinking in terms of nested *genba*, we can identify places to look at for developing analytical frameworks to evaluate the politics of language. In the end, hip-hop in Japan produces no single, linear progression toward localization (or toward global convergence), but, rather, competing styles that are enacted through language. This contingent view of language politics may help us see beyond some of the stereotypes that see (and hear) all uses of English as evidence of "American influence." In fact, we need a sense of the speakers' *genba* to even understand what they are saying in English.

CHAPTER 6

WOMEN RAPPERS AND THE PRICE OF CUTISMO

The relative scarcity of women rappers in Japan presents an analytical puzzle. Given that Japanese record company executives regard women consumers and artists as the key to many major pop hits, why have there been so few women emcees? Except for Yuri, of East End X Yuri—regarded by many hip-hop musicians as a negative example, embodying what is *not* hip-hop but merely pop—male emcees and deejays dominate the story of hip-hop in Japan. Some specialty music magazines tend to exclude women emcees from the category of "real" hip-hop, thereby to some extent creating an artificial blind spot, but this cannot serve as the whole explanation. Quite simply, far fewer women rappers than men have been making albums. In this regard, hip-hop is somewhat unusual, a veritable macho island in a sea of cute stars. Is there something about hip-hop ideals as expressed in nightclubs and record companies that hinders women's participation as rappers? If so, what does this suggest about the dynamics of hip-hop, gender, and globalization in Japan?

When I ask Japanese artists and music magazine writers why there are so few women rappers, most of them simply shrug their shoulders. Some suggest that "hip-hop is just a manly thing [*otokorashii*]" and leave it at that. In some ways this response accurately reflects the numerical dominance of men in hip-hop, whether on stage in clubs, in the specialty hip-hop magazines, and on radio shows presenting the latest rap music. Two books that examine the history of Japanese hip-hop include interviews with over twenty people, all of whom are men (Gotō 1997; Krush et al. 1998). Another overview of the scene circa 1996 lists 125 active Japanese groups and solo artists, including both rappers and deejays (Egaitsu 1997a). Of these, only eight included women (two mixed groups, three all-female groups, three solo women).[1] In the early 2000s, the Japanese rap groups who achieved some success in sales were almost exclusively groups of men, such as Rip Slyme, Kick the Can Crew, Scha Dara Parr, Rhymester, King Giddra, and Ketsumeishi. But as we saw in chapter 4, women make up the majority of the fan base of certain hip-hop groups, especially those in the party-rap vein, such as Scha Dara Parr, Dassen Trio, and EDU. Even these groups feature all men. Gender is clearly a key dimension for understanding which Japanese hip-hop groups achieve success, and yet the importance of the female fan has not (yet) translated into a sizable presence of women rappers onstage.

The idea of the pyramid of the music scene, whereby artists move up depending on their ability to pass through industry gatekeeping (discussed in chapter 3), provides a partial explanation for the imbalance. If we distinguish between fans' power and record-company power, we are reminded that artists must pass through record-company gates in order to get recording contracts, album releases, and access to media promotion. The majority of these gates are controlled by men, and their prejudices regarding what a rapper should be undoubtedly play a role. Like their male counterparts, even some of the women in record-company executive suites have at times reinforced the notion that hip-hop should be hard core (haado koa) and can prefer tough, masculine performance styles.[2]

In the first years of the twenty-first century, however, a few women participating in Japan's hip-hop scene have managed to navigate a path between both cute and macho stereotypes. Whether or not this foretells of a broader change in gender norms in Japan is beyond the scope of this chapter. Instead, I offer a more limited ethnographic look at the musicians Ai, Hime, and Miss Monday to discuss the ways they have carved out a space for themselves in a world dominated by men both on stage and in the corporate suites. In contrast to the carefree party-rap vibe, the more recent female artists engender a space that is neither macho in the battling-samurai mode nor stereotypically feminine cute. This is significant because in parallel to a kind of machismo common among male rappers, many women singers in Japan's pop music world are expected to conform to a particular type of feminine cuteness, which I propose calling "cutismo." In contrast, the more recent female hip-hoppers discussed here represent for women (*onna daihyō*) in a way that rejects images of feminine vulnerability. (Such an attitude is not unique to women in hip-hop.) In addition, a few women have played important roles in promoting the music in record companies. I discuss in particular Riko Sakurai, who was a top executive from the launch of Def Jam Japan in 2001 until late 2003.

In chapter 2, we saw how the machismo of battling heightened the aesthetic stakes between the different groups and families, and how the character of these battles shifted over time as the contexts around the music changed. As the hip-hop scene evolved from asking the question, "What is hip-hop?" to wondering, "What is *Japanese* hip-hop?" to exemplifying diverse regional, class, and stylistic variations along numerous lines, so, too, have women hip-hoppers gradually taken more diverse stances toward feminine ideals. Yet the relative scarcity of female emcees also means that, like it or not, they are interpreted as women rappers more than, say, Saitama rappers or Hachioji rappers (i.e., different regions around Tokyo). Women in Japanese hip-hop, both on stage and behind the scenes, face a somewhat different set of challenges than those confronting men. But in ways similar to the operation of the star system for male rappers, women musicians who have risen to prominence have become a standard against which other female artists are forced to define themselves. In this sense, cutismo exacts a price on all women in the music business, even those who resist the stereotype. We can see this through examples of Yuri and in the R & B styles of Utada Hikaru. Yet three b-girls—Ai, Miss Monday, and Hime—suggest possibilities for alternative formulations of the feminine hip-hopper.

Cutismo in Rap and the Pop Music Imaginary

Ichii Yuri was a singer with a revolving-door girl group called Tokyo Performance Doll. (There were other regional versions of the "performance doll" brand, for example in Osaka and cities in Asia.) Pop idols are a remarkably successful industry in Japan, premised on the notion that the singer need not be exceptionally talented, but is, rather, just a "normal girl" (*futsū no ko*). Thus the cuteness of an idol singer should not be equated with either beauty or virtuosity, but rather with an approachable intimacy. Tokyo Performance Doll (TPD) provides just one example of the kind of girl group in which the performers are not only interchangeable but also replaceable. Yuri had been part of TPD for a while and was seeking to do something a little different. She thought rap might be just the thing.

The group East End was originally composed of the rapper Gaku, DJ Yoggy, and the DJ/producer Rock-Tee. In 1992, they released their first album, *The Beginning of the End*, on the independent label File Records. As part of the marketing blitz that followed their success with Yuri, Gaku and Yoggy tell the story of how the collaboration developed (East End X Yuri 1995). Since the sales of their first album were only moderate, File Records told East End it would be hard to release another album. Meanwhile, Yuri and Gaku were friends. When Yuri was preparing for a solo show, she wanted to try rapping, so she began practicing with Gaku. In February 1994, Gaku performed with Yuri for a part of her show. Impressed by the combination, File Records decided to sign them together for a minialbum. Here we see elements of both gatekeeping and cutismo. East End on their own faced obstacles, but with the pop star Yuri, they got a second chance. At first, DJ Yoggy was skeptical about working with an idol singer: "Basically, at the time I thought 'idol = puppet' [*ningyō*]. Idols don't perform live. But for us, we always performed live" (32). Yoggy here referred to the fact that idols often lip-synch their lyrics in shows and emphasize dancing and costume changes rather than the music. But when Yoggy discovered that Yuri could indeed perform live, he came around. The story of what happened next gives some insight into the opportunities and risks involved in moving up the pyramid from indies to majors.

In June 1994, East End X Yuri released *Denim-ed Soul* on File Records, a minialbum with four songs. The back of the CD showed East End as five guys (two dancers plus Yoggy, Gaku, and Rock-Tee) along with Yuri. The single "Da.Yo.Ne." moved up the charts. The group was then picked up by Epic Sony, a major label, which released their full album *Denim-ed Soul 2*. All the photos, as well as the logo, on this album featured only Yuri and two East End members (Yoggy and Gaku), thus shedding the two dancers and the producer Rock-Tee. It is not uncommon for groups to lose members as they move up the pyramid, and though each group has its own reasons, one imagines that corporate marketing strategies play a role. (Years later Rock-Tee explained to me that he left because of "artistic differences," but he declined to elaborate.) The singles "Maicca" and "Da.Yo.Ne." both sold around a million copies. The record company also had "Da.Yo.Ne." remade by other groups, each translating the slang term (roughly, "yeah, you're right") into a variety of local dialects (Kansai, Hiroshima, Hokkaido, etc.). This kind of marketing strategy is precisely what makes record companies vulnerable to the charge that they will try any gimmick to sell a few CDs. It also enmeshed East End X Yuri more deeply in the world of commercial pop.

Moving up the pyramid of a music scene from the independent level to a major label also meant that for East End X Yuri success was now defined by much larger returns. The Faustian bargain of becoming pop stars fell harshly on them. Their next single "Ne" was released in the fall of 1996, but it failed to live up to sales expectations, despite a TV commercial tie-up with a trendy car. Rumors placed sales at around seventy thousand, which would have been enormous if they had remained with their indie label, but it was deemed a complete flop after their previous hits. Epic Sony let the group go: the pyramid is not only a ladder to the top but can also be a slippery slope down as well. Yuri went on to be a TV talent (i.e., a celebrity talking head on game and talk shows). Yoggy reportedly ran a flower store for a while. Gaku struggled for years to make it back into the recording studio. In fact, the Funky Grammar Night freestyle session discussed in chapter 3 was one of his first forays back onto stage after he had gone big and then crashed. One hip-hop artist commented that Gaku was caught in an impossible situation. He had lost credibility in the club scene because he had joined the world of pop idols. At the same time, no record company wanted to be associated with a failed has-been. One aspect of the music scene's pyramid is that people's location is very visible. Artists know where their sales stand in relation to others, and few report being completely satisfied. As we can see with East End, even artists who achieve million-sellers are not guaranteed smooth careers. In the end, Gaku managed something of a comeback, releasing two more solo albums, but only years later.

The movement of stars up and down the pyramid also influences the ways record companies judge the excitement of particular genres and styles (see Negus 1999). Overall, the East End X Yuri moment for Japanese hip-hop set in motion major-label signings of party-rap groups (like Now, a three-woman group), but the failure of their (and others') follow-ups also may have poisoned the well for cute party rap. Still, the hits of Yuri's group reflected broader trends linking cutismo and consumerism. Although the experiment failed for J-rap (in the eyes of record companies), the formula of cute consumption more generally thrives in Japan.

Cutismo, Pop Music, and Women Consumers

Outside of hip-hop, women singers from other genres compete powerfully with male-oriented groups. Indeed, the best-selling artists in Japan's pop music history are women, namely, Utada Hikaru and Hamasaki Ayumi. One could argue that even the edgy, masculinist styles of groups like Kishidan (a "yankee," i.e., young tough group, albeit with a humorous side) achieved their success by drawing female fans. Whenever I spoke with major-label record-company executives, they would always identify young women as the driving force behind all kinds of hit products. On the streets of Shibuya, it is the young girls in their school uniforms who are the focus of TV interviewers tracking the latest fads. Moreover, viewing women as the touchstones of trendiness tends to become a kind of self-fulfilling prophecy, producing a gendered bias in a feedback loop of artists, record companies, media, and fans.

It is important to note, however, that there is no single image of femininity that dominates such trends, especially perhaps in the world of popular music. As discussed in earlier chapters, the history of popular music in Japan is characterized by shifts in production methods, fan attachments, and genre trends. The anthropologist James Stanlaw (2000) has drawn attention to the language and gender dimensions of some of these changes as well. In the late 1970s and early 1980s, the girl group O'nyanko Club (Kitten Club) performed titillating songs like "Don't Take Off My Sailor Suit!" (a reference to the school uniforms worn by junior and senior high school students). Notably, the lyrics were written by in-house writers (presumably men). Stanlaw identifies a trend in which some female singers like Yuki (of the Judy and Mary Band) and Yuming (aka Matsutoya Yumi) shed vestiges of pop-idol femininity in favor of more forthright, even tomboyish, lyrics, often using English words. Stanlaw argues that the use of English lifts these singers out of their Japanese context and can ease some of the constraints they may feel when using traditional Japanese language or themes. This is a provocative contention, and it may well reflect the experience of these songwriters, but I would also suggest that the dynamic relationship between language use and larger performance contexts should be considered as well.

For example, the dominant mode of "fashionably cute" recognized by record companies in the mid-1990s grew in part out of shifts in the music market toward a greater emphasis on women consumers. As mentioned before, the writer Kōtarō Asō (1997) pointed to how CD players, karaoke boxes, and trendy dramas drew large numbers of women consumers to the recording industry. He argued that this constituted a key factor in the explosion of million-selling hits in the mid-1990s: girls and young women drove these music booms. Whether or not this accurately reflects market dynamics, the belief itself can become a kind of self-fulfilling prophecy. The feedback loops of marketing, sales, observation and reporting, and new production reinforce networks enmeshing young women in music trends. If Japanese popular culture stands for one thing in a global imaginary, it may well be the cult of the cute. Asō's analysis gives a very explicit example of how record companies actively theorize the power of cute in its ability to draw a certain kind of female consumer. In the next chapter, I will examine how the mapping of nonfan consumers, such as "the kind of woman who buys Ayumi Hamasaki" (a pop star), reproduces a power of cute defined by cross-product synergy, using artists to sell soap to sell magazines to sell TV shows.

Yet if this power of cute accrues to certain kinds of products such as trendy, drama-ending theme songs or karaoke-friendly pop hits, does that mean that women who express their cutismo also attain power? Not necessarily. Consider Sharon Kinsella's definition of Japan's idea of cute: "*Kawaii* or 'cute' essentially means childlike; it celebrates sweet, adorable, innocent, pure, simple, genuine, gentle, vulnerable, weak, and inexperienced social behavior and physical appearances" (1995, 220). While it might seem that this lionization of a feminine ideal could empower young women, the catch-22 is that women and girls have been encouraged not only to idolize cute but also to become cute. This means that "young people became popular according to their apparent weakness, dependence and inability rather than their strengths and capabilities" (226). This illustrates how cutismo as a source of women's power is in many ways a self-defeating proposition.[3] Because cute "power" depends on weakness, vulnerability, and a lack of responsibility, there are limits on how much authority one can achieve by using it.

Another media phenomenon linking cutismo to capitalism occurred in the mid- to late 1990s in the sensationalism surrounding the commodification of high school girls' sexuality. News reports about high school girls who would go on "paid dates" with older men reflected a different use of the cute, one that seemed potentially more self-directed than serving tea as an "office lady." Schoolgirls were quoted calling themselves "brand-name" items, paid by salarymen to go to dinner or to sing karaoke.[4] The moral panic that ensued generated its own advertising, both for the girls who participated in this phenomenon and, perhaps more centrally, for the (male-dominated) media outlets that covered the sensational stories with arguably more attraction than abhorrence (Iida 2000). The media storm, too, revolved more around the public's condemnation of the girls' material motives than around questioning the salarymen's actions in paying for the services. As John Treat points out more generally, young women (or *shōjo*) were not respected for their ability to produce: "The role of the *shōjo* in this [Japan's] service economy was not to make the products but to consume them" (Treat 1996b, 281). Cutismo is an all-consuming power. Yet even in consumerism, some resistance to dominant norms appears. For example, Laura Miller (2003) argues that high school *kogal* (small gal) use writing on top of small photo prints (which they trade among themselves) to question the feminine roles assigned to them by the adult world. Laura Miller draws our attention to their communication within peer groups, as opposed to in the mediated world of magazines and television. These brief examples are meant to be suggestive of some broader contexts for understanding gender in popular music.

The Japanese R & B Boom and Women's Voices

In the late 1990s, a Japanese R & B boom led by women singers helped to bring (male) Japanese hip-hop into mainstream consciousness. Sparked by female artists like Misia, Utada Hikaru, and groups like Double and Sugar Soul, this "new R & B" (*nyū aru ando bii*) was characterized by melodic and attractive young women singers. The music tends to be bass heavy with an emphasis on the rhythms and always with a token DJ scratch solo. As these singers and groups produced hit songs, they often recorded remix versions with Japanese rappers accompanying them. Zeebra appeared with Misia and Sugar Soul, Rhymester with Double, Muro with Misia, and so on. One of the intriguing contrasts with the earlier J-rap boom begun with East End X Yuri and Scha Dara Parr is that the more recent artists hail from the underground scene rather than the party-rap world. As we saw in chapter 4, however, the underground-party divide of the mid-1990s was as much about the gender of the fans as about the musical style. In the late-1990s, this gender divide shifted to characterize production: now male rappers were contrasted with female R & B singers. I would argue that this reinforced the gendered bias equating rap with men. We can see this in the media. For example, a writer for *Remix*, a "club and street sounds magazine," compares the flighty fad of Japanese R & B with what he calls the "mature foundation" of hip-hop: "Now that it seems the so-called Japanese R & B/melody-oriented songs are starting to fade, we've reached the stage where there will be some natural weeding out. . . . But there's no worry about that for Japanese hip-hop, because the scene itself is supported by people choosing the authentic over the fake. Now more than ever, true ability and originality will distinguish those artists who preserve 'realness' [*riarusa*]" (Kinoshita 2000, 14–15). Although couched in language contrasting "mere fads" with "true ability," the masculinist sensibility in evaluating the music is worth noting. Although the women singers may be more popular, they are, according to this line of thinking, less real. Yet it was the new R & B boom that brought a variety of the underground hip-hop artists into the national spotlight. In the late 1990s, it was the resolutely masculine, outsider, tough-guy stance of Zeebra, Muro, and Rhymester that provided a striking contrast to the melodic and feminine world of Japanese R & B. An intriguing example of the pairing of female singing and male rap featured a newcomer singer, Rima, with the rapper Umedy. Together they reworked a 1970s pop song ("Yoake no skat") that revolved around a popular theme from classical Japanese drama, dating back to the 1600s: love suicides (*shinjū*). This suggests a more complex interaction than Stanlaw's association of English with new feminine ideals. Even traditional Japanese themes can be reworked to speak to changing norms. What became emphasized in this duet was the masculinity of rapping and the femininity of singing.

The best-selling album in Japanese pop music history also illustrates the kind of cutismo (rather than tomboyishness) that can emerge even with a mixing of English and Japanese. The debut album *First Love* (1999) by R & B singer Utada Hikaru set a postwar record for album sales, topping more than 9 million copies. She is a remarkable singer, raised both in New York and Tokyo, bilingual, and with musical parents. She appeals to a deep pop sensibility. One thing that stands out in her early lyrics—for example, in the song "Addicted"—is the vulnerability at the core of *kawaii*. She longs for a man who does not return her calls, and it pains her. She wants to meet him and acknowledges in the bilingual hook, "I may be addicted to you" (*kimi ni* addicted *ka mo*). The music video, shot in Taiwan, revels in pan-Asian imagery—red dragons, paper screens, silhouetted break-dancers, a hundred bicycle-riding, Walkman-listening Asian youth—a kind of global consumer *kawaii*. Utada defined the pinnacle of Japanese pop music in the late 1990s with a style that drew on hip-hop production methods of sampled, bass-heavy music. While this became a standard by which other female artists would be judged, other women in the music industry were forging different models for success. Intriguingly, the way in which Utada represents a kind of standard J-R&B language, in part due to her commercial success, might be seen as mirroring the social processes that reinforce ideas of standard women's language.

In addition to contrasts between English and Japanese, we might also consider how ideas of "women's language" relate to certain kinds of lyrics. When male emcees say "hip-hop is a manly thing" as a way of explaining the scarcity of women emcees in Japan, they are partly referring to stereotypes of gendered language use. As we have seen, hip-hop stresses self-emphasis (*jibun shuchō*). The language scholar Masayoshi Shibatani (1990, 374) notes, in contrast, that "women's speech is characterized by softness and politeness, . . . [which] derives from the less frequent use of Sino-Japanese forms in preference to native Japanese forms and from the general avoidance of the rough forms used by men." In this sense, women tend to be regarded as "more Japanese" than men, at least in terms of their language use. But such generalizations have little explanatory power if they are not put into specific locations and historical contexts. As the anthropologist Mariko Tamanoi (1990) shows, women's voices have the potential "to explode order and to restore contradiction and diversity in the anthropology of Japan" (309) because overall claims about Japanese identity too often elide the gendering of mainstream stereotypes.

So-called women's speech is one domain where assertions of a timeless, universal Japaneseness must constantly be called into question. According to the linguistic anthropologist Shigeko Okamoto (1995), women's speech was particularly encouraged during the Meiji era and is a construct based largely on the speech style of middle- and upper middle-class women, particularly those who expressed the soft-spoken, indirect, and refined ideals of "Yamanote language," which refers to the area of Tokyo regarded as more effete, and which contrasts with the rough, direct, and vulgar style of *shita-machi kotoba* (downtown language). The disciplining of women's language coincided with government efforts to promote the feminine ideal of the good wife and wise mother and was thus both related to class and normative. In the late 1980s and early 1990s, young women were frequently castigated in the popular press for their supposedly vulgar language. Yet based on recordings collected in 1992, Okamoto found wide variation in the use of feminine speech among college students. She argues that women use speech strategically to communicate pragmatic meanings and images of self. Masculine speech by women is thus not degenerate or vulgar so much as "meaningful choice based on their understandings of themselves . . . situated in specific interpersonal relationships and sociocultural contexts" (317). In some ways, this kind of research points to a *genba* notion of cultural value by highlighting the situated and conjunctural character of language choices. Thus we can come to a deeper understanding of song lyrics by attending to the strategic uses of different kinds of language, not just English versus Japanese, and by mapping a shift in how popular female artists construct their performative personas. A possible transformation can be seen both in executive suites of record companies and onstage.

Post-cutismo in the Executive Suites and Onstage

One woman's career path illustrates how the chances of succeeding as an executive in the music business depend on navigating multiple kinds of bias. Riko Sakurai's success demonstrates the improvisatory and entrepreneurial skills needed to rise in the music world. When I first met Riko in 1996, she was working as an MTV-Japan VJ, introducing US hip-hop to a Japanese audience. In 2001, she helped launch Def Jam Japan and soon oversaw a stable of six artists and a staff of around thirty people. In 2004, she helped coordinate Utada Hikaru's debut English-language album in the United States on Island/Def Jam in New York—a remarkable achievement for a woman who grew up in a town of twenty thousand inhabitants a couple hours from Tokyo.

In the fall of 1996 in a coffee shop in Shibuya, Riko told me her story. Her mother was a banker and her father a member of the Communist Party in Japan. Though he was a candidate in every election, he never held office. Nevertheless, Riko says her family was discriminated against because of her father's politics. She received no birthday-party invitations from neighborhood friends; the police tapped their phone; they were blackmailed. Riko attended International Christian University in Tokyo, where she learned English and studied sociology. She was also part of Galaxy, a soul music "circle" (college student club) based at Waseda University. The members met weekly to discuss the latest music and to gossip about their friends. Their big project was to hold a dance party at the annual school festival. Of the fifteen or so members, she was the only woman. "At first, they didn't think a woman could talk intelligently about music," she explained, but even so, she managed to hold her own within the group. Quite a few music groups emerged from friendships formed in Galaxy, including Rhymester, Mellow Yellow, and DJ Ben. "Now it's famous, so it's cool to be a member, but back then, we weren't cool," said Riko.

Riko graduated from college in 1993. She applied for a job at one of the largest marketing and research firms in Japan and made it to the second round of interviews. Riko explained that at the follow-up interview with a vice president, he had only one question: " 'What does your father do?' I made something up, but they had already hired a private investigator, and they knew. They didn't care anything about who I was, only what my father did. I knew I needed to find something different." Riko eventually landed a job with the public broadcasting company NHK ("they are government run, so they can't hire investigators"). At the same time, she worked part-time as the tour manager for De La Soul, Run-DMC, and A Tribe Called Quest when they came to Japan. It was this work that led to an offer to become an MTV-Japan VJ. She sees hip-hop as teaching the younger generation to express themselves and to have their own opinion. Judging from the faxes the show received, "Teenage girls are most interested in my show. They say they like that I express my own opinion. That's rare on television." Riko looked down on the women announcers on NHK news shows: "They are just passive Muppets. They teach women to be victims." Riko presented the MTV show for seven years and also had a show on one of Tokyo's most popular FM stations, J-Wave.

For two years (1999–2001) Riko also wrote a column about hip-hop for the *Asahi* newspaper, the second largest daily in Japan. Her final column included these thoughts about hip-hop and Japan:

In Japan, where the negative aspects of group consciousness are so strong, where people get carried along by the mass trends and worry too much about what others think, the hip-hop world's posture is especially important. Because the challenge is to avoid acting out like children or isolating oneself, and rather to find the stance that will help you lead your life. I'm not a rapper, but my aim is to use the ideal of "self emphasis" to keep moving forward. (Sakurai 2002, 8)

She clearly drew on these ideals when she helped launch Def Jam Japan in 2001. Def Jam is, of course, one of the most powerful labels in the hip-hop world in the United States, and the company has branched out with some overseas ventures. Under the umbrella of Universal Music, Def Jam Japan was ostensibly headed by someone else, but Riko was given free rein to choose the first artists to support.

Although most of the earliest artists signed to Def Jam Japan were men —Dabo (of Nitro Microphone Underground), Sphere of Influence (Zeebra's younger brother), Tokona-X (of M.O.S.A.D.) and S-Word (pronounced "sword") —the one woman Riko produced deserves special attention. Ai is a singer in the R & B vein, not a rapper, but with her first release, she took a very different path than that followed by the Japanese R & B then dominating the charts. During a visit to the Massachusetts Institute of Technology (MIT) in October 2003, Riko described meeting Ai while dancing at a club. She noticed that Ai had marks on her arm; it turned out she was in an abusive relationship. There on the dance floor, Riko and Ai connected, even though Ai's background had little in common with that of Riko. According to the biography posted on Def Jam Japan's Web site, Ai was born in 1981 in Los Angeles, learned singing in a gospel choir, and is fully bilingual. Her mother "half-Japanese, half-Italian," and her father Japanese. When Ai was four, he was transferred back to Japan, and she spent her youth going back and forth between Kagoshima and Los Angeles. She studied dance in Los Angeles and even appeared in one of Janet Jackson's videos.

In a personal communication in October 2003, Riko told me that Ai's 2003 debut single "Last Words" was hailed by Chikada Haruo (one of the original rappers with Vibrastone in the 1980s), who for several years has been writing a weekly column about hit songs called "Kangaeru hitto" ("Thinking about Hits"). He called it a new moment for Japanese R & B because unlike the longing, vulnerable, dependent image that characterized most of this genre, Ai's lyrics encouraged making a clean break. Her last words? "Get the hell out of my life." She provides one example of the ways that being a b-girl has transformed into something quite different from the models of both Yuri and Utada. In this, she shares something with two other women emcees from Japan.

A woman rapper who calls herself Miss Monday illustrates that at least one major record label is willing to support an emcee who does not rely on cutismo. Miss Monday identifies herself as representing women (*onna daihyō*), but her perspective does not translate into a simple ideological program, and it grows out of years of work in the music business. She might be viewed as a freeter who kept at her musical career for years before finally getting her big break. I have known Monday since the fall of 1995, when I began attending a weekly Thursday night event at a club in Harajuku called Grass. At that time, she was part of a three-woman group called Now. Monday and Yuka were dancers who backed up the rapper Baby Setsu. As mentioned before, their style tended toward the *kawaii* end of the spectrum, with love songs about pagers and convenience stores. They signed a two-year contract with a major record label as part of the wave of signings following in the wake of East End X Yuri's million-selling hits. But after East End X Yuri's poor sales in the fall of 1995, Now were called into the record company's offices and told the company was reneging on their two-year contract after only one year. Over the next few years, Monday worked with Umedy (a rapper with EDU) to keep active in the music scene while living at home and working part-time. She continued to practice as a singer and rapper, eventually landing a contract with the independent label Id Records. In 2000, nearly six years after Monday was scouted by Umedy (he saw her group dancing in a Tsukuba shopping mall), Id released her first solo album (a minialbum).

Miss Monday's indie EP was well received. She was picked up by the major label Epic Sony, which released her full-length debut album *Free Ya* in 2002. This was followed by another solo album titled *Natural* in 2003. The title track of *Natural* encapsulates Monday's unassuming yet assertive style in which she describes her indifference to all the times people have told her "it can't be done" (*muri*). In this she is "representing for the ladies," but in a style she contrasts with the brash, masculine b-boyism ideology we heard espoused by

Rhymester in chapter 2. In an e-mail communication of February 2004 she said to me,

Although I do sing a song called "Guide for Lady MC," actually it's not that I'm trying to represent [*daihyō*] for all women rappers. For emcees, there's always the sense that you have to say "I'm number one!" but I'm really not that type. What I want to say is, "Even if you're a girl, do what you want to do." It doesn't have to be hip-hop. You can be a mechanic or a truck driver. My attitude is, together as women let's challenge ourselves to do what we want.

It is a post–Japanese R & B moment in that she does not spend time lamenting lost opportunities or unrequited loves, but rather expresses a desire to do more for herself.

Although sales of Monday's first solo album were only around twenty thousand, her second album sold over thirty thousand. This growth in sales was all the more impressive because sales in the record industry as a whole were dropping sharply at the time. Monday now tours regularly, performing with the American artists The Pharcyde and Ja Rule, for example, when they came to Japan. Only five feet tall, Monday is small, with a quick smile and a warm, lively personality that her representatives say make her popular at the record-company offices, where she apparently provides a sharp contrast to the stereotype of surly, unresponsive male rappers. Monday draws a largely teenage girl crowd. Her videos have no sex kittens, the male break-dancers stay in the back, and it is Monday's message that is in the front.

Hime offers another example of a solo female rapper from the early 2000s and something of a foil to Miss Monday. Hime's solo debut, titled *Hime hajime* (*Hime's First*), was released by DJ Honda's label in October 2003. DJ Honda has a store in SoHo in New York City and offices in Tokyo and Seoul, so his support of a female rapper is only one aspect of his contributions to a more complex future for transnational hip-hop. Hime, whose stage name translates roughly as "princess," grabbed attention in 2003 among free-paper and some underground hip-hop magazine writers. Born in 1979, she represents for Hachioji (in western Tokyo), as well as calling herself, like Monday, representing for women. She is notable for her explicit uses of Japanese clichés in her music, such as describing how to write the kanji for *hime* ("with woman on the left, giant on the right"). She calls herself the voice of the "Japanese doll" and even has a kind of fight song for so-called yellow cabs. *Yellow cab*, as Karen Kelsky (2001) has explained, is a derogatory term for a Japanese woman who will pick up anyone. Hime rejects that slur, proposing instead that being a yellow cab means that women are in the driver's seat.

Hime also appreciates the traditional rhythms of the Japanese language. Here again we see the importance of locating generalized features of so-called women's language (e.g., that women speak in more traditional forms) in specific contexts. Hime's use of Japanese clichés is provocative in a club setting where the latest slang from MTV tends to be most valued. In contrast, after a show in Ebisu in July 2004, Hime talked about how she likes to write haiku. Explicitly Japanese imagery and sounds permeate her songs. In the song "If the Peony Stands," she calls herself a "female samurai," striking out with her sword, sitting beneath cherry blossoms, rapping about Japan's four seasons.

a sober girl not caring about rank	*shirafu de bureikō na reijō*
neither old or new, an apprentice geisha	*konjyaku towazu suru oshaku*
like a flower, watchful underwater	*shakuyaku no fūbō suimenka de shūtō*
a flower's life is short, time tells	*hana no inochi hakanaki jiki ni hakarai*
challenge yourself in battles	*idomu tatakai*
hey heads, skip the excuses	hey heads, *doke kuchi toke*
gorgeous, the Japanese doll talks back	*inase ni tōru Japanese doll mono mōsu*

Although the verses work in rhyming patterns, that is, the imported rap poetics, Hime uses an ancient poetry form, the thirty-one-syllable tanka, for the chorus.

this sound,	*kono oto to*
giri and ninjo	*giri to ninjō*
the spirit of harmony	*wa no kokoro*
will the surprise attack	*kishū suru ka na*
come from the peony?	*shakuyaku no hana*

—Hime (2003) "Tateba shakuyaku" *Hime hajime* (DJ Honda Recordings, DHCA-1, Tokyo)

Hime says she is a "Japanese doll," but one who talks back, even as images of cherry blossoms falling on her black hair evoke a certain degree of femininity. What highlights the complex mixture of hip-hop and Japan, however, is the sampling she employs. The song opens with the sound of a *taiko* drum and what sounds like a traditional narrator of kabuki or bunraku saying "yo." Not only does Hime use poetics of classical Japanese poetry by creating the chorus in tanka form she says in a later verse, "It is the spirit of the language in the 5-7-5-7-7 form [5-7-5-7-7 *no kotodama*] that will lead others to raise the white flag." Because Hime focuses on male rappers ("lots of fists," as she says earlier in the song), her use of the term *kotodama* offers a suggestive lesson for Japan studies.

Rethinking Japan Studies: The Spirit of the Language in Different *Genba*

The term *kotodama* deserves some comment because it provides insight into an ongoing debate between those (often Japanese) commentators who emphasize the uniqueness of the Japanese language and those (often Western) Japan studies scholars who critique assertions of uniqueness by showing the social constructedness of ethnic essentialism. For example, Roy Andrew Miller (1982) has pointed out that the term *kotodama* has been used by *Nihonjinron* writers to suggest that the Japanese language (*koto*) has abiding within it a unique spirit (*tama*). Roy Miller points out that such assertions of uniqueness were used to pursue militarist nationalist policies in the period leading up to World War II. Hence, in his view (and I agree), claims of uniqueness are often used to discipline segments of Japanese society, not unlike criticisms of women who use supposedly vulgar (i.e., masculine) language.

Yet Hime's use of the word shows that the term *kotodama* can be used for progressive cultural interventions as well. In attempting to carve out a space for her voice in the male-dominated world of Japanese rap, she is playing with traditional clichés. Using tanka poetry forms alongside reworkings of the idea of the yellow cab, Hime shows that we must locate the constructedness of essentialism in particular *genba*. The term *kotodama* itself need not reinforce a nationalist uniqueness. In the case of her lyrics, she implies that the magic of the Japanese language endures even when performed in a rap song, a borrowed form made her own through clever word play. This, I would argue, constitutes a progressive use of the term. This means that Japan studies critiques that aim to point out the constructedness of Japanese identity may be able to sharpen their point of attack by specifying in greater detail the evolving contexts in which such constructions take place. For me, the idea of the *genba* provides a way for theorizing such contexts.

In the collective, improvisational, and performative character of Hime's rap, we can see this particular moment for women in Japanese hip-hop. Hime still feels she must identify herself as a female rapper, yet she, like Miss Monday, experiments with a range of symbolic resources that speak to a feminine stance beyond cutismo. She negotiates the seeming discordance between woman and emcee by drawing on recognizably Japanese images — the yellow cab, the woman samurai, and even the apprentice geisha (*oshaku*). To the extent that this represents one response to the global machismo prevalent in hip-hop, Hime shows some tendency to battle with male emcees on their own turf by asserting her own autonomous control.

Conclusion

What can we say about the gendered dimension of transnational popular culture? The relative absence of women in Japanese hip-hop is important to keep in mind because it serves as a reminder that no matter what voices are brought to the fore through the music, there will be other voices that are ignored, marginalized, or excluded. Nevertheless, the artists Hime, Miss Monday, and Ai illustrate some of the ways women in Japanese hip-hop today have shed some of the ideals of cutismo in favor of following their own directions. They show how solo female artists are getting a chance to create full-length albums and, moreover, that they can adopt some of the tough, in-your-face style that characterizes Japanese male rappers. This is not to say that they are treated in the same way as male rappers. When I asked Monday what it was like to be signed to a major label, she complained that the company representatives frequently asked her to pay more attention to her appearance, to wear more makeup, and generally to try to act more cute.[5]

Women are central to popular culture in Japan, indeed, by most reckonings, they are its leading edge. It is young women especially who are generally viewed as the driving force in any new fad, including ones in popular music. Yet there persists a peculiar conservatism among the men who control entertainment companies, as if they could see only what has been successful in the past. What was last popular often seems to drive executives' expectations of what will prove popular next. With East End X Yuri, the party-rap flavor driven by playful youth slang became a model of cute success. But when Riko Sakurai at Def Jam Japan recognized Ai's potential, she took Japanese R & B in a new direction. Miss Monday and Hime, too, offer post-cutismo role models for young girls in Japan. In some ways, then, the story of women in Japanese hip-hop is revealing of the possibilities that remain untapped, of the ways that the political and artistic potentials of hip-hop have not yet been fully realized. Despite the catch-22 that dogged women emcees early on, some new artists and women executives hold out the promise that, as Hime says in her lyrics, the surprise attack may come from the peony.

The medium isn't the message, the moola is the message.

—Henry Louis Gates Jr., "Net Worth"

CHAPTER 7

MAKING MONEY, JAPAN-STYLE

How can we understand the role of business interests in the development of hip-hop in Japan? Some might argue that it all comes down to the money. After all, who would be putting on the shows, making the CDs, opening record stores, starting magazines, if it were not for all the money to be made? I would argue that a different contention more accurately reflects the development of Japan's hip-hop scene. Namely, that without artists committed to recording more albums, putting on shows, and reaching out to wider audiences, there would be no money to be made from hip-hop in Japan. In other words, to understand the business of hip-hop, we need a new perspective on markets not as a sum of economic activities, but as one dimension of broader cultural movements. In some ways, this in itself is a common understanding of culture industries. Here, however, I zero in on the disjunctures between conceptions of cultural markets held by artists and industry executives to show how record companies' presumption that economic success derives from big hits among nonfan consumers disguises more fundamental, one might say *genba* dynamics, of the music industry.

This chapter focuses on the motivations that drive artists in their careers. I consider, for example, the practical decisions they make in navigating paths through a fickle entertainment industry. As we will see, what motivates Japanese hip-hop artists is not making money per se, but other goals, most notably, achieving support for upcoming projects, building a reputation, and extending fan support. Through a look at negotiations with producers, we see how for artists there is no dividing line between culture and market. They are in a real sense artist-entrepreneurs because their business is their art and vice versa. In contrast, industry perspectives tend to formulate the music market as a hit-driven enterprise dependent on million-selling albums and lucrative celebrity synergies. From an industry perspective, the culture of hip-hop is irrelevant in part because the majority of mass consumers tend not to be devoted fans following artists in the clubs. One sense in which the recording industry is viewed as hit-driven comes from the fact that 90 percent of new album releases fail to turn a profit. I would argue that a success rate of 10 percent versus the failure of 90 percent is too simplistic a model for understanding the complex sum of interactions that produce the larger music scene. Moreover, the sharp decline in million-selling albums from the mid-1990s to the present shows that the industry may need to reformulate its strategies for success. I suggest a more nuanced understanding of the market, one which considers artists' careers and extends the notion of *genba* to see what it takes not only to move the crowd but also to move the market in new directions.

The economic analyst Harold Vogel argues that economics explain entertainment industries: "It is *economic forces*—profit motives, if you will—that are always behind the scenes regulating the flows and rates of implementation [of new forms of entertainment]" (1994, xvii). In fact, there are a number of reasons to doubt that economic forces drive hip-hop in Japan. Historically, as we saw in chapter 2, major record labels were skeptical of the very idea of Japanese hip-hop for the first decade of the music's emergence in Japan. The genre was recognized as potentially lucrative in the eyes of major labels only after a couple of million-selling hits in 1994–95. Hence, major entertainment companies came late to the game and still only support a small fraction of active hip-hop artists. In chapter 3, I proposed viewing the overall music scene in terms of a pyramid, with fans and potential artists at the wide base, performing and minor recording artists occupying the middle levels, and megahit stars at the top. One of the features of this pyramid is that most of the activities of artists remain largely invisible in terms of overall sales figures. Amateur recording artists, and even most independent artists, collectively constitute only a small fraction of overall sales. Nevertheless, they form the base out of which large companies select the kinds of artists they see as having strong sales potential. By drawing attention to the pyramid structure of a music scene, I want to suggest that the characterizations of the music industry we get from overall sales figures and portraits of megahit stars give a distorted picture of the music market.

The ethnographic portraits below provide a way of grounding some recent insights from studies of cultural economy. Scholarship in cultural economy aims in part to move beyond the idea that markets are embedded in socio-cultural contexts (Du Gay and Pryke 2002; Ohmann 1996). Instead of viewing markets as operating within but separate from cultural processes, we can achieve deeper insights by considering how economic discourses "format and frame markets and economic organizational relations, 'making them up' rather than simply observing or describing them from a God's-eye vantage point" (Du Gay and Pryke 2002, 2). This viewpoint is analogous to the view of globalization proposed in this book, namely, that global flows are not so much localized by their performance in *genba*, but rather that artists in the *genba* actualize the intersection of and negotiations between the global and the local. By analogy, the hip-hop culture market is actualized through the performance of cultural and commercial processes together. We can see this in the details of artists negotiating with producers.

In this chapter, I contrast artists' perspectives on their careers with an industry perspective that focuses primarily on sales by megahit stars. I begin by looking in detail at the negotiations of Rock Steady Crew Japan with producers who wanted to make a break-dance video for retail sale. RSC Japan's views of the substance of hip-hop culture form the basis of their business negotiations and show one way that business and culture must be viewed in tandem. Then I look at some features of the mass market for music, where success is measured in sales, artists' power arises from celebrity status, and fan participation is reckoned in terms of purchase points. The decline in record sales and the especially sharp drop in million-sellers suggest that the record industry could benefit from rethinking the dynamics that build vibrant music scenes. I then discuss the ups and downs of a decade-long career in music. Umedy, who began his career as a rapper, has managed to consistently reinvent himself in ways that illustrate how the creativity required to succeed in the music business depends on more than musical talent.

An Ethnographic Approach to Cultural Economy

An ethnographic approach to cultural economy should begin by examining the ways markets are constructed out of everyday discourses and practices. By starting with the particulars of diverse actors' commitments and aims, and then working outward to understand how markets develop through everyday interactions, we can gain the tools to understand how media businesses develop where, literally, no markets have gone before. Such an ethnographic approach draws into question whether it is possible to distinguish economic forces from cultural forces, a distinction highlighted by the tensions between music conceptualized as artistic creation and music understood as commodity. Often associated with Theodor Adorno and the Frankfurt School (Longhurst 1995), this conceptual bifurcation persists in consumers' perspective on the music business and in the recurring valorization of independent artists in smaller-circulation media outlets (e.g., specialty magazines, free papers, Web sites). In theory, music is "ideological where the circumstances of production in it gain primacy over the productive forces" (Adorno 1976, 223). This dichotomy between the more *economic* "circumstances of production," associated with the recording industry, and the more *cultural* "productive forces," associated with the rap artists, is partly what fuels our enduring interest in underground groups. They are assumed to be, and often are, less susceptible to the pressures of major entertainment companies. The problem with this formulation is that it assumes an opposition between artists' and corporate producers' desires, which may not always be the case.

Business negotiations illustrate how understandings of hip-hop culture and the market must be considered together to grasp what it takes to produce a meaningful product. I say *meaningful* rather than *successful* because market success is only one of the key measures that artists focus on. An ethnographic perspective thus illuminates the making up of markets because depending on one's location—indie artist, pop star, freelance producer, major label director—markets are viewed differently, particularly in terms of the purposes they serve. An unsigned artist desires a contract not only to make a record but also to break into the scene and gain access to promotion channels in magazines, radio, TV, and so on. Established stars face a different range of concerns, such as protecting their stardom and managing their exposure. Where we begin our analysis of the music industry thus influences what we see.[1]

In practice, the pyramid of a music scene does not exist ready made, but is built up from the bottom through persistent efforts of artists, both to hone skills and to develop opportunities to perform, record, promote, and—if they are resourceful and lucky—to profit from their efforts. In this respect it is important to underscore that most hip-hop groups began long before they were "discovered." The break-dancing group Rock Steady Crew Japan serves as a good example. Rather than starting with record companies and their discovery of new talent, I focus here on the entrepreneurial side of hip-hop creativity from a middle-level artist's perspective, that is, a group with an established track record but without star power (yet?). In particular, to what extent are notions of hip-hop culture integral to b-boys' conception of the market?

Rock Steady Crew Japan and the Video Proposal

Rock Steady Crew Japan (RSC-Japan), a hip-hop collective that centers around break dancing but also includes rappers, DJs, and graffiti artists, is led by Crazy-A, an elder statesman of the Japanese hip-hop scene and one of the pioneers of break dancing in Yoyogi Park back in early 1984. His group, originally known as the Tokyo B-Boys, became the Tokyo-based collective associated with New York's Rock Steady Crew, one of the original, and most successful, break-dancing groups.[2] Crazy-A makes a living recording, performing, and organizing events. In 1998, he began organizing B-Boy Park, an outdoor festival drawing upward of ten thousand people and held annually each summer in Yoyogi Park, the same Tokyo park where he began. While most of this book has focused on rappers, studying RSC-Japan gives us a chance to consider some of the business challenges facing a b-boy.

In the summer of 1997, I visited Crazy-A's office, then located in a nondescript but classy condo about a mile from Shibuya station. I had come to watch some videos of the early days of break dancing in Japan, but was also allowed to observe RSC-Japan's negotiations with two freelance video producers who had come with a proposal from a major record company. The proposed project aimed at producing a video featuring RSC-Japan to be sold in stores.

The collaborative setting for RSC-Japan reminds us of the supportive network that families can provide in forming an institutional structure separate from the corporate offices of entertainment companies. I arrived at around 7 p.m., and it seemed as though everyone was just getting down to work. A couple of graphic-design artists (a man and a woman) were working on a magazine ad for an upcoming Tokyo B-Boy's anniversary show. In an adjacent room, DJ Beat was working on some new songs using his MPC (midi processing center). While work went on, I sat on the overstuffed leather couch with a cup of buckwheat tea watching the early days of break dancing portrayed in video clips from 1984–85. Cell phones were ringing, and in the then early days of ring tones, Crazy-A's, oddly enough, rang "We Wish You a Merry Christmas." Crazy-A, speaking on the phone, said that an appointment for 11 p.m. worked well with his schedule. His early meeting at 8 p.m. was with the video producers. They arrived on time with briefcases and dressed casually in slacks and button-down shirts (no suits).

Defining Success

This meeting is instructive because it shows how the meaning of success for RSC-Japan revolved more around establishing their reputation than in garnering major sales. Strong sales could help their reputation, but if commercial success led to the group being viewed as a sellout, that is, performing just for money, it could pose substantial risks as well. The group's effort to navigate between these competing concerns illustrates that there is no clear line between the productive forces (cultural creativity) and circumstances of production (economic expectations). Rather, the dynamics of media businesses, as of businesses more generally, emerge from conventions decided by debates that usually operate in a context of uncertainty about success, and even differing understandings of what success might mean.

Succeeding as a dance group poses particular challenges. While hip-hop music has become big business—rap in particular, and more so than deejaying—dance has been less easy to capitalize on. As one RSC-Japan member lamented, "You can't copyright a great dance move."[3] Dance schools are booming in Japan, but lessons and live performances simply do not offer the possibility of the massive financial returns comparable to a hit single or platinum album. Crazy-A once suggested the creation of a professional sports league for break dancing, akin to Japan's soccer or baseball leagues, as a way to take the dance business to the next level. Producing a video would be a way of gaining exposure and making some money for future projects the group was planning, such as an RSC-Japan store. Nevertheless, making a video for sale did have its risks.

The meeting began with RSC-Japan's Char, a lively straight-talking assistant in a Puma trainer jacket and white shorts, introducing himself to the two video producers. He said that he would be conducting the negotiations, but that Crazy-A, seated next to him, would make any final decisions. Throughout the conversation, Crazy-A sat silently, observing without emotion. The two producers sat down and received their tea from the woman doing graphic design (even this world has its office ladies who serve tea, though here she was dressed as a b-girl in baggy jeans and floppy hat). The producers brought out the proposal. What transpired was a far cry from the coolheaded, nonconfrontational, virtually nonverbal negotiating style that is the stereotype of Japanese businessmen (e.g., in Michael Crichton's xenophobic novel *Rising Sun*).

The exchange cut to the core of how these b-boys view hip-hop culture in relation to business. The idea pitched was to make a break-dance video for the retail market, not for broadcast. Things got off to a bad start, however, when the producers offered nothing toward RSC-Japan's production costs. Char objected, "We have to practice for several days, develop a routine, get people together. It's like making a song; there are production costs." The two free-lancers asked that they just be heard out, so that they could present the contract proposal as a whole, and then discuss the details. But Char was incensed. Clearly, there was a fundamental misconception of what RSC-Japan was all about and talking about contracts and details was putting the cart before the horse.

Do the Producers Understand Hip-Hop Culture?

Initially, one of RSC-Japan's main concerns was whether the group's image portrayed through the video would effectively convey their deep engagement with hip-hop culture. Char gave an example by explaining what they would look for in a director. If they were going to do a photo shoot of RSC-Japan, they would never allow it to be done in a studio. "Hip-hop is a culture of the street. It was on the street at Hokoten [in Yoyogi Park on Sundays] where Crazy-A perfected his style. When Akira [Crazy-A] started, he would have to pay his respects to the Yakuza thugs [*chinpira*] who controlled where people could set up. It was always outdoors that the breakers battled." Crazy-A spoke up, "Even when African American b-boys came from the States, I wouldn't lose," he said, thus emphasizing the battling aspect of success. Char continued,

So before we take any photos, we'd want to know, is this [director] the kind of guy who would come out with us and bomb [that is, spray-paint graffiti] on a subway train? If you get caught, that's a ¥200,000 [$1,700] fine. Would this director be the kind of guy who says, "Oh yes, I'm sorry, it was wrong," or would he say, "Yeah, I had them write that. I think it's cool." That's the kind of thing we need to know before we take part.

Char laid out the terms they would need before even considering working with the record company. Either the record company would come forward with a lot of money to produce the video and pay the dancers, or they would give the video a strong promotional push in an effort to sell upward of a hundred thousand copies. The former scenario seems like the perfect example of being a sellout, but there is another way to think about Char's logic. Henry Louis Gates Jr., writing about the "bling-bling" character of celebrity advertising, notes that conspicuously expensive production values in videos or commercials lend a sense of importance to a product, even if there is little obvious connection between the celebrity and the product being endorsed. Viewers are likely to think, "Why would they spend all that money for an endorsement if they didn't believe in their product? It must be important." This is what

Gates means by "the medium isn't the message, the moola is the message" (1998, 60). A group like RSC-Japan could justify, in their own minds at least, producing a high quality video as a way to demonstrate their importance.

Alternatively, Char would want the producers to press for a hit. The producers, ignoring the idea of providing a large sum upfront to RSC-Japan, responded that a hundred thousand units was well beyond the anticipated sales, and hence beyond the anticipated promotion budget. They were hoping for something more in the range of thirty thousand. (It is reasonable to assume that they were doubling their true sales projections to flatter RSC-Japan.) But Char noted that the middle ground—producing a moderately successful video for moderate production fees—would be the most risky for RSC-Japan. The record company would be able to test the market for a breakdancing video, but it was a potential disaster for the dance group. Char explained that the greatest danger was that RSC-Japan would be seen as merely taking some money from a major record company in the interest of, well, simply making some money. This could lead to accusations that RSC-Japan was selling out. "For [the record company] small sales would mean little, but for us, it could mean the end. Rumors spread quickly, and we would no longer be able to perform. We'd be left with nothing to do but give dance lessons." I played a small part in the negotiations when Char pointed out to the producers that "someone from America is even studying Crazy-A's history. That's how important he is to the hip-hop scene."

These negotiations made clear that "being hip-hop," however it is interpreted, is not external to business considerations, nor is it relevant only to the artists and the fans.[4] I observed about a dozen business negotiation sessions like this one. It was clear that the artists' association with the culture of hip-hop—that is, their aesthetic and political commitments—always proved central to the apparently "purely business" strategies discussed. The argument that ultimately everything comes down to money not only neglects other important motivations but also provides a skewed portrait of how culture industries necessarily work.[5] Char's logic reflected the need to guard RSC-Japan's reputation regardless of this particular project's success or failure.

At the end of the meeting, after almost an hour of Char's browbeating —during which the producers could hardly get a word in edgewise—Char apologized "if I was too direct." The producers said, no, no, it was very instructive. They pocketed their proposal and, somewhat sheepishly, said thank you "for the lesson" (benkyō ni narimashita). In a stark reminder that this was still Japan, everyone, including Char and Crazy-A, then finished with the standard closing, "I humbly request your benevolence in the future" (kore kara mo yo-

roshiku onegai shimasu), and while sitting, they all bowed to each other. The negotiations done, the four of them started chatting, and it seemed to me that this was where the real business began. RSC-Japan had a stake in being tough up front, but they were also open to media promotion that worked in their favor, building their status within the scene and attracting enough capital to keep other projects going. A week later, I saw one of the producers at a club event, and though he was embarrassed about the meeting, he also said he still hoped to work with RSC-Japan in the future, acknowledging that he would have to come with a better proposal.

Some people are likely to dismiss artists' invocation of hip-hop culture as little more than a rationalization for activities that ultimately have an economic explanation. But from RSC-Japan's standpoint, protecting the culture was intimately connected to building the business. The group members were willing to forego making the video to protect their reputation. For Crazy-A and RSC, the practical considerations for staging events, performing, and recording media projects can seem to outweigh the larger abstractions—respecting black culture, keeping it real—but it would be a mistake to conclude that hip-hop ideologies are used merely as afterthoughts or rationalizations. On the contrary, artists' discourses aimed at constructing a meaningful commitment to hip-hop in Japan constitute the market because that is how they decide to market themselves. RSC-Japan recognized that above all, their viability depended on their reputation among their fans, a "commodity" more fundamental than a video in stores. How does this vision of the market contrast with more economic views of Japan's recording industry?

Japan's Recording Industry

Conceptualizing Japan's recorded-music market in terms of sales data makes artists' individual concerns vanish. Instead, we see the prominence of big hits in terms of their ability to generate income. In this section, I briefly consider some of the distinctive features of Japan's recorded-music market before turning to the ways a focus on celebrities and hits provides a very different conception of music cultures, especially compared to the perspectives of artists. As in our exploration of the diversity of globalization processes, we can see how the business emerges out of competing and contradictory discourses. I would argue that we cannot speak of a market for recorded music in singular terms.

The distinctiveness of the market in Japan emerges in a variety of ways, including the relative strength of national artists, the particular range of genres, the presence of rental CD shops, and the low rates of unauthorized online music sharing. From the end of World War II through 1967, Western music (*yōgaku*) outsold Japanese music (*hōgaku*), but from 1968 on, music by Japanese artists led in sales (Kawabata 1991, 334). Since then, Japanese musicians have generally increased their market share such that over the past decade, recordings by Japanese artists sell at two to three times the rate of those by Western artists (RIAJ 2003, 5). What are the most recent figures for leading genres? The Web site of the Recording Industry Association of Japan (www.riaj.com) gives a breakdown of new releases by key genres (all formats). In 2004, new releases were led by so-called new music (*nyū myūjikku*; generally emphasizing rock singer-songwriter types) with 3,299 releases. Next came pop music (*kayōkyoku/poppusu*; all other pop music including hip-hop and R & B) with 1,966 releases. This is followed by *enka* (an older generation's popular music with some traditional styles of vocals) with 1,721 releases. The remaining number of Japanese music releases total 2,295, of which about one-third are from anime TV and film shows (796 releases), followed by classical music and various other genres. It should be clear that the Japaneseness of Japan's music market arises from the ethnicity of the artists rather than the styles of the music.

Japan's support of a wide range of national artists contrasts with the worldwide market for recorded music, which is dominated by US artists. However, US music exports are gradually losing their luster. In 1987, American artists accounted for half of global music sales, but by the mid-1990s, that figure was down to one-third, and there are reasons to believe the trend toward more locally produced music will continue (Dwyer, Dawson, and Roberts 1996, 48). In spite of the massive concentration of the global recording industry in the hands of a few multinational giants—Sony-BMG, Universal, Warner, EMI—we also find localizing tendencies that one would expect under more flexible regimes of accumulation. Interestingly, the nation of origin of each major label's headquarters is seldom credited as the origin of the music, unlike, say, Japanese cars, which remain "Japanese" even if they are manufactured largely in North America. No one thinks of Michael Jackson's music as Japanese because Sony for a time produced his music.

Two other aspects that distinguish Japan's music market are rental CD shops and low rates of online piracy. These characteristics further demonstrate that abstract markets do not operate separately from their concrete settings. In Japan, recorded music sales rose steadily during the postwar period, peaked in 1998, and then began a sharp decline that continued through 2004. The start of the decline coincided with the emergence of Napster in 1999, but there are reasons to think that online piracy offers only a partial explanation for the decline in sales. As I discuss elsewhere (Condry 2004), online piracy is less prevalent in Japan than in the United States. In Japan, most young people access the Internet using cell phones, which as yet tend to have neither broadband connections nor substantial hard drives. In addition, ubiquitous CD rental shops make it relatively easy and inexpensive to sample new music without relying on unauthorized downloads. CD prices are high in Japan, generally between ¥2,500 and ¥3000 (US $23–27), but renting a CD is very cheap, generally around ¥300 ($3). The widening availability of CD burners contributes to this "sneaker net" for passing around music and also limits the attractiveness of online file sharing. This suggests that the lack of online piracy arises less from a national respect for copyright than from the combination of a business setting in which rental shops make it easy for consumers to sample music cheaply and a technology environment dominated by Internet-ready cell phones that make downloading over peer-to-peer networks unfeasible.

This section provided a sense of the production side of the recording industry. What can we say about the ways consumer patterns drive the markets?

Consumer-Driven Markets

In media industries, where viewership ratings and sales figures are watched like sports scores, the power of consumers appears paramount. What does this idea of consumer-driven markets mean?[6] The economists Carl Shapiro and Hal Varian explain that while the old industrial economy was driven by supply-side *economies of scale*, the new information economy is driven by demand-side *economies of networks* (Shapiro and Varian 1999, 173). The differences between these two regimes of accumulation are profound. Improving profitability in manufacturing requires streamlining processes of production. Information-based businesses necessarily strive to produce not only commodities; perhaps more important, they aim to produce a desire to consume. As Walter Benjamin (1969, 237) once observed, "One of the foremost tasks of art has always been the creation of a demand which could be fully satisfied only later."

In addition, industrial, resource-based economies tend to follow principles of *diminishing returns*, whereas information-based economies are often characterized by *increasing returns*. What does this mean? Diminishing returns tend to produce a stable equilibrium among competing industries. For example, in the competition between hydroelectric power plants and coal-powered plants, each industry will use up easily available resources first until a stable equilibrium is reached.[7] In contrast, the dynamics of information-based economies depend on networks and positive feedback for success.[8] Positive feedback magnifies the effects of small economic shifts, such that over time one technology is likely to destroy the competition (e.g., in the ways VHS videocassette recorders beat out the Betamax format).[9] As interoperable networking increases, so does the value of the technology or product. A single fax machine is worthless, but the value of fax machines increases as more people use them. Such dynamics apply to commercial phenomena, like cell phone networks, as well as non-commercial networks, like online peer-to-peer software networks.[10] Value increases as more people use the product. Unlike resource-based regimes, network economics predicts that between two competing technologies, in many cases one product will "lock in" and drive out the competitor.

If we combine the idea of lock-in with the performative logic of the *genba*, we have an explanation for why among several faddish phenomena that differ little, one explodes in popularity while the others languish. We see this in the music world with the "one-in-ten" success rate. It can also be observed in children's games, for example, in the ways Pokémon trading cards can mean everything to a certain cohort—until they move on and then the next thing (e.g., Yu-Gi-Oh) takes over. What the *genba* adds is a way to see how the success of the cards depends less on the character of the product than on the sociability of consumption. The anthropologist Anne Allison (2003) has discussed the Pokémon market—which includes trading cards, television shows, and film—along with a wide range of character goods. Because playing Pokémon revolves around the idea that you "gotta catch 'em all," she shows how a key element of the phenomenon's influence arises from the integration of play with consumption (394).[11] This means that the logic of the market is also the logic of the game, and thus both build on each other to produce expanding networks of influence. The game reinforces the market, which in turn reinforces the game, a classic example of network effects. A focus on the *genba* of the market draws attention to these particular social interactions more than the sum total of sales. Certain kinds of markets seem to rely on these dynamics more than other kinds of markets, though I see it as a spectrum of possibilities rather than as a simple binary. For example, the value of Pokémon trading cards clearly does not reside in the quality of the paper or the exquisiteness of the drawing. The value emerges because peers might desire the same rare card and because that card gives a player power in a Pokémon game. Lock-in also helps explain the phenomenon of the recording industry's paucity of big hits (though very lucrative) and a majority of less-than-stellar-selling albums.

Mapping Megahits through Categories of Consumers

Like other information-based industries—software, movies, pharmaceuticals —music is relatively expensive to produce (the first copy) and especially inexpensive to reproduce (subsequent copies). This is one factor that makes the recording industry a hit-driven enterprise. Large profits are generated most effectively by big hits, and this encourages consolidation among producers, distributors, retailers, concert promoters, and media outlets. To the extent that each of these corporate actors can amplify the network effects, the more successful they are likely to be. Record companies reinforce network effects by rewarding those who achieve certain kinds of success, primarily, strong sales. Major record companies with the resources to respond quickly to rapid explosions in demand are best poised to exploit the whims of music consumers. When an album explodes in popularity, the economies of scale in CD production are extremely lucrative. Although studio production and marketing costs are substantial, the price for pressing one CD (including the media, recording, plastic case, and the printed material) is about $0.75 in the United States. A record company then sells the $15 retail CD to a record store for about $8 (Vogel 1994, 143). Book publishing presents a useful comparison. Manufacturing a hardcover book (printing and binding) costs about 10 percent of the retail price, for example, $2.50 for a $25 book (Auletta 1997, 54), which is about double the rate for a CD ($0.75 for a $15 CD, so about 5 percent of retail goes toward manufacturing costs). These figures highlight the extreme moneymaking potential of hit albums. On the other hand, record companies have great difficulty predicting what will become a hit. Despite impressive marketing resources, almost 90 percent of record company releases fail to turn a profit, a rate that is even worse than the US movie industry's 60 to 70 percent failure rate (Vogel 1994, 143, 27). Since record companies generally do not pay out for failures, one worries that there is a self-serving dimension to the companies' claims of high failure rates. But it also points to a fundamental uncertainty experienced by record companies, a sense of helplessness vis-à-vis the fact that everything depends on the consumer. How are consumers imagined?

One common way of mapping consumers is in terms of their affiliation with particular star celebrities. A magazine called *Data Watch* illustrates some of the key features of consumer mapping: the centrality of replaceable, megahit celebrities; a mass of nonfan consumers with different tastes; and a network of media (radio, magazines, live spots, television, etc.) connecting the celebrities and consumers in synergistic marketing networks.

Data Watch is published by Tsutaya, the leading big-box media retail and rental conglomerate in Japan. The company calls its stores Culture Convenience Clubs (in English). They trade in CDS, DVDS, and videos (for sale and rental), and also books, magazines, and video games (for sale). According to the masthead, *Data Watch* culls information from its database of 18 million club members (almost 15 percent of the population), 1,400 stores, and 4 million online club members.[12] The winter 2004 issue promised a portrait of the "real market" (*riaru maaketto*) of music by analyzing the characteristics of the consumers who bought the year's top-selling CDS. The level of detail in *Data Watch*'s consumer profiles is eerie. What percentage of people who purchased Avril Lavigne are single and have a *koibito* (boyfriend/girlfriend)? Thirty percent. What percentage of people who purchased Eminem go to karaoke several times a month? Twenty-six percent. One can compare these figures for each artist, regardless of genre or nation of origin, side by side, in a veritable supermarket of data. The logic of this data analysis begins with celebrity success, then associates purchases with types of fans. The resulting taxonomy gives a sense of how difference is imagined in these media worlds. Consumer tribes exhibit patterns of purchasing that are then related to lifestyle. It is lifestyle imagined as a series of purchase points.

In this view, the fan-celebrity connection itself is paramount, while the substance of that relationship is largely ignored. In other words, we learn the top magazines for female Rip Slyme fans, but not why they care. Instead, we observe how different artists attract different kinds of consumers who then can be used to capitalize on other kinds of products.

By extension, what Tsutaya sells is not just the CDS to the consumer but also information about consumers to the record companies, magazines, and other media outlets.[13] To consumers, Big Brother is convenient and saves them money. Rewarded with discounts, new release information, and special giveaways, consumers welcome the intrusion.

The *Data Watch* magazine is notable for focusing entirely on the very top tiers of the music pyramid. This gives a skewed understanding of the soil required to cultivate the next big stars. We see this clearly in an article that provides a summary analysis to the *Data Watch* issue on the music market, "Are Today's Music Consumers Really 'Music Fans?'" According to the article, the answer is no. The analyst points out that the bulk of consumption comes from

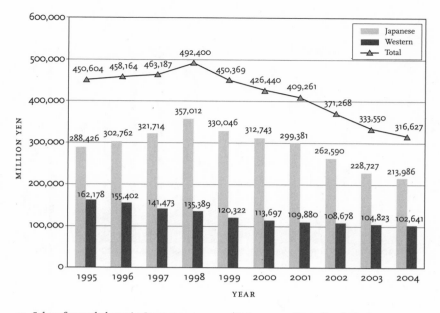

13. Sales of recorded music, Japan, 1995–2004. (Data source: Recording Industry Association of Japan.)

people who rarely go to concerts and who, in general, do not know much about music (Muraoka 2004, 62). For some reason, they made a particular purchase, but their lives revolve only partly around music. Nightclubs provide a symbolic counterpoint. Musicians focus on the *genba* not because the fans there are the ones who will buy the most albums, but because there is an intensity of interaction that brings the music to life. Yet there are reasons to think that the industry marketing strategies that focus on megahits are faltering and that a deeper consideration of the *genba* dynamics may be needed to reverse the recent downturn in sales.

Declining Sales and an Even Sharper Decline in Million-Sellers

The sharp drop in million-selling albums in Japan since the mid-1990s suggests that the focus on casual nonfan consumers and megahit stars may be a strategy in need of revision. In 1998, 14 percent of the units of overall album sales came from albums that sold over one million copies. In 2004, only 6 percent of overall album sales came from million-sellers.[14] The reasons for the decline in overall sales and in sales of million-sellers are complex. Since

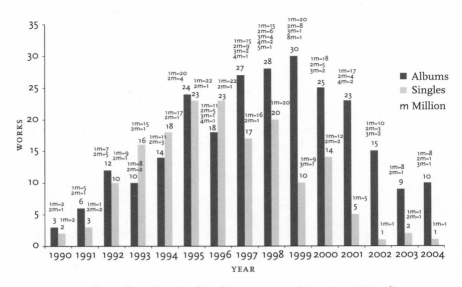

14. Japan's million-selling albums and singles, 1990–2004. (Data source: Recording Industry Association of Japan.)

the late 1990s, typical music consumers are spending more on cell phones, video games, and DVDs, while the ease of getting music online or from friends burning CDs has increased. Yet whatever the reasons, the recording industry is facing an environment where the potential of megahit stars is reduced. As a result, building core audiences who will buy albums even in an environment in which they can get copies for free (online or CD-R) or cheaply (rental shops) becomes more important than ever.

The declining returns from million-sellers indicates that record companies may have something to gain from focusing on *genba* dynamics for building core, as opposed to mass, audiences. Without access to a wider range of proprietary data to connect the dots, this suggestion is necessarily speculative. But with the declining ratio of million-sellers to overall sales, the kinds of celebrity-consumer mapping we see in *Data Watch* is less representative of the overall market in 2004 compared to a decade before. The recording industry may have something to gain by shifting its attention from the nonfan consumers to the audience of consumers who are also fans. In that case, the *genba* may provide a better model of interaction than the array of purchase points we get from *Data Watch* and overall sales figures.

For the artist-entrepreneur who must convince the record company gatekeepers that he or she can resonate with both the clubbers and the mass market, negotiating these contrasting images of the market poses challenges.

Given that so few artists are able to muster a big hit, how do artists manage to stay in the business? By, I would suggest, being creative in their art and their business.

Ups and Downs of a Career in Music

The pyramid structure of a music scene, described in chapter 3, can give the impression that the best artists move smoothly up the pyramid, beating out less talented rivals until they eventually reach the top. It is safe to say that not a single musician experiences his or her career in this way. Not only do most fail to reach the upper echelons of success but the paths are almost always rocky, circuitous, and characterized by ongoing uncertainty and numerous ups and downs. A personal biography can give a sense of the ways artists navigate between their times in clubs and recording studios and their (hoped-for) success in the market.

One artist in particular has remained a close informant over the years I have been studying hip-hop in Japan, and his experience gives a detailed look at the complexity of making a living in the music business. In this section, I put the challenge of making money into motion, showing some of the ways that the business negotiations, such as we saw with RSC and the images of markets and fans examined in the last section, contextualize the day-to-day and year-to-year efforts of a musician-entrepreneur. Like other musicians who have managed to stay in the business over many years, Umedy combines a keen artistic sensibility with an energetic entrepreneurial spirit. He illustrates a scrappy attitude and persistence that characterizes many of those who manage to stay in the music business. Most musicians spend their careers working other jobs as well. I met artists who work for record companies, do graphic design, or are employed by clothing stores either as buyers or as sales clerks. I also met cooks, waitresses, sewer workers, and even a private investigator trying to make it in the music business.

Umedy spent his high school years in Fukushima, a medium-sized city several hours north of Tokyo. Growing up, he mostly listened to Japanese pop music, but an album by Run-DMC sparked his interest in rapping, and he practiced by mimicking the lyrics. When he began college in Tsukuba, about an hour from Tokyo, he met his fellow swim-team member DJ Etsu, who had been collecting hip-hop records throughout high school. Together, they started organizing parties, with Etsu as DJ and Umedy rapping. By the end of college, they were organizing a Sunday afternoon event at a shopping mall: renting a room, charging admission, and performing. "This is when I realized I could make money at this," Umedy recalled.[15] He was scouting talent to include in this Sunday event when he discovered the young women, then just finishing high school, who would later record as the trio Now (Baby Setsu, Yuka, and Monday, later Miss Monday). Umedy, his brother Taka-C, and DJ Etsu formed the group EDU, and they continued to perform in small club events for no pay, though they made some money if they organized the event (i.e., rented the club and then risked losing money if they could not get enough people to come). After college, Umedy organized events, wrote for a swim magazine, volunteered part-time as a swim coach, and kept performing and networking as part of EDU. Through club events he met Cake-K, a rapper with the group B-Fresh. Cake had a small studio set up in the kitchen of his tiny Tokyo apartment, and together they self-produced a compilation album they called *Kitchens*. Sales were marginal, but they used the CD as a demo to help them get live performing gigs.

EDU's club shows led to their first break. The tenth floor of a Roppongi building, R? Hall, often held hip-hop events, and it was there that EDU's show was noticed by a scout for the artist-management company Amuse.[16] The scout invited EDU to perform on a late-night TV battle-of-the-bands show. Although EDU lost in their first effort, Umedy says that so many people sent postcards objecting to the judges' decision, that they were given another chance. On their second try in December 1994, they won. The prize was a recording contract with Avion, a record label within the larger company JVC Victor. They also received a small monthly salary from Amuse. Umedy says this salary was always termed a "loan." In the end, Umedy says they never received any royalties from their debut album because all income went to pay back the loan.

The record company's idea for promoting EDU hinged on the cuteness of having two brothers as rappers. Their first album, *Do You Love Kiss*, aimed to bridge hip-hop styles with pop-music emotionality. It sold well enough for a newcomer album, reportedly around twenty thousand units, and Avion planned a second release. Troubles arose, however, when Umedy's brother Taka-C decided he wanted to aim for a more underground sound and left the group. Umedy found another rapper to join the group, but to no avail. According to EDU's manager at JVC Victor, the departure of Taka-C proved a debilitating blow. As two brothers they drew the attention of teen fashion magazines, but now, Victor could not see how to promote EDU. Umedy was let go by both his record label and the artist-management company.

Umedy brainstormed a next step, struggling with the tensions involved in being an entrepreneur in the music business.[17] Umedy pursued several

15. Miss Monday, DJ Etsu, Umedy at club Core in Roppongi, 2000. Photo by the author.

avenues at once, with the aim, above all, of "staying in the news," as he said, by continuing to perform and produce. A producer friend offered some slots on the *Best of Japanese Hip-Hop* series, and Umedy's Kitchens family eventually contributed three songs to three different albums with productions by Now, Climax, DJ Etsu, and DJ Kool K. Through connections made at Amuse, Umedy also hosted a weekly radio show.

Umedy's main project, however, was a self-produced album called *Kitchens 2*. A clothing store called Ghetto Japan contributed money to the project in exchange for a logo on the CD and periodic appearances in the store by Etsu and Umedy as DJs. Umedy kept costs low by recording exclusively in the apartment of Cake-K. They even used a closet-sized recording booth for the vocals, which clearly became uncomfortably hot. The main outside expense was the track-down (mixing of the songs) at another friend's apartment-studio. Umedy and fellow Kitchens family members distributed the album to record stores themselves, and after about six months, they had managed to sell almost all of the two thousand copies. There was some grumbling among the compilation's other artists that most of the money went into the Kitchens coffers to support future projects, but most agreed that keeping active and generating news (*nyūsu*) was the key to continuing their musical careers. Meanwhile, they shifted the location of their weekly event. The Kitchens groups ended their Thursday night appearances at the club Grass ("only our friends come; it's meaningless because there's no promotion," said Umedy at the time). They moved to a Roppongi club called Rowdy, where crowds of two hundred or so came to see them on Saturday nights through 1997. Again, we see the determined effort not so much to make money, but to keep active and use that activity to promote the work.

The *Kitchens 2* album eventually caught the eye of another major label, and in the spring of 1998, Umedy was recording again. Meanwhile, Now, the three-woman group that included Miss Monday, managed one more release with a new label (East/West). It was not a huge hit, in part because the record company was struggling financially and could not adequately promote the album. The record company soon went out of business, and Now disbanded. Setsu was fed up and broke off contact with the group. Yuka went to work selling clothes at a department store in Shinjuku. Monday kept working on music with Umedy and the other handful of Kitchens artists. Hers is the success story related in the previous chapter. Umedy, on the other hand, faced difficult choices. By the late 1990s, he was regarded as too old (late twenties) in the eyes of record companies to be a new star. So he refocused his attention on Monday's career. He provided rap support at her shows and helped with the negotiations for her new albums. Umedy worked more on producing tracks, artist management, and searching out new talent such as Bigga Raiji in the Japanese reggae scene.

This brief look at Umedy's life gives another perspective on the ways markets are made out of diverse practices and particular ideas about what it means to be a hip-hop artist. Umedy's efforts cannot be reduced to making money; rather, they revolve around building a reputation, developing a network of business associates, and pursuing projects that further his artistic as well as business goals. Part of what explains Umedy's longevity in the scene is his ability to establish his expertise at designing new tracks and convincing record company executives that he has the proper *genba* experience to be trusted. Let's take a look at how he accomplished this.

In chapter 3, I argued that the control record companies can exert over artists has more to do with gatekeeping than with forcing artists to conform to certain styles. A meeting, which I observed on July 11, 2000, between Umedy and a company executive at Id Records provides an example of how this gatekeeping occurs. The company was planning to release Miss Monday's first solo album. Umedy met with the director, Otsuji-san, to determine the types of songs that would be used for the album's singles. Although some consumers suspect that record companies force artists to produce particular kinds of tracks, the negotiations conducted by Umedy show that so-called corporate control can be a fraught process of negotiation.

Umedy began the meeting by playing songs he had picked out from ten recent releases of American hip-hop and R & B groups: Busta Rhymes, Jurassic 5, Lucy Pearl, Ruff Ryders 2, Mary J. Blige, and so on. Umedy had picked out one song from each of the albums for Otsuji-san to hear. He played about a minute from each of the selected tracks and talked through his ideas while the music played. Jurassic 5 is West Coast underground, he explained, but Busta, though it sounds more hard core, is very much "major." Otsuji-san struggled to decide on the best styles, and they kept going through the albums. Umedy described the producers and the styles, linking Busta and Ruff Ryders with a new release by Zeebra ("Based on a True Story"): "This is the kind of song he was thinking about when he produced the album," explained Umedy.

A notable difference in levels of understanding of music production became clear as the meeting went on. It seems one of Umedy's goals was to demonstrate his particular expertise as a musician with a sense of club audiences. Otsuji-san was drawn toward the harder Busta-type sound, with the deep enveloping bass and edgy rhythms, but then Umedy showed him how Monday's quick delivery style, a kind of reggae skat, would sound. Umedy did this with nonsense sounds, sometimes ending with the ironic phrase, "*iwana-kute mo ii*" (you don't have to say it). Clearly, Umedy had this overlay in his head all along, but Otsuji-san, now hearing the difference between Busta's rap on the album and the style that Monday would do, became even more confused. They went back through the albums.

In the discussions of different styles, they were both obviously concerned about the potential for club play. "This kind of track might be played at Harlem after Rhymester's 'B-Boyism,' but that other style is more likely to follow Zeebra," Umedy pointed out. To illustrate the connection he was trying to make, Umedy rapped some of Rhymester's lyrics over the top of the Jurassic 5 song. Later, Umedy explained to me that what Otsuji-san, and music executives generally, tend to aim for is something between the "white" of light pop and the "black" of hard-core underground. One of the goals for promoting Monday was to have a somewhat underground sound get her noticed in the free papers, perhaps even in *Blast*, the main hip-hop magazine at the time. Getting club play would be a great help. Here we can see some of the ways the overall market is imagined in terms of paths through the *genba* of the specialized listeners. In other words, despite *Data Watch*'s conclusion that mainstream success depended on nonfan consumers, both Umedy and Otsuji-san agreed that the path to major success for Monday would be facilitated by a song that could appeal to core, even maniac (*maniakku*), club audiences.

In the end, they decided that Umedy would make three tracks. One was to be a mix between the styles of Lucy Pearl's "I Wanna Dance Tonight" and a Jurassic 5 song, but would have reggae lyrics and rhythm over the top. A second track would be in the vein of Busta Rhymes, with the hope that it might have enough of an underground sound to be played at Harlem. The third track would be straight dance-hall reggae. Umedy's goal here was to make a song that could be pressed on seven-inch vinyl and be distributed to DJs for underground buzz. Finally, Umedy played a few tracks he had produced to give a further sense of the sound he could do and the way he thought about producing "something like something else," namely, with a different chord progression but the rhythm (bass and percussion) in much of the same flavor. In August 2001, I asked Umedy whether he felt it limited his creative possibilities to try to create similar tracks to other songs. He laughed, and said, "I am not good enough to copy it exactly, so what comes out is very different anyway."[18]

Both the overlaps and the disjunctures with the *Data Watch* vision of the market are telling. Hit albums are valued in both, but in music production, a sense of the core sounds prove important as well. Indeed, club play and attention by specialty magazines were also viewed as critical for breaking Monday into the mainstream. This preproduction step involves negotiating musical ideas through songs from the contemporary US market, while also attending to Japanese groups that have had some success: Zeebra, Rhymester, Buddha Brand. This helps us see the articulations between foreign and domestic, between mass and underground, that reproduce the larger dances of homogeneity and difference within Japan's hip-hop world. Intriguingly, differences between Umedy and the record company representative in levels of musical sensitivity also entered into the negotiation process.

By the summer of 2004, Miss Monday's career had taken off, and Umedy was right there with her, albeit more behind the scenes than next to her on stage. He was promoted to Miss Monday's manager, while also producing songs for her third solo album (her second solo album with the major label Epic/Sony). Umedy has largely given up his dream of being the lead star on stage, but both he and Monday have remained in the music business through their determination, many years of practice, and a combination of artistic skill and entrepreneurial acumen. Only about half of the artists who appeared on the self-produced CD *Kitchens 2* are still active, and none is as successful as Monday or Umedy. One lesson, however, is that making money was in many ways secondary to keeping active and keeping the publicity going in ways that could convince record companies that the musicians have a future.

Conclusion

Commercialism does not drive hip-hop in Japan. The idea that it all comes down to the money misconstrues the dynamics of hip-hop's expansion. Artists' efforts precede market exploitation. Moreover, locating a driving force in capitalistic dynamics neglects the motivations that drive musicians forward in their careers despite low odds of success. Indeed, market forces in the music world are so complex and unpredictable that record companies say only one in ten albums succeeds, though we must be sensitive to how this reflects a somewhat idiosyncratic understanding of success. Granted, this view of the market can be regarded as self-serving for record companies because contracts with artists do not pay out if the album does not succeed. In addition, if we examine the discourses of commercialism and culture as conceptualized by those who make up Japan's hip-hop scene, we find no single market in which artists find a niche. Instead, we see artists' careers develop, if they do, through business opportunities that enhance their reputations, productivity, and fan bases. Similarly, when producers imagine markets, they can make assumptions with respect to successes elsewhere, as when Umedy and Otsuji-san reviewed the latest releases from the United States, but their interpretations necessarily verge on guesswork. In this sense, media markets themselves are in fact made up of contradictory discourses.

The particulars of hip-hop culture do go into constructing the common ground on which producers and artists meet and debate. We can identify differences in constructing cultural markets by examining how artists conceive of the projects. For example, in looking at how artists approach negotiations with producers, we can see how the break-dance crew RSC Japan did not try to separate the business of hip-hop from the culture of hip-hop, but rather asserted that success is driven by the latter. They wanted a director willing to spray-paint a train. In contrast, Umedy was willing to navigate between the major sound of Busta Rhymes and an edgier dance-hall–reggae style in order to move Miss Monday's sound in new directions. Both examples illustrate the performative character of cultural economy, where the construction of markets happens not so much in the imagination as in the collective practices of all the players — artists, fans, record companies, and the media. The value of seeing these evolving, interactive, and conflicted aspects of commercialism and hip-hop globalization is that they bring into focus the improvisatory character of staying active artistically and staying in the news. In contrast, record companies and other major media outlets (like Tsutaya's stores and magazines) tend to focus almost exclusively on the very top of the music pyramid, calculating the diverse media synergies possible among celebrities (e.g., which artist is best for selling which magazines). In contrast, I argue that more can be learned about the core conditions that drive music scenes by examining interactions in the *genba* levels of the pyramid. It is here that hip-hop in Japan found fertile soil for cultivating succeeding generations of musicians.

CONCLUSION

LESSONS OF HIP-HOP GLOBALIZATION

Although many styles of hip-hop have gone from the United States to Japan, is there anything Japanese hip-hop has of importance to contribute to American audiences? The view of New York City's Ground Zero from the ashes of Hiroshima suggests that there is. In a 2002 music video, the group King Giddra rapped about the aftermath of 9/11 using images of Hiroshima after the atomic bombing.[1] The linkage of images shows how world politics can be reimagined through the lenses of different *genba*, that is, specific locations that teach us about the intersections of wider forces. As Zeebra intones at the opening of the song, "It is time to rethink world peace," and his group does so by thinking about civilians caught in wars' firestorms. Each of the three artists who make up King Giddra offer a particular take on "911," as they call it. Zeebra's lyrics express sympathy for New Yorkers, describe the shock of watching "live on CNN," witnessing "a wound in world history." But he also questions the response of the U.S. government and media.

Is this terrorists against a nation? No,	*Kore wa terorisuto tai kokka? Iya, chigau*
that's mistaking one part for the whole.	*ichibu no hōdō dake de mimachigau.*
The media's strategy: push good and evil	*Sonna media senryaku yuragu zen'aku*
and I see an atom bomb that fell in	*ukabu genkaku wa ochita genbaku*
the past	

—King Giddra (2002) "911" *Saishû Heiki* (video) (Defstar, Japan, DFVL-8052)

Although television networks broadcast the tragedy of 9/11 worldwide, viewers responded and interpreted it differently depending on their location. For example, some American commentators likened 9/11 to Pearl Harbor in the sense that both events were surprise attacks. Some Japanese bristle at the suggestion, pointing out that Pearl Harbor was an attack on the U.S. military, not on civilians. Moreover, while American commentators called the site of the World Trade Center towers Ground Zero, Japan has two locations known as ground zero: Hiroshima and Nagasaki.

The music video created for King Giddra's "911" track opens with an image of ground zero Hiroshima. At the center of the picture, the government building now known as the Peace Dome figures prominently. Although it was located close to the epicenter of the blast, the building remained standing while everything around was flattened and incinerated. It stands as a testimony to the destructive power of technology and the resilience of the Japanese people in the face of adversity. At the start of the video, the image of the destruction of the building and the surrounding area of Hiroshima is doubled, so that two images of the Peace Dome side by side recall the look of the Twin Towers after they fell. From this Hiroshima ground zero location, we see how a Japanese response to 9/11 carries special weight.

In his verse, K Dub Shine addresses civilian casualties and political infrastructures.

civilization and justice, mixed with hypocrisy	*bunmei to seigi, gizen, gocha maze*
as a cold wind blows on Afghan refugees	*afugan nanmin ni fuku tsumetai kaze*
it's always civilians who are sacrificed,	*gisei wa itsu mo shimin no hō e kuru*
even so, Bush sleeps in his bed tonight	*kon'ya mo* Bush *wa beddo de nemuru*

—King Giddra (2002) "911" *Saishû Heiki* (video), (Defstar, DFVL-8052)

Shine's emphasis on the civilian tragedies points to a consonance between ground zero Hiroshima, New York, Afghan refugees, and the countless others caught in the cross fire of larger political and military conflicts. In addition, King Giddra's rap underscores an affinity between African Americans as disenfranchised citizens in the United States and Japanese youth unable to see their concerns adequately addressed in their own political system. Such artists also are involved in the work of imagining new transnational connections through vehicles of popular culture. In this regard, the supposedly ephemeral side of popular culture may be better viewed in terms of its immediacy in responding to world events.

Paradoxes of Hip-Hop in Japan:
Neither Disappearing nor Localizing

It may seem strange to think that hip-hop in Japan has anything important to teach us about globalization. There are those in Japan and the United States who view Japanese rappers as a transient fad, likely to disappear once the next big thing comes along. They note that young Japanese have little, if any, first-hand experience with African American struggles or artistic commitments, that is, the root forces that animate hip-hop in the United States. Does this not prove that hip-hop in Japan is driven by entertainment companies, media outlets, and fashion industries eager to hype the latest cool fad? The history of hip-hop in Japan suggests otherwise, because early on, entertainment and media industries showed only lukewarm interest. During the first decade of hip-hop's emergence in Japan, from the mid-1980s to the mid-1990s, the power brokers in music magazines and record companies were generally skeptical that hip-hop would ever take root. They noted that the language was ill suited to rap, that Japan had no street culture, and that youth were imitating "black style" without understanding rap's deeper significance (see chapter 1). There were plenty of reasons why hip-hop should have disappeared in Japan, but it did not do so. One paradox of hip-hop in Japan is that it was not supposed to mean anything to young Japanese, yet it does. They should not be hip-hop, yet they are. It is precisely the enduring growth of hip-hop in Japan in the midst of widespread assumptions that it would quickly disappear that makes the phenomenon so instructive about processes of globalization.

The vibrant, expanding scene of hip-hop in Japan shows that some understandings of globalization are in need of revision. To the extent that we conceive of transnational flows primarily in terms of multinational corporations, powerful media, communications technology, or government actors, we fail to recognize the diversity of paths that can lead to global cultural connections. For example, we expect the global presence of companies such as Coca-Cola, McDonald's, and Disney because they have the backing of enormous, institutionally solid, multinational corporations. We can understand how diasporic communities around the world bring the cultures of their homelands to their new residences. But *hip-hop* in *Japan?* Its emergence and staying power cannot be explained by the strength of corporate giants or of migratory communities. Instead, I would argue, Japanese hip-hop points to the power of *genba*, the actual sites where the gamut of participants in the scene perform, socialize, and network. I argue that these performance sites constitute a key path through which cultural globalization travels.

Put another way, a primary lesson of hip-hop's spread in Japan is that the sparks that initially inspired young Japanese found fuel to burn by passing through *genba*. In nightclubs, the intense musical experience—enlivened by the crowded space, sexually charged dancing bodies, enormous sound systems, freestyle battles on stage, and the like—generated social and artistic networks that gradually built the scene (see chapters 2 and 3). These sites encouraged the social organization of families of hip-hop groups around similar aesthetic and political commitments. They battled for audiences, legitimacy, and financial support for their artistic projects. As the scene developed, hip-hop moved into the realm of media, passing through the *genba* of recording studios, and from there into the broader realm of the entertainment industry (*gyōkai*). Recording studios are sites where the processes of rehearsal and performance crystallize into a commodity form. Studios also constitute places where artists are socialized into the business of being a professional, learning standards of quality, the limits of mass media–appropriate language, and the legal risks of sampling copyrighted works. The *genba* I have focused on for this research—nightclubs and recording studios—are connected to diverse businesses and hence do not constitute a realm of civil society beyond the reach of capitalism and state power. But we can see how, as sites of performance, *genba* encourage the focus of energy and attention to produce something (live shows, recorded music) whose character cannot be reduced to political-economic interests. In this sense, hip-hop in Japan is a cultural and artistic movement that illustrates the diversity of globalization processes.

A second seemingly paradoxical feature of hip-hop in Japan involves the manner in which the scene has developed. Neither the phrase *global homogenization* nor the term *localization* accurately describes the changes in the scene over the years. Instead, we see both deepening connectedness (to the global scene) and widening diversity (both within Japan and worldwide). Deepening connectedness appears in the increasing velocity with which popular styles circulate. Both major and underground artists from the United States tour the globe more widely now than in the past. Dominant musical styles of American track-makers like Timbaland and Swizz Beats find proponents in other countries as well. The fairly unidirectional character of this flow (United States to the rest) may be shifting as foreign artists gradually find audiences outside their own countries, for example, with Akon, a Senegalese rapper popular in New York. In March 2005, Japanese rappers performed with Korean rappers partly through the support of the Japan Foundation (Japan Foundation 2005). In addition, Puerto Rico's Spanish-language reggae/rap style reggaeton was in early 2005 a staple on English-language hip-hop radio stations in the United States and was also featured prominently in Tokyo's hip-hop specialty stores. Japanese rappers occasionally record overseas as well. Japan's Lil Ai appeared, rapping in Japanese, on a song by the New York City rapper KRS-One ("Let's Go" from *The Beef* [2003] soundtrack). In 2005, the anime TV show *Samurai Champloo* aired on the Cartoon Network in the United States with a Japanese hip-hop soundtrack. The first appearance of Japanese hip-hop in the United States may have been when Scha Dara Parr and Takagi Kan appeared on a De La Soul album (*Buhloone Mind State*, 1993).

This deepening integration among international scenes, however, has not entailed homogenization. Instead, we find that such global crosscurrents are accompanied by a widening diversity among artists, fan groups, and media. If anything, the differences between Japan's various rap styles are becoming more, not less, pronounced. When we hear Hime, the female rapper discussed in chapter 6, using an eighth-century poetic form in a rap song, we can see how aesthetic choices for rap artists keep extending the frames of reference for what can be included under the rubric of hip-hop. The widening diversity is also visible in the fact that in the early 1990s, Japan's Tokyo-dominated hip-hop scene had fewer artists and styles than in the circa 2005 scene. Now, we find everything from gangsta rappers (though they would call themselves hard core) to samurai rappers, party rappers, conscious rappers, women emcees, and regional varieties from Sapporo to Nagoya to Osaka to Okinawa. I have argued that this widening diversity is apparent in the variety of ways issues of race, fandom, language, gender, and markets function within the scene as well (see chapters 1, 4, 5, 6, and 7, respectively).

One way to understand the seemingly contradictory trends of global connectedness (e.g., the globalization of Timbaland-style tracks) and widening diversity (e.g., samurai rappers and *gyangustaa* boys) is to remind ourselves of the pyramid structure of a music scene (chapter 3). Using this metaphor, we can see how over time, Japan's hip-hop scene has grown taller with the appearance of more megahit groups like Kick the Can Crew and Rip Slyme. At the same time, a more expansive base includes a widening diversity of regions, classes, and ethnicities in Japan's scenes. Globally, too, we see a wider base and taller peak of hip-hop artists around the world. More artists in more places are developing their own scenes, while top artists reach for higher sales spikes, at times thanks to their support in foreign countries. Given the tendency for industry gatekeepers to take cues from styles that are already popular, demonstrated in chapter 7, homogenization may accurately characterize the range of styles at the top levels. But it would be a mistake to generalize

from what appears in mainstream hip-hop to characterize the diversity of artists lower down the pyramid. In this respect, relatively unpopular groups may
be representative of potentially powerful movements even if they have not
achieved strong sales.

Clubs as *genba* of cultural production are crucibles where intersecting
power forces converge to create spaces for a variety of aesthetic and political
struggles through music. That is one reason why I have highlighted battles
as providing the most insight into the development of the scene. From this
perspective, it is not surprising that we find in Japan neither straightforward
global homogenization nor an unambiguous localization of hip-hop in dance,
rapping, deejaying, and visual art. Shifting contexts and widening battles
among groups feed the fire of hip-hop in Japan through aesthetic conflicts
that also promote a variety of political subjectivities. Rap in Japan includes
hard core, party rap, rock rap, free-jazz rap, and spoken word rap. Whether in
samurai gear or thug wear, everyone stakes a claim to being authentic or good
(and among their fans they earn it). Thus global/local oppositions are better
transposed into questions of how artistic sensibilities and political subjectivities are enlivened through different kinds of performativity, whether onstage
or in the marketplace. In other words, because homogenization and diversification proceed simultaneously, we should be less concerned with whether
global or local forces are winning and more concerned with mapping the particular potentials of different kinds of global connectedness. What are the
potentials for change?

Has Hip-Hop Changed Japan?

Gauging the impact of hip-hop on Japan requires considering carefully what
we might mean by cultural influence. I would caution readers to be wary
of descriptions that emphasize something like a culture clash. For example,
when I mention to Americans that I study hip-hop in Japan, I often hear,
"How strange. I would have thought Japanese culture and hip-hop couldn't
go together." We heard this kind of explanation from Riko Sakurai as well
(chapter 6), discussing the clash between self-emphasis and a Japanese tendency to worry about what others think. Such representations assume cultural difference in terms of national character, that is, as a static, unchanging
essence, albeit often with internal contradictions. (Are the Japanese Zen aes-
thetes or samurai swordsmen?) From this perspective, the reserved, polite,
soft-spoken culture of Japan contrasts with the image of an in-your-face, ag-

gressive, loud, and funky black culture of rap. But there is never a static notion of Japaneseness, nor a single meaning of hip-hop.

Images of a culture clash give an ahistorical picture of hip-hop's impact in Japan because the genre has passed through several distinct eras. In the mid-1980s, it was indeed the "shock" of difference, experienced initially through breakdancing and graffiti in film and live performance, that inspired the first generation of hip-hoppers. But it was a shock without a deep understanding of hip-hop. After the first J-rap hits of the mid-1990s, party rappers and underground hip-hoppers debated in interviews, onstage, and on CDs about what constituted the best way to make hip-hop *Japanese*. Each camp drew on alternative views of Japaneseness, thus calling into question any overarching definitions of how national identity and hip-hop ideals intersect. Party rappers pointed to their wider audiences as proof that a carefree, playfully critical stance was most appropriate to Japan. Underground rappers tended to focus more intently on the darker side of Japanese society and on themselves. After 1999, the growing diversity of the scene made it even more difficult to define any single Japanese approach.

If we think about the influence of hip-hop in Japan in terms of diverse, competing *genba*, we can see how the influence of hip-hop on Japan depends not on the character of hip-hop vis-à-vis the character of Japan, but rather on the performative impact of different styles, that is, on the extent to which particular artists are able to move the crowd. The impact of hip-hop on Japan, therefore, is best conceived in terms of providing a space, that is, a *genba*, where the diverse participants—rappers, fans, writers, record executives—meet to perform, network, and socialize. Depending on what aspects of hip-hop we consider in Japan (dance, rap, deejaying, graffiti, fashion, etc.), the kinds of influence extend in different directions as well.

At the same time, we should be cautious about assigning causation to hip-hop in the context of broader changes in Japanese society. People who reached Japan's age of adulthood (twenty) around the year 2000 were children during the booming bubble economy of the 1980s. Starting in 1992, the economy went into a long-term recession, which became known as the lost decade (*ushinawareta jūnen*). In post–bubble economy Japan, young people faced shifting national terrain. Unemployment among youth grew sharply during the 1990s. Young people's transition from school to work grew problematic. Hardworking students found fewer decent jobs. Promises of lifetime employment grew scarcer, while so-called *freeter*, who work in low-end part-time jobs, grew increasingly prevalent. In short, the promises of middle-class

Japan were disappearing, but to be replaced by what? As we saw, these developments appeared in rap lyrics as well (chapter 3). In 1995, Zeebra of King Giddra rapped about the ways the credentials society crushes the dreams of children. In 2001, Kan of MSC rapped about the desperation of a salaryman fearing unemployment. It is difficult to imagine that hip-hop "caused" any youth to reevaluate their life goals. Going to clubs, however, embodied a movement against the mainstream and probably did encourage certain directions of thinking about what goals are most important, such as emphasizing leisure, performance, consumption, and speaking out.

At the same time, in Japan's youth culture the glass is both half empty and half full. By the beginning of the twenty-first century, youth's creative power as consumers was being heralded as a key to developing Japan's high-end content industries. If entertainment businesses in music, anime, and manga are part of what will become an engine of growth for Japan's exports, youth will surely prove a critical linchpin of the process. The global spread of anime is even leading to a new appreciation of formerly unappealing *otaku*. These cross-cutting forces contextualized the club scene where students and *freeter* were the most committed participants. Clearly, gauging cultural influence requires a nuanced sense of the location of actors in the scene.

The idea of the *genba* draws attention to particular nodes of power energized by performative dynamics, making up culture and markets as they go. The use of the term *culture* here points not to overarching patterns of a particular social group or place, but to patterns of meaning that guide human activity. Hip-hop lives in Japan as long as it means something to people. It means something to people when they write rhymes, program beats, write on the concrete, dance in the street. But meaning also arises from the character of debates about authority itself. One political consequence of hip-hop aesthetics in Japan involves how the idea of *genba* implies an ontological questioning of governmental and corporate authority. Part of what makes hip-hop in Japan exciting is the idea that young people can be empowered by finding their own stance and developing their own politics, even outside the halls of power.

The sense of self-actualizing *genba* is part of what Utamaru promotes in the title track to the album *Uwasa no shinsō* (*Truth behind the Rumors*, 2001). While "outsider geezers" (*gaiya no yaji*) criticize Japan's hip-hoppers, Utamaru says "ignore them" to build up one's own sense of status and meaning that does not depend on approval from the elites.[2] On this album, we hear echoes of Utamaru responding to the criticisms his group received for the cover of their 1999 album *Respect*, which featured them in military uniforms (see chapter 1). Part of the criticism revolved around the idea that hip-hop relates to a particular original place (*honba*) and that therefore Japanese youth have no authority to speak within hip-hop. In Rhymester's 2001 song, Utamaru responds by denying the existence of any *honba*, asserting instead that all performative locations are a kind of *genba* (place of actualization).

there is no *honba* beyond this *genba*	*kono genba igai ni honba nante sonzai shinai*
no value in listening to	*gaiya no yaji wa kiku ni*
to out-of-touch old folks	*hotonda atai shinai*
want to rid yourself of an	*konpurekkusu*
inferiority complex?	*maji dasshitai*
then see others' criticisms	*tanin no hyōka nante no wa*
as a sign of changing times	*sore koso jidai shidai*

—Rhymester (2001) "Uwasa no shinsô" *Uwasa no shinsô* (Sony Ki/oon, KSCL-430)

The idea that there is no *honba* besides this *genba* conceives of influence in terms of performance, not of some unassailable essence. This conception points to an understanding of power as emerging from moving the crowd, that is, from energizing and being held accountable to some larger, social network.

Is Hip-Hop in Japan a Movement for Positive Change?

Can we draw some tentative conclusions about hip-hop's overall influence in relation to the themes of each chapter of the present book? How does it score? Is racial discrimination lessened? (A little.) Do *genba* performances give underground artists a fighting chance to compete with heavily marketed pop stars? (Sort of.) Do the battles among groups, families, and styles eventually separate the good from the bad and lead upward toward some kind of progress? (Yes and no.) Do fans find meaning beyond *otaku* isolation? (Yes.) Is language enriched by expanding Japanese to include hip-hop and hip-hop to include Japanese? (To some extent.) Do women's uses of hip-hop empower them in a man's world? (They might.) Will commercialism ultimately kill hip-hop? (I doubt it.) In each chapter, I develop more nuanced answers to these questions. Here I would like to try to draw together some of these themes in more general terms.

In the abstract, I propose thinking about the overall scorecard in terms of battles within and between *genba*. When performances can move the crowd (energize fans, persuade record executives, make news), then influence expands outward to reach even broader audiences. We cannot talk about influence without some sense of the feedback loops connecting different locations. In Japanese hip-hop terms, this has entailed succeeding eras in which *underground* and *pop* have meant different things, and so the larger contexts in which battles proceeded shifted as well. In the early days of Japanese rap, that is, the late 1980s, Itō Seikō set up the battle as avant-garde rap versus overly managed and commercialized rock. After the hit singles by East End X Yuri and Scha Dara Parr, the underground tried to establish their legitimacy, despite smaller sales, in terms of their deeper connection to hip-hop ideals (opposition, self-emphasis, keeping it real) while party rappers focused on Japaneseness in terms of carefree, lighthearted, pleasurable music. In some ways, Rhymester's song "B-Boyism" in 1998 marked a watershed. The song became an anthem to protecting one's own aesthetic stance as a core value of hip-hop, both encapsulating the history of battles within the Japanese scene and offering a reason why there could no longer be a single scene.

In the years since then, we can witness a growing diversity between scenes in Japan regionally and in terms of the aesthetic and political stakes of the music. Along with diversity comes the increasing compartmentalization of different styles. Some groups care about hip-hop's connection to African Americans, while others brag that they only listen to Japanese hip-hop. So, in general, the influence of hip-hop on understandings of race, gender, and language continues to evolve in contradictory ways. Some Japanese hip-hoppers do use the music as a gateway to a deeper understanding of race issues. As yet, however, hip-hop's popularity has not deeply altered the racism against African Americans in Japan. One hopes that when hip-hop fans reach higher levels of status in corporate and government sectors, racism against African Americans will decrease. I would say that hip-hop has had a greater effect on drawing attention to ideas of race within Japanese society, raising issues of racism against Okinawans, Korean Japanese, and *burakumin*, for example. In addition, the advent of Japanese hip-hoppers who perform with Korean emcees both in Korea and Japan suggests that the emergence of cross-Asian *genba* may eventually lead to deeper connections between the so-called Japanese race and Chinese and Korean others. In terms of women's empowerment, the recent examples of the female hip-hoppers Ai, Hime, and Miss Monday show that gender is finally gaining wider treatment within a Japanese rap scene largely dominated by men. If some of these straight-talking women achieve mainstream success, it may be possible to point to hip-hop as a vehicle for gender equality in Japan. Their influence up until 2005, however, seems largely confined to their fans, a substantial, but not widespread, effect. Will hip-hop change the Japanese language? The influence of hip-hop on the Japanese language seems to me rather slight. Young people do adopt new slang and drag out the pronunciation of certain syllables to give some Japanese words a black English sound (like *ku RAA bu* for "club"), but the rhythm and rhyme added to Japanese words tends to be confined to lyrics within songs. Rap's influence on the Japanese language is most pronounced in unsettling ideas for Japanese uniqueness that rely on images of the Japanese language as timeless and unchanging.

Whether the underground will ever defeat pop depends very much on what counts as winning. If artists can content themselves with the satisfaction of performance in clubs and the ability to release albums to the public, then most artists in the underground scene have already won, thanks to a widening array of clubs and the declining cost of making albums using new digital technologies (like Pro Tools recording software for the Macintosh). If all underground artists want to be huge megahit stars, history suggests that most will be disappointed. Yet with the Internet now an increasingly important medium for music distribution, the power of major entertainment companies may decrease. Since major labels tend to focus on achieving megahits, the underground scene may find new opportunities by building on live *genba* performances to develop self-organizing, collaborative communities online. An online dis battle between Dev Large of Buddha Brand and K Dub Shine in 2004 provided a window on the potential for new kinds of musical battles over the Internet.

The battles among hip-hop groups will undoubtedly keep evolving. Again, the question of whether "good hip-hop" or "bad rap" will win out depends very much on competing definitions of success. The sharp decline in million-selling albums and singles since 1998 may mean that the recording industry should turn its attention to devoted fans rather than pursuing the whims of vaguely interested consumers (see chapter 7). I would also argue that the power of fandom is increasing in Japan, where hopes are being placed on content industries to help lead Japan to a new era of economic prosperity. In this sense, not only can fans find satisfaction beyond *otaku* isolation but they should occupy a more central place in efforts to promote Japan's economic growth and political influence by enhancing its international status as a cultural superpower.

The intersection of markets and overt political messaging in popular culture is complex. In general, what appears at the top of the music-scene pyramid tends to be less political, less oppositional, but a big hit could conceivably make top-level executives more open to supporting more political music.[3] Commercialism seems unlikely to kill hip-hop in Japan, though worries about this possibility are an eternal source of concern among artists and fans in every music genre. Commercial success leads to greater visibility of some styles (especially the party rap vein in Japan in the mid-1990s and underground collaborations with R & B artists in the late 1990s). But because commercial success inspires both imitators and opponents, in the end, it is not commercialism, but a more generally declining interest that will relegate hip-hop to the realm of nostalgia. Judging from the ubiquity of rock bands in Japan today, I expect hip-hop to endure in the country for decades to come, at least in terms of hip-hop in the form of a rapper with a microphone, a DJ scratching music, and background tracks programmed from samples and synthesized sounds.

Rethinking Soft Power: Japanese Rappers Criticize US Militarism

A focus on *genba* also suggests a way of extending the insights of the idea of soft power. In particular, we can see that assessing the soft power of cultural forms depends on the content more than the origin of the style. In this sense, soft power depends on "keeping it real," that is, linking the words to specific actions. As readers may recall, soft power refers to the attractiveness of a nation's culture, politics, and ideals (Nye 2004). The theory of soft power suggests that when Japanese adopt (and adapt) hip-hop style, they will view America's national interests in a more sympathetic light. Examples of Japanese hip-hop songs that question American government policies, however, show that we must examine the content of popular culture in addition to the style if we are to gauge influence. That is one reason I provided so many examples of lyrics in this book, namely, to evaluate the messages, not just the form, of hip-hop in Japan.

Take, for example, Rhymester's song "911 Everyday" from their 2004 album *Gray Zone*. In the song, Utamaru and Mummy-D rap about watching television coverage of distant disasters. It disgusts them and makes them feel helpless. Some parts of the song question whether US foreign policy is living up to its ideals of spreading democracy and freedom. In particular, they voice skepticism about the United States' use of military power, especially when the Bush administration's arguments about the existence of just cause for toppling Saddam Hussein were based on falsehoods about weapons of mass destruction: "here it comes, the 'just cause' / cluster bombs, bunker busters / raining death's agony on people" (ima nara tsuite kuru daigi meibun / kurasu-taa, bankaa basutaa / kaki kesareta tami no danmatsuma) (Rhymester [2004] "911 Eburiidei" *Gray Zone*, Sony Ki/oon, KSCL-850). When Rhymester played this song on a Tokyo radio show, Utamaru told me in a personal communication July 2, 2005, they received faxes from Japanese journalists who had worked in Iraq. The reporters praised them for addressing issues of militarism and for speaking more forthrightly than the journalists had been able to do in their newspapers.

Rhymester's song questioning the Iraq war as seen from Japan also suggests a way to extend thinking about cosmopolitanism as a feature of globalization. Cosmopolitans tend to be defined in terms of an outward-looking subjectivity, a sense of ethical connection to broader humanity (Hannerz 1996; Tomlinson 1999). A *genba* perspective shows that one can draw on global imagery and yet come to very different conclusions about how this imagery should be interpreted. Mummy-D criticizing the bunker-busting bombs of the Iraq war shows that life in a post–9/11 world assumes a particular cast depending on one's location.

The idea of soft power is extremely important; it demands attention be paid to the global, public image of the hard power of economic sanctions and military actions. In this regard, Guantánamo Bay and Abu Ghraib excesses caused damage to America's national interest that outweighed the benefits of any supposed intelligence gathered in the process. We might ask what kinds of cultural exchange can lead to greater sympathy among the people of the world to develop more democratic institutions and processes for dealing with the challenges of a globalizing world. Hip-hop offers a channel for speaking truth to power and more broadly has provided a way for hip-hoppers to imagine themselves as part of a global cultural movement. As Mummy-D says later in the song, the young generation must transcend the limitations of the United Nations and media agitation by using their imagination. Hip-hop proves to be a vehicle for doing just that.

Genba Limits and Possibilities

What are the limits of the *genba* concept? To what extent is a farm a *genba*? A factory? A television studio? A fitness club? McDonald's? Disneyland? An advertising agency? A hostess club? A baseball stadium? A fish market? A confectionary factory? An anime studio? The usefulness of the concept does not arise from a capacity to categorize types of *genba*, but rather from the possibility of drawing attention to the performative character of the social interactions in the different spaces. I leave it to other researchers to decide whether the concept of *genba* has any usefulness for their work, but I would suggest a few ways the idea might be extended and also point out some limitations.

In some ways, the idea of a *genba* applies most directly to cultural events and media gaining their force from the social activities that build up some kind of scene or movement. The parades of fashion mavens in the Harajuku section of Tokyo clearly depend on the see-and-be-seen character of fashion, from the junior high schoolers cruising Takeshita Street to the hipper late-teens/early-twenties set that cruises Ura-Harajuku (back-Harajuku). A sense of participation, yet ultimate difference from the others, animates the scene. We could distinguish among different music scenes—rock, J-pop, noise, hard core (underground noise rock), punk, salsa, jazz, *enka*, techno, house, drum 'n' bass, and so on—in the sense that some styles (or perhaps more accurately, different eras of different styles) depend on *genba* to a different degree. Yet because they all develop distinctive networks around and through sites of live performance and recording, the idea of *genba* may provide useful ways of conceptualizing musical developments beyond a contest between indigenous and Western features. In contrast, writing a book can be a more solitary activity, depending less on *genba* than, say, producing a magazine. Some *genba*, such as those for films or anime, require larger groups of people to produce the work. Meanwhile, movie theaters do not provide the same interactive participation as do nightclubs (the movie cannot see you, for example), though one can imagine opening night at Cannes as a *genba*. I would point out that what makes Cannes more of a *genba* than a multiplex in a mall is not the presence of powerful elites, but rather the fact that collaborative, networking, and performative aspects of the event are heightened. Even in situations where styles of consumption are presumably standardized, consumer practices can nevertheless be transformative, as we learn from James Watson's (1997) edited volume on McDonald's in East Asia.

Clearly, the *genba* concept cannot explain every aspect of globalization. The business negotiations discussed in chapter 7 have a performative character to them, but they differ substantially from club performances in the sense that accountability is more binary in structure. The record company executive and artist negotiate a contract and proceed on those terms. The expanding, performative power of a new album comes later. The artist's performance in a studio is assembled, fine-tuned, and then moves through broader networks of retail and media. Understanding the forces that lead to media booms requires moving beyond the corporate offices into the realm of feedback loops among artists, record companies, fans, and media.

The idea of the *genba* as a path of cultural globalization seems somewhat less applicable to so-called low-end service and information work increasingly outsourced to places like Bangalore, India (Friedman 2005). We can think of assembly-line factories, call centers, database input centers, and so on as varieties of *genba*, but they are much more centrally controlled than the *genba* of hip-hop in Japan. This suggests that we need to specify the populist features of sites of performance to evaluate the kinds of influence they have. *Genba* differ in terms of how much room there is for improvisation, individual performance, mobility, dialogue, and discipline.

As a research tool, the notion of *genba* provides a way to approach the multitude of possible sites to examine a system of circulation. When I began my research, people agreed: Go to the *genba*. That's where the action is. So even though only some of the key activities that sustain artist-entrepreneurs pass through *genba*, they do provide a focus of attention and energy that serve as a starting point for analysis. The analytical concept of *genba* draws attention to the sociable side of global cultural movements. The circulation of media depends on building collective energy, not only on filling a niche. Anthropology draws attention to the word-of-mouth level of globalization. Thus the concept of *genba* offers a different model of social organization, of defining authority and success, one that depends not on turning a profit, but on moving the crowd. This points to an alternative to some multinational brand-name corporations as a path to extend the reach of cultural globalization.

The story of hip-hop in Japan helps us see that the music and the understandings of hip-hop culture were initially driven by the persistence of deeply committed individuals and groups. We can also see the importance of *genba* for providing a focus, a place where something is actually produced, and where people are enlivened by that production. I believe artistic and cultural movements have a large role to play in encouraging the more democratic and progressive features of globalization. Some aspects of Japanese hip-hop show great promise, particularly as a youth-oriented movement that prizes speaking out, opposition, and a playful contestation of the status quo. Such skills not only develop strong artists, they also energize *genba* where people can work collectively toward a better future. In this respect, hip-hop Japan suggests some promising possibilities for generating new forms of cultural connection across national borders.

NOTES

INTRODUCTION: HIP-HOP, JAPAN, AND CULTURAL GLOBALIZATION

1 These lyrics, although the words are spoken on the album by ECD, are credited to Egaitsu Hiroshi, a writer and deejay. The lyrics appear on ECD (1997) the "Intro" *Big Youth* (Avex/Cutting Edge, CTCR-14075).

2 "*Genba*" is pronounced with a hard "g" as in "given," and following Japanese usage connotes either singular or plural.

3 Some people complain that studies of hip-hop tend to put too much emphasis on rap to the exclusion of the other elements. I agree that entire books could, and I hope will, be written on Japan's break-dance, deejay and graffiti scenes. My choice of topics is not meant to suggest that rapping is the most important part of hip-hop. Rather, I find rap particularly instructive because it is the most commercially successful aspect of hip-hop and because it involves a deep engagement with language. Although I have titled the book "hip-hop Japan," and in part I aim to provide a broad-based overview, I am acutely aware that this monograph captures only a small fraction of hip-hop's diverse manifestations.

4 Manhattan Records, Dance Music Records (DMR), and Cisco Records all have specialty hip-hop shops within a block of the Tokyū Hands Department Store in Shibuya, and there you can find flyers to upcoming events. To get to Cave the first time, you have to decipher the somewhat cryptic map on a flyer, though the neighborhood police box (*kōban*) can also be a source for directions.

5 The book's title is inspired by Nelson George's (1998) *Hip-Hop America*. Following George, I attempt to link thinking about the culture of hip-hop with that about the

broader social settings and business interests. Other important works examining hip-hop in the United States include Baker 1993, Boyd 2002, Fernando 1994, Forman 2002, Forman and Neal 2004, Kitwana 2002, Potter 1995, Rivera 2003, Rose 1994, and Schloss 2004.

6 The majority of these studio visits occurred at Crown Records in Akasaka (Tokyo), where I witnessed the making of several volumes of the compilation series *Best of Japanese Hip-Hop* and *Best of Japanese DJ*.

7 From February 1996 to February 1997, I also attended monthly editorial meetings of *Remix* magazine, which covers a range of club music genres (house, techno, art rock, jazz and hip-hop).

8 Compare, for example, two music videos on *Future Shock Visual Tracks First Edition* (Polystar, 2001, PSVR-5085). The video by Ozrosaurus, "Rollin' 045," shows the group in lowrider vehicles popular in their home area of Yokohama (telephone area code 045), while in the next video, "Hip Hop 2 Zero 00 featuring Rino," Soul Scream uses samurai swords to fight ninja.

9 The interpenetration of commercial and underground is partly inspired by Dick Hebdige's (1979) work on subculture. However, in contrast to his argument that punk style was increasingly appropriated into dominant culture, I place more emphasis on the persistence of the underground hip-hop scene, even in the context of increasing commercialization.

10 That is, if the last line was, as might be expected, "K-O-H-E-I Japan," it would rhyme with *jikan*. By using "Japonica" he disrupts both the rhyme and the meter. That makes the last line operate like the punch line of a joke.

11 In the volume edited by William W. Kelly (2004), my own chapter on fans, which was slightly revised and included here, is susceptible to this criticism as well, namely, that it adopts primarily a national frame of reference.

1. YELLOW B-BOYS, BLACK CULTURE, AND THE ELVIS EFFECT

1 The song "B-Boyism" also appears on the 1999 Rhymester album *Respect* (Next Level/File Records, NLCD-026).

2 Criticisms of African American rappers who are not "real" are provocatively portrayed by the emcee Gift of Gab from the duo Blackalicious. In one of his songs, he debates an imagined fan who wishes for more real rhymes. He raps, "but that won't sell 'cause you got to keep it real / so that we can feel where you're coming from, because these streets is ill, / so if you ain't killing niggas in rhymes your whole sound's just bubblegum." / I said I won't contribute to genocide, I'd rather try to cultivate the inside / and evolve the frustrated ghetto mind, / the devil and his army have never been a friend of mine." Blackalicious, "Shallow Days," on *Nia* (Quannum Projects, 1999, MWRII2CD).

3 See Koshiro 2003 for an analysis of African American literature's deep and enduring impact on modern Japan.

4 KP rap about relations between North and South Korea on the album *Neverland* (Toshiba—EMI, 2003, TOCT-0909).

5　As Kelsky 2001 shows, some Japanese women escape oppressive gender relations in Japan through their relationships with Western men.

6　For the tribute song, see DJ Krush featuring MC Boss, "Candle Chant," on *Zen* (Sony Records, 2001, SRCL-4995).

7　Lafura Jackson's story is told in a book written by his mother; see Eguchi 2001. A provisional translation is also available: Yoshiko Jackson and Lafura Jackson, "Lafura Jackson a.k.a. A-Twice: The Life of a Rap Artist" (2002).

2. BATTLING HIP-HOP SAMURAI

1　See Kick the Can Crew, "Mikoshi Rockers (feat. Rhymester)," on *Vitalizer* (Warner Music Japan, 2002, HDCA-10084).

2　The character of the battles in Japan unfolds in *genba* that contrast in diverse ways with hip-hop in other countries. See for comparison a growing number of studies examining hip-hop in other countries (Durand 2002; Fernandes 2003; Japan-Foundation 2005; Maxwell 2003; Mitchell 2001a; Mitchell 2001b; Perullo and Fenn 2003; Prevos 1996; Urla 2001; Weiss 2002).

3　Yamada Yōji gained fame for his Tora-san series of films. *Twilight Samurai* revolves around a group of samurai who tally the substantial holdings of their regional lord. These samurai entertain themselves with geisha at night and ridicule a fellow samurai they call "Twilight" because, as a poor widower, he must go home at dusk to care for his young daughters. Meanwhile, the townspeople are struggling through poverty and famine. In one of the film's most affecting motifs, dead children float by on the river. When their bodies get caught on the reeds by the riverbank, farmers matter-of-factly push them along. Thus we see the limits of assertions of a singular way of the samurai.

4　This narrative draws heavily on Hosokawa, Matsumura, and Shiba 1991.

5　What is Western? What is Japanese? Kawabata (1991) states, "The current standard for classifying *hōban* [Japanese records] and *yōban* [Western records] is three-fold: first the nationality of the original record; second, the performers' nationality; and third, the language of the song's lyrics. There is really no strict distinction." It is worth noting that the distinction between domestic and import is determined by where the CD is manufactured, not by the nationality of the artist or group. Most so-called Western music sold in Japan is *kokuban* (pressed in Japan). This domestic press usually includes a bonus track and translations of the lyrics and liner notes into Japanese, but costs about twice as much as an import ($25–30 for the domestic press versus $15 for an import). One would imagine sharp competition, but imports are seldom available except at the enormous Tokyo retailers like Tower Records, HMV, and Wave. The rapid growth of the mail-order business of record and CD sales in the 1990s may mean more listeners are benefiting from the import prices.

6　One could argue that language differences, a relatively closed media market in the United States, and the sheer dominance of American popular culture globally precludes Americans from wide experimentation with foreign popular culture, but none of that explains why manga and anime have managed to become major business in the United States, while Japanese music has not. There are already some important studies of Japanese popular culture success outside of Japan (Allison 2003; Belson and Bremner 2004; Iwabuchi 2002; Tobin 2004), but the question of the slow flow of J-pop music to the United States is a subject for another project.

7 As Cornel West (2004, 22) says, globalization is inescapable; the question is whether it will be an American-led corporate globalization or a democratic globalization. The answer, of course, is that globalization is and will be both corporate led and potentially democratic. This points us toward what is perhaps the more important question, namely, what kinds of social structures and motivations can drive democratic globalization? What kinds of organizing principles besides corporate capitalism can encourage transnational cultural movements? The early years of hip-hop in Japan offer some lessons.

8 A video of *Wild Style* with Japanese subtitles was rereleased in September 1996 through the record company Vortex (MLK-001). It also had a brief run as a midnight show at the Parco Department store in Shibuya around the same time.

9 In the winter of 1997, live bands were banned from playing at Hokoten. However, the area continues to provide a gathering place for fan groups, but there are fewer musicians than in the past. The so-called rock 'n' rollers still come every Sunday wearing jeans, leather jackets, and boots, and sporting greased-back Elvis hairdos, to do a kind of twist to American rock of the 1950s and 1960s. Female fans of various bands also gather nearby and engage in costume play (*kosu pure*) wearing lacy bridal-style gowns (white, black, or red), black lipstick and eye makeup, and colored, tormented hair. We see here the links between street-parade fashion (as *genba*) and street stages (as *genba* as well).

10 Ozawa Kenji, "Kon'ya wa boogie back feat. Scha Dara Parr" on *Life* (Toshiba-EMI, 1994, TOCT-8495).

11 Both songs appear on the album East End X Yuri, *Denim-ed Soul II* (Epic/Sony, 1995 ESCB-1590).

3. *GENBA* GLOBALIZATION AND LOCATIONS OF POWER

1 Ginsburg, Abu-Lughod, and Larkin (2002, 3) raise key questions regarding media power, broadly defined, in an important edited volume. The ethnographic studies of media included in the volume suggest a broad range of methods for unraveling diverse dimensions of power: in the ways media can enable cultural activism (Ginsburg 2002; McLagan 2002; Turner 2002); in the ways television shows that aim to promote national ideals are nevertheless creatively reinterpreted, often against the grain, by diverse audiences (Abu-Lughod 2002; Mankekar 2002; Wilk 2002); and in the ways technologies such as radio and cinema, which may be presumed to play similar roles everywhere, are in fact diversely appropriated in different settings (Larkin 2002; Spitulnik 2002). Of particular interest for understanding Japanese hip-hop are the considerations of the social sites of production. In the examples of Latino advertising in the United States (Davila 2002) and of the transposition

of Hollywood story lines to Bollywood extravaganzas (Ganti 2002), we see how final products result from a complex mix of institutional structures, ideas about audiences, experiences of the producers, and channels of distribution.

2 Recent years have witnessed an increasingly flexible understanding of fieldwork sites in Japan anthropology. I have been inspired by important works that explore such sites as a fish market, a hostess club, a confectionary factory, and an advertising agency (Bestor 2004; Allison 1994; Kondo 1990; Moeran 1996). Here, too, the anthropologists consider the setting and work outward to analyze broader cultural conceptions of markets, sexuality, crafted selves, and publicity.

3 Gupta and Ferguson (1997, 39) argue that it is important to see anthropology's distinctive trademark not as a commitment to "the local," as in the people of some local community, but rather to emphasize anthropology's "attentiveness to epistemological and political issues of location." They put it this way: "Ethnography's great strength has always been the explicit and well-developed sense of location, of being set here-and-not-elsewhere. This strength becomes a liability when notions of 'here' and 'elsewhere' are assumed to be features of geography, rather than sites constructed in fields of unequal power relations" (35). Gupta and Ferguson stress the importance of foregrounding questions of "location, intervention, and the construction of situated knowledges" (5) and of focusing on "shifting locations" rather than "bounded fields" (39). This approach offers a way of focusing cultural research across boundaries and through transnational connections.

4 For those who would prefer an English-language phrase to capture the idea of *genba*, I would suggest *focus location* because *genba* refers to locations (not just physical or geographic sites, but social and cultural positions as well) where people's attention and energies focus on getting something done. Thus *genba* globalization refers to the processes by which the global refracts through focus locations and thereby is put back into the world.

5 JET stands for Japan Exchange and Teaching Program. Run by Japan's Ministry of Education, the program sends thousands of English-speaking college graduates to teach in Japan's junior and senior high schools. I was based in Kurikoma near the northern edge of Miyagi prefecture, in a town of 16,000, surrounded by rice fields.

6 Japanese youth have long complained about the pressures of their credentials society in which the status of one's school and one's company construct the primary measures of success. In 1961, for example, Nakagawa Gorō produced the folk song "Jukensei burūsu" ("Exam-Student Blues"), which satirizes the pressures on parents and children to succeed in an educational arms race. See also Field (1995), which analyzes what the author calls the "disappearance of childhood" as the young are turned into laborers supporting cram schools and the educational-testing industry.

7 MSC, "Shinjuku Underground Area" on *Matador* (Blues Interactions, 2003, PCD-5846).

8 This is the official translation. See the Prime Minister of Japan's official Web site: www.kantei.go.jp/foreign/policy/titeki/kettei/030708f_e.html). Accessed July 12, 2004.

9　The general consensus among the artists and record company people I spoke with while doing fieldwork from 1995 to 1997 was that sales of 100,000 albums constituted a hit, at least for a group that had not yet had massive sales. Given the decline in total sales since then, I adjusted this hit level to 80,000 to arrive at this figure.

10　A more complete picture of the music scene would include a wider range of actors including artist-management companies, publishing divisions, booking agents, and so on. The four-part schematic diagram is meant to remind us that binary relations (artist–record company, artist-fan, artist-media) operate in a fluid context.

11　See *Top 100* for a list of all the top-selling albums of 2002, including Rip Slyme (2002) *Tokyo Classic* (Warner Music Japan, WPC7-10147). Oricon is the company that tracks album sales in Japan, publishing the weekly *Oricon* trade magazine for record companies and a consumer version called *Za ichiban* (*The Number One*). Rip Slyme finished number 9 in the year-end album top one hundred chart, which lists the albums that appeared in the top one hundred between December 3, 2001, and November 25, 2002. Rip Slyme posted sales of 922,760 albums during that period; total sales were likely somewhat higher. The figures for singles, karaoke requests, and sales come from this same issue of *Oricon*.

12　According to *Top 100* Dabo's album *Hitman* sold 41,610 copies in the first two months after its release on September 25, 2002 (2003, 112). Total sales are likely higher, but I could not access that data.

4. RAP FANS AND CONSUMER CULTURE

1　This also appears in the video *Thumpin' Camp: Legend of Japanese Hip-Hop* (dir. Akishima Takashi, 1996, Cutting Edge, CTVR-94001).

2　The show at the Japan Society of New York City in the spring of 2005, curated by Murakami Takashi, for example, brought some self-styled *otaku* art to the United States. See also Murakami 2005.

3　This information was taken from the RIAJ Web site at www.riaj.com/data/others/million_q.html (accessed April 27, 2005). See chapter 7 for more discussion of these trends in megahits, and a detailed chart of the numbers of million-sellers.

4　Evidence for the deepening of the niche scenes appears in an increasing number of record releases, as well as in overseas tours by representative acts. DJ Krush and Urbarian Gym's T.O.P. Rankaz (hip-hop) appeared in New York. Chelsea (reggae) tours in Jamaica. Ken Ishii (techno) is gaining increasing international fame.

5　Examples of families circa 1996 include the Funky Grammar Unit (Rhymester, East End, Mellow Yellow), Kaminari (Rino, Twigy, You the Rock, DJ Yas, and others), the Little Bird Nation, which is the "LB" of the party rap festival (Scha Dara Parr, Tokyo #1 Soul Set, Dassen Trio, and others), and a less central (but more familiar to me) collection called Kitchens (EDU, Now, Cake-K, and others).

6　In the early 1980s, the Ministry of Health and Welfare approved the use of unheated blood products for Japanese patients, despite warnings of the danger of contamination by the virus later identified as HIV. Over four hundred people, mostly hemophiliac children, were infected with HIV as a result. In the spring of 1996, news reports broke the scandal by showing collusion between a pharmaceutical company called Green Cross and the Health Ministry to suppress a report warning of the blood transfusion dangers.

7   For example, Asō (1997, 19) reports that up until the appearance of these pre-idols in the late 1960s, the informal forms for *me* (*boku*) and *you* (*kimi*) were never used in lyrics.

8   At club events, too, DJs spinning after 3 a.m. will often play rare or relatively unknown old soul, jazz, and funk albums as "sample time" (*neta taimu*).

9   Miyadai points out that initially the idea of *otaku* connoted a kind of person without good interpersonal skills, but as groups of people began to consider themselves *otaku* who faced unfair discrimination, the term took on the connotation of a cultural type (from *jinkaku ruikei* to *bunka ruikei*) (Miyadai 1994, 162–66).

10 Three *s*'s because of the Japanese words for these items: *sentakuki, suihanki, sōjiki.*

11 In considering criticisms of fans, it would be important to include outsiders' criticisms, but interestingly, few of the latter exist. Except for the dismissive attitude articulated in the phrase "they're just imitation New Yorkers," expressed by music industry folks skeptical of Japanese rap, there are few outside criticisms of Japanese hip-hop fans. This seems to support Miyadai's claim that outsiders have no feeling one way or the other about other islands in space.

5. RHYMING IN JAPANESE

1   The concept of dialogue gives a sense of the multiple dimensions of cultural stakes. Mikhail Bakhtin argues persuasively that meaning does not arise out of a one-to-one relation, as if hip-hop or Japaneseness could be reduced to a single set of ideas or expressions. Bakhtin (1981, 276) encourages us to see that meaning arises out of dialogue. In his words, "no living word relates to its object in a *singular* way: between the word and its object, between the word and the speaking subject, there exists an elastic environment of other, alien words about the same object, the same theme. . . . It is precisely in that process of living interaction with this specific environment that the word may be individualized and given stylistic shape." It is worth noting that even the intent of the speaking subject cannot fully determine the meaning of words, and this abstract formulation has practical consequences for understanding how censorship, free speech, co-optation, and resistance operate in uneasy tension in popular culture. Bakhtin gives us another perspective on the idea of *genba* as a location where words are actualized, where the consequences of hybridity are experienced less as a mixture than as a performance in time, a grounding of the "elastic environment," the "living interaction" in a setting open to ethnographic examination.

2   The significance of the debates around Japanese hip-hop can be viewed in light of a range of scholarship showing that ideas about how communication works, and to what purpose, are culturally variable and need to be discovered rather than simply assumed (Woolard and Schieffelin 1994). Judith Irvine and Susan Gal (2000, 35), for example, draw attention to the ideological aspects of linguistic differentiation by analyzing the conceptual schemes people use to "frame their understandings of linguistic varieties and map those understandings onto people, events, and activi-

ties." They call these schemes ideologies because they are suffused with political and moral issues and are subject to the interests of their bearers' social position. The challenge is not only mapping the structure of such ideologies but also analyzing their consequences. Irvine and Gal identify three semiotic processes that can help us understand the relationship between language use, ideologies, and politics: *iconization*, by which linguistic features are taken to stand for social groups as a whole; *fractal recursivity*, which involves the projection of an opposition, salient at some level of relationship, onto some other level; and *erasure*, which, in simplifying the sociolinguistic field, renders some persons or activities invisible (37–38).

3 Whether Itō is giving a historically accurate depiction of the adoption of the Western calendar is not important for my point. One could easily argue that various top-down forces in the Japanese government and in the West forced the Japanese people to use, at least in some settings, a Western calendar. My point in using Itō is to highlight an alternative model of how cultural patterns spread, one that focuses on grassroots dynamics working in tandem with larger political economic forces.

4 It is worth clarifying the two different meanings for the word *producer*. In a recording studio, the producer guides the assemblage of the track and vocals using the mixer (or a computer). The term *producer* is also used to describe the track-maker, that is, the musician who brings the track to the studio.

5 Their name is an acronym. *D* stands for Delight, the bar that the leader JJay founded and runs (it is also the place where the group members first met). *E* stands for Epicenter, aka JJay; JJay's given name is Junji. *S* stands for Shima, one of the rappers, whose full name is Shima Hiroki. *D* stands for Drunkk, the other rapper.

6 The studio is a place for professionals, as MA$A reminded musicians on numerous occasions. For example, when a DJ adding a scratch solo to a song asked if he could keep the first part and then just fix the second half, MA$A told him simply to redo the whole thing, rather than fiddling with the recording computer: "After all, you're a pro" (*purō da kara*).

7 "Punch in" refers to recording just a section of a verse or line by punching the record button on and off over an already recorded tape while the tape is running.

8 Interestingly, the term Otaki uses to describe making rock grow in Japan, *dochaku*, is also the word Roland Robertson used to coin glocalization. See chapter 3 for more discussion of so-called glocal/grobal debates.

9 Irvine and Gal (2000) call this "fractal recursivity," whereby a distinction at one level, between American dialects, is transformed into a linguistic distinction at another level—between artificial, TV-ready Japanese and earthy, regional, organic Japanese.

10 Cake-K dubbed this video for me. I do not have the source information. According to Cake-K's label, the video was produced in 1991.

11 Cool-K, featuring Umedy (EDU) and Baby Setsu (Now), "One Mo' Night (Pickles Mix)," on *Best of Japanese Hip-Hop Vol. 7* (Crown Records, 1996, CRCP-20142).

12 The lyrics are mostly in English: "*Naiyō* nothing / everybody watching." Scha Dara Parr, "Watch or Not Such a TV," on *Big Project of Scha Dara* (File, 1990, 23MF020D).

13 The lyrics were reprinted in the August 2002 issue of *Blast* magazine (*Blast* editors 2002). I gratefully acknowledge the help of Furukawa Kou in providing me with a

copy. The details of the story about the removal of King Giddra's songs from store shelves are taken from this issue of the magazine.

14 The lyrics were published in *Blast* in August 2002 (*Blast* editors 2002).

6. WOMEN RAPPERS AND THE PRICE OF CUTISMO

1 Some of the women listed are part of groups with more men — East End X Yuri (two men, one woman) and Jupiter (a production group run by men featuring women singers). There were three all-female groups — Melon, Orchids, and Section S — and three solo artists — Hac, Sugar Soul, and Rim.

2 Okada Makiko, a woman who played a leading role in developing new artists through the Next Level imprint of the independent label File Records, preferred a style with some edge, for example, at least according to some of the artists who brought demos to her. For whatever reasons, she did not promote women rappers.

3 Similarly, the sociologist Yuko Ogasawara (1998) regards the freedom (i.e., lack of authority) of office ladies (or OLS) in a Japanese bank as a source of their power. She shows that men must curry favor with women in order to move up the corporate ladder, and hence women are not simply powerless. Yet she also shows that when women resist their subordinate positions in dead-end jobs, epitomized by serving tea to the men, they reinforce the stereotype that women are too emotional to be given responsibility. This shows that whenever speaking of power, we must consider the limits as well as the potentials.

4 In the film version of Murakami Ryū's novel *Love and Pop* (1996), the schoolgirls who sell their companionship to older, lonely men appear above all to be bored. It is work to hang out with boring older men. The girls may earn money and clothes, but they are paid for a reason. The film *Bounce Kogals* (dir. Harada Masato 1997) underscores the onerousness of the job when it depicts a girl whose assignment is to listen to an older man brag about his conquests of rape and murder during World War II.

5 Monday also faced negative fan reactions on 2 Channel, a popular Web site for exchanging views on popular culture, where some people called her a lesbian or expressed a desire to have sex with her. She shrugged those reactions off and focused instead on how fans tended to fall into two categories: those that like her lyrics and those that appreciated the deeper (i.e., less pop-oriented) hip-hop sounds. She said she intended to push both lyrics and deeper hip-hop sounds for her third album, later released in 2005.

7. MAKING MONEY, JAPAN-STYLE

1 In his study of Tsukiji, the Tokyo fish market that is the largest in the world, Theodore Bestor points out that the debate over how to interpret markets tends to counterpose *formalist* interpretations, which emphasize rational choice in terms of quantifiable calculations, against *substantivist* interpretations, which focus on the socially and culturally embedded contexts of exchange. He finds, however, that the distinction blurs in everyday practice. For although the fish traders themselves are

formalists in their descriptions of exchange rates, transaction costs, and so on, "to work in a market*place*, on some level one must be a substantivist: one must intuitively engage in exchange that is embedded in social context and know that assessments of advantage and reciprocity can be simultaneously calculated in financial, cultural, and moral currencies" (2004, 308). He adds, "To be sure, buy low and sell high is always good formalist advice. But buy from whom? Sell to whom? When? Where?" Answering these questions requires a substantivist perspective.

2 Rock Steady Crew, the original group from New York City, is led by Crazy Legs and has offshoots in cities around the world. The original New York crew was featured in numerous early films including *Wild Style* (dir. Charlie Ahearn 1982) and *Flashdance* (dir. Adrian Lyne 1983).

3 The New York dancer who invented the so-called Campbell Lock was able to receive trademark protection for his particular dance pose. This rare example aside, intellectual property regimes seem ill suited to developing business models for dance styles (Ananya Chatterjee, personal communication, February 2005).

4 As Keith Negus (1999) has expertly described in tracing the interplay between corporate cultures, music genres, and artists' positions, these limitations are clear to people up and down the corporate ladder.

5 Angela McRobbie (2002) offers cogent lessons for considering how this transforms "the social" into "work," because what constitutes work is almost everything in an artist's social life. Mirroring the expansion of *freeter* employment, she also notes that jobs in entertainment businesses are "permanently transitional," which produces disembedded and highly individualized personnel (97).

6 There is a striking convergence in analyses of millennial capitalism in that both cultural studies and economic theory highlight the increasing importance of consumers. As Jean and John Comaroff point out, consumption has become a prime mover in social theory: "The invisible hand, or the Gucci-gloved fist, that animates political impulses, the material imperatives, and the social forms of the Second Coming of Capitalism" (2000, 294). Similarly, Daniel Miller (1997) offers trenchant critiques of ideas of so-called pure capitalism that ignore the local tendencies of consumers and producers.

7 The economist Brian Arthur (1994) points out that in markets characterized by diminishing returns, competition leads to a relatively stable and efficient equilibrium. Consider, for example, competition between coal and water plants to produce electric power. As coal-powered plants gain in market share, the price of coal gradually goes up, making water-generated electricity more competitive. As more hydroelectric dams are constructed and the sites easiest to exploit are used first, engineers must seek more expensive dam sites, and the use of coal becomes increasingly economical. Over time, the two technologies achieve an equilibrium of the market share that reflects the most efficient use of available technology and resources. Thus competition among firms in resource-based production is expected to produce a stable equilibrium characterized by an efficient distribution of resources. Diminishing returns makes this work.

8 Shapiro and Varian point out that networks come in several forms: physical networks such as telephone, railroad, and airline networks; high-technology networks

such as compatible fax machines, modems, and e-mail; virtual networks such as the network of Macintosh users, the network of CD machines, or of Nintendo-64 users. The idea is that as these networks grow, positive feedback reinforces the gains of networks in ascendance, at times tending toward monopoly, though often creating unstable monopolies or oligopolies in the end.

9 The VCR market is one of the classic examples because the VHS format eclipsed the arguably technologically superior Beta format. As the VHS format gained increased market share, it benefited from increasing returns. That is, as more people bought VHS players, video outlets became more likely to stock VHS-format prerecorded videos, film distributors became more likely to produce them, and the value of owning a VHS-format player increased. These are called network effects as advantages accrue to one format because it is embedded in a specific network, whereby increasing use generates increasing value. Over time, the roughly even market shares of Beta and VHS fluctuated due to external circumstance, "luck," and corporate maneuvering (Arthur 1994).

10 Peer-to-peer networks are a case study of network effects. As a widening array of music listeners moves their music collections onto hard drives, the library expands while the particular network used to connect them has continually migrated from one to the next: Napster, Kazaa, eDonkey, Bit Torrent, and beyond.

11 For example, within the Gameboy world of Pokémon and Yu-Gi-Oh, players must buy things from stores within the game to move up the levels. Yet it is also notable that many parents rationalize the effects in a positive light, noting that the fixation on Pokémon cultivates interests beyond materialism, including reading, organizing, gathering information, math, exchanges, calculation, strategy, and storytelling. Anne Allison says, "The fact that 'getting' is the very logic of the Pokémon game, however, may be one sign of further progression of the entwinement of play in commodity acquisitiveness. . . . While cuteness may bring postmodern relief, then, it comes at the expense of a cascading commoditization" (2003, 393). One wonders as well which is more frightening, that children find it natural to visit stores inside their video games, or that parents can see in this consumerism a mechanism to encourage their kids to learn skills on the way to adulthood, such as reading, calculating, sharing, and trading. This is a sign that the logic of parenting—how can I get my kids to pay attention to books?—becomes smoothly interwoven with consumerism.

12 Tsutaya's ability to gather information is enhanced because it is a club, similar to Blockbuster or Hollywood Video in the United States, and so it has fairly detailed information about each consumer, including cell-phone numbers, e-mail addresses, workplace, home address, phone numbers, age, occupation, marital status, education, and so on. *Data Watch* also included results from e-mail surveys. One thing that makes this kind of surveillance easily acceptable is that with each purchase or rental, consumers are offered the chance to use their point cards to accumulate credit toward a discount on a later purchase. This rewards people who do most of their shopping in one chain while building a database of customers' habits. In the summer of 2003, I met with a vice president at Tsutaya who described how the Tsutaya point card could now be used in some convenience stores and gas sta-

tions, thus providing an even more detailed portrait of people's daily shopping habits, and he explained that further tie-ups were being negotiated.

13 One expects that *Data Watch*, more than being aimed at a mass market, is aimed at showing what more specialized information Tsutaya can sell to record manufacturers. Potential marketing synergies are clearly a focus of the data. For each artist's consumers, we learn the top ten magazines, segregated by gender, associated with the people who purchased a particular artist's CD. For Rip Slyme and Hamasaki Ayumi, three of the top ten magazines bought by the male consumers were *manga*, but for the women, fashion magazines led. For Eminem fans, the men tended toward fashion magazines and viewed themselves as more "classy" (*share*) than average, more likely to buy CDs they learn about from magazines, as compared to TV shows, which dominated as the information source for the other artists. For Eminem, the caricature of the common kind of fan shows a boy with brown-dyed hair and heavy headphones and the caption: "His whole body is Nike!" The fans for the Chinese women's group Joshi Nijū Gakubō viewed themselves as "the normal type," who tended to care less about fashion and who seldom went to hot spots or live shows. Hamasaki Ayumi's female fans were more likely to dress fashionably, seek out the latest hot spots, and, according to the caricature, they regarded the appearance of their fingernails as vitally important. Putting the consumer first in this sense means knowing them according to their consumption habits.

14 The percentages are approximate because publicly available RIAJ data shows only the number of albums selling more than a million, and higher sales are marked in 1 million increments. The calculations are as follows: In 1998, million-sellers accounted for 42 million CD albums out of a total (Japanese and Western) of sales of 302 million (13.9 percent). In 2004, million-sellers produced 13 million in sales as part of a total of 220 million albums sold (5.9 percent). The sales figures and million-sellers data are taken from the Recording Industry Association of Japan Web site: www.riaj.com/data/album/album_m.html (sales figures); www.riaj.com/data/others/million_q.html (million sellers). (Accessed April 27, 2005.) The original was in Japanese.

15 Interview with the author, October 6, 1996.

16 It is worth noting the difference between a record company (*kaisha*) and an artist-management company (*jimusho*) to get a sense of the different aspects of selling music and musicians. Record companies are generally involved only in producing and selling records, while the management company more generally develops the artists. Iguchi on behalf of Amuse, for example, manages the artists' schedules, sells artists or groups to record companies, promotes the artists, goes to live shows, and helps produce radio and TV programs. According to Iguchi, the record company is the "father" (who controls making records and has the authority, *shudōken*), while the management company is the "mother" (who raises the artist, *sodatsu*). Only artists signed to a major record company tend to belong to a management company. At independent labels, artists usually act as their own managers.

17 In the spring of 1996, he invited me to attend a business meeting with Monchi Tanaka, an active producer of hip-hop and R & B albums in Japan, including the compilation series *Best of Japanese Hip-Hop*. They met at Tanaka's Shibuya

studio overlooking Yoyogi Park in a room with case after case of records lining the walls. While Tanaka chain-smoked, they discussed the pros and cons of different options. Umedy floated the idea of producing his next album by himself and hand-delivering the album to stores. Tanaka acknowledged that some record stores tended to be receptive when independent artists delivered their own CDS. With self-produced albums, the artists would recoup a large percentage of sales revenue (50 percent of retail rather than the 1–2 percent of retail with a major label release). Since Umedy had access to most of the necessary equipment at Cake-K's apartment-studio, he could produce the entire album, except for the final track-down, on a shoestring budget (still a couple of thousand dollars). The dream of self-produced/self-distributed albums using personal computers and the Internet is a recurring image of entrepreneurial-minded artists, but as yet there have been very few examples of success using this route. Major labels' marketing muscle and distribution networks remain necessary for widespread success. I expect Internet distribution to open some more possibilities for independent success, but there have been few examples so far.

18 Personal communication, August 2001.

CONCLUSION: LESSONS OF HIP-HOP GLOBALIZATION

1 The lyrics are taken from this video as well.
2 The phrase *gaiya no yaji* deserves a further note because it draws into focus several themes from different chapters. The term *gaiya* means "outside the field," or "someone who has no direct relationship to the thing." We can hear echoes of the idea of *otaku* "islands in space," such that outsiders fail to grasp the solidity of the social worlds within the islands. *Yaji* is a blunt word for older men (politicians, corporate leaders), thus, old and out of touch, offering little of value to artists and their peers. I would also note that this song appears on the album produced after Rhymester were attacked for dressing up in military uniforms for their 1999 album *Respect*.
3 It is something of an overgeneralization, but I think the politics of record companies are best characterized not in terms of partisan electoral politics, but rather in terms of the power of hits. Hypothetically, if there were a song calling for the assassination of a major political leader that became a huge hit, I could imagine conversations in the record company executive offices that included the question, "Where is our assassination song?" That may be extreme, but I believe it captures something of the conservative logic of major entertainment companies. The logic is conservative not vis-à-vis liberal, but rather in paying close attention to recent major successes.

REFERENCES

Abu-Lughod, Lila. 2002. "Egyptian Melodrama: Technology of the Modern Subject?" In *Media Worlds: Anthropology on New Terrain*, ed. Faye D. Ginsburg, Abu-Lughod, and Brian Larkin, 39–57. Berkeley: University of California Press.

Adorno, Theodor W. 1976. *Introduction to the Sociology of Music*. Trans. E. B. Ashton. New York: Seabury.

Allinson, Gary D. 1997. *Japan's Postwar History*. Ithaca, NY: Cornell University Press.

Allison, Anne. 1994. *Nightwork: Sexuality, Pleasure, and Corporate Masculinity in a Tokyo Hostess Club*. Chicago: University of Chicago Press.

———. 2003. "Portable Monsters and Commodity Cuteness: *Pokémon* as Japan's New Global Power." *Postcolonial Studies* 6 (3): 381–95.

Aoyagi, Hiroshi. 2000. "Pop Idols and the Asian Identity." In *Japan Pop! Inside the World of Japanese Popular Culture*, ed. Timothy Craig, 309–26. Armonk, NY: M. E. Sharpe.

Appadurai, Arjun. 1996. *Modernity at Large: Cultural Dimensions of Globalization*. Minneapolis: University of Minnesota Press.

Arthur, W. Brian. 1994. "Competing Technologies, Increasing Returns, and Lock-In by Historical Small Events." In *Increasing Returns and Path Dependence in the Economy*, ed. Arthur, 13–32. Ann Arbor: University of Michigan Press.

Askew, Kelly, and Richard C. Wilk, eds. 2002. *The Anthropology of Media: A Reader*. Malden, MA: Blackwell.

Asō, Kōtarō. 1997. *Breeku shinkaron* (Theory of Increasing Music Hits). Tokyo: Jōhō Sentaa Shuppankyoku.

Atkins, E. Taylor. 2001. *Blue Nippon: Authenticating Jazz in Japan*. Durham, NC: Duke University Press.

Auletta, Ken. 1997. "The Impossible Business." *New Yorker*, October 6, 50–63.

Baker, Houston A. 1993. *Black Studies, Rap, and the Academy*. Chicago: University of Chicago Press.

Bakhtin, Mikhail. 1981. "Discourse in the Novel." In *The Dialogic Imagination: Four Essays*, ed. Michael Holquist, trans. Caryl Emerson and Holquist, 259–422. Austin: University of Texas Press.

Baran, Madeliene. 2002. "Copyright and Music: A History Told in MP3's." Illegal Art: http://www.illegal-art.org/audio/historic.html.

Barrett, Stanley, Sean Stockholm, and Jeanette Burke. 2001. "The Idea of Power and the Power of Ideas: A Review Essay." *American Anthropologist* 103 (2): 468–80.

Befu, Harumi. 2001. *Hegemony of Homogeneity: An Anthropological Analysis of "Nihon-jinron."* Melbourne: Trans Pacific.

Bell, MC, and Cake-K. 1998. "B-Fresh." *Woofin'*, October, 112.

Belson, Ken, and Brian Bremner. 2004. *Hello Kitty: The Remarkable Story of Sanrio and the Billion Dollar Feline Phenomenon*. Singapore: John Wiley and Sons.

Benjamin, Walter. 1969. "The Work of Art in an Age of Mechanical Reproduction." In *Illuminations*, ed. Hannah Arendt, trans. Harry Zohn, 217–51. New York: Schocken.

Bestor, Theodore. 2004. *Tsukiji: The Fish Market at the Center of the World*. Berkeley: University of California Press.

Blast editors. 2002. "King Ghidora: 'Unstoppable' or 'Stoppable'." *Blast*, August, 114–21.

Bourdieu, Pierre. 1984. *Distinction: A Social Critique of the Judgment of Taste*. Trans. R. Nice. Cambridge, MA: Harvard University Press.

Boyd, Todd. 2002. *The New H.N.I.C. (Head Niggas in Charge): The Death of Civil Rights and the Reign of Hip Hop*. New York: New York University Press.

Brannon, Mary Yoko. 1992. " 'Bwana Mickey': Constructing Cultural Consumption at Tokyo Disneyland." In *Re-Made in Japan: Everyday Life and Consumer Taste in a Changing Society*, ed. Joseph J. Tobin, 216–34. New Haven, Conn.: Yale University Press.

Bynoe, Yvonne. 2002. "Getting Real about Global Hip-Hop." *Georgetown Journal of International Affairs* 3 (1): 77–84.

———. 2004. *Stand and Deliver: Political Activism, Leadership, and Hip Hop Culture*. Brooklyn, NY: Soft Skull.

Chikushi, Tetsuya. 1986. "Young People as a New Human Race." *Japan Quarterly* 33 (3): 291–94.

Ching, Leo. 1996. "Imaginings in the Empires of the Sun: Japanese Mass Culture in Asia." In *Contemporary Japan and Popular Culture*, ed. John Whittier Treat, 169–94. Honolulu: University of Hawai'i Press.

Chūsonji, Yutsuko, ed. 1996. *Wild Q*. Tokyo: Magazine House.

Clammer, John. 1997. *Contemporary Urban Japan*. Oxford: Blackwell.

Comaroff, Jean, and John Comaroff. 2000. "Millennial Capitalism: First Thoughts on a Second Coming." *Public Culture* 12 (2): 291–343.

Condry, Ian. 2004. "Cultures of Music Piracy: An Ethnographic Comparison of the US and Japan." *International Journal of Cultural Studies* 7 (3): 343–63.

Cornyetz, Nina. 1994. "Fetishized Blackness: Hip Hop and Racial Desire in Contemporary Japan." *Social Text* 12 (1): 113–39.

Craig, Timothy, ed. 2000. *Japan Pop! Inside the World of Japanese Popular Culture.* Armonk, NY: M. E. Sharpe.

Dale, Peter N. 1986. *The Myth of Japanese Uniqueness.* London: Croom Helm.

Davila, Arlene. 2002. "Culture in the Ad World: Producing the Latin Look." In *Media Worlds: Anthropology on New Terrain*, ed. Faye D. Ginsburg, Lila Abu-Lughod, and Brian Larkin, 264–80. Berkeley: University of California Press.

De Vos, George, and Hiroshi Wagatsuma. 1966. *Japan's Invisible Race: Caste in Culture and Personality.* Berkeley: University of California Press.

Dower, John W. 1986. *War without Mercy: Race and Power in the Pacific War.* New York: Pantheon.

———. 1999. Embracing Defeat: Japan in the Wake of World War II. New York: Norton.

Dreisinger, Baz. 2002. "Tokyo after Dark." *Vibe*, August, 130–38.

Du Gay, Paul, and Michael Pryke, eds. 2002. *Cultural Economy: Cultural Analysis and Commercial Life.* London: Sage.

Durand, Alain-Philippe, ed. 2002. *Black, Blanc, Beur: Rap Music and Hip-Hop Culture in the Francophone World.* Lanham, MD: Scarecrow.

Dwyer, Paula, Margaret Dawson, and Dexter Roberts. 1996. "The New Music Biz." *Business Week*, 48–58.

East End X Yuri. 1995. *Sony Magazines Presents East End X Yuri.* Tokyo: Sony Magazines.

ECD. 1997. "Represent Nippon (14): Bokutachi wa risk o shotte yatte iru" (Represent Nippon [14]: We're Taking Risks to Do Hip Hop). *Black Music Review*, February, 62–63.

Egaitsu, Hiroshi. 1997a. *Hip Hop Best One Hundred (Best Album Series).* Tokyo: Bad News.

———. 1997b. "Japanese Hip-Hop Scene Chronology." *Groove*, April 1, 34–35.

———. 2002. "Hippu hoppu o ikiru jidai no toujou" (The appearance of the generation the lives hip hop). http://www.bounce.com/contents/tokushu/feature/20020124_japanesehiphop (accessed Oct. 1, 2004).

Eguchi, Yoshiko. 2001. *Lafura, nijū yon–sai no yuigon: Aru rappaa no shougai* (Lafura, a Twenty-Four-Year-Old's Last Request: The Life of a Rapper). Tokyo: Poplar sha.

Fernandes, Sujatha. 2003. "Fear of a Black Nation: Local Rappers, Transnational Crossings, and State Power in Contemporary Cuba." *Anthropological Quarterly* 76 (4): 575–608.

Fernando, S. H., Jr. 1994. *The New Beats: Exploring the Music, Culture, and Attitudes of Hip-Hop.* New York: Anchor.

Field, Norma. 1989. "*Somehow*: The Postmodern as Atmosphere." In *Postmodernism and Japan*, ed. Masao Miyoshi and H.D. Harootunian, 169–88. Durham, NC: Duke University Press.

———. 1995. "The Child as Laborer and Consumer: The Disappearance of Childhood in Contemporary Japan." In *Children and the Politics of Culture*, ed. Sharon Stephens, 51–78. Princeton, NJ: Princeton University Press.

Fiske, John. 1992. "The Cultural Economy of Fandom." In *The Adoring Audience: Fan Culture and Popular Media*, ed. L. A. Lewis, 30–49. London: Routledge.

Forman, Murray. 2002. *The 'Hood Comes First: Race, Space, and Place in Rap and Hip-Hop.* Middletown, CT: Wesleyan University Press.

Forman, Murray, and Mark Anthony Neal, eds. 2004. *That's the Joint: A Hip-Hop Studies Reader*. New York: Routledge.

Fowler, Edward. 1996. *San'ya Blues: Laboring Life in Contemporary Tokyo*. Ithaca, NY: Cornell University Press.

Friedman, Thomas. 2005. *The World Is Flat: A Brief History of the Twenty-first Century*. New York: Farrar, Straus and Giroux.

Frith, Simon. 1996. *Performing Rites: On the Value of Popular Music*. Cambridge, MA: Harvard University Press.

Fujita, Tadashi. 1996. *Tokyo Hip Hop Guide*. Tokyo: Ohta.

Ganti, Tejaswini. 2002. "'And Yet My Heart Is Still Indian': The Bombay Film Industry and the (H)Indianization of Hollywood." In *Media Worlds: Anthropology on New Terrain*, ed. Faye D. Ginsburg, Lila Abu-Lughod, and Brian Larkin, 281–300. Berkeley: University of California Press.

Gates, Henry Louis, Jr. 1998. "Net Worth." *New Yorker*, June 1, 48–61.

Genocchio, Benjamin. 2004. "For Japanese Girls, Black Is Beautiful." *New York Times*, April 4.

George, Nelson. 1998. *Hip Hop America*. New York: Viking.

Ginsburg, Faye D. 2002. "Screen Memories: Resignifying the Traditional in Indigenous Media." In *Media Worlds: Anthropology on New Terrain*, ed. Ginsburg, Lila Abu-Lughod, and Brian Larkin, 39–57. Berkeley: University of California Press.

Ginsburg, Faye D., Lila Abu-Lughod, and Brian Larkin, eds. 2002. *Media Worlds: Anthropology on New Terrain*. Berkeley: University of California Press.

Gotō, Akio, ed. 1997. *J-Rap izen: Hippu-hoppu karuchaa wa koo shite umareta* (Before J-Rap: This Is How Hip-Hop Culture Was Born). Tokyo: Tokyo FM Shuppan.

Grieco, Elizabeth M., and Rachel C. Cassidy. 2001. *Overview of Race and Hispanic Origin 2000: US Census Brief*. Washington, DC: US Census Bureau.

Gupta, Akhil, and James Ferguson. 1997. "Discipline and Practice: 'The Field' as Site, Method, and Location in Anthropology." In *Anthropological Locations: Boundaries and Grounds of a Field Science*, ed. Gupta and Ferguson, 1–46. Berkeley: University of California Press.

Hall, Stuart. 1997. "The Local and the Global: Globalization and Ethnicity." In *Culture, Globalization, and the World-System: Contemporary Conditions for the Representation of Identity*, ed. Anthony D. King, 19–39. Minneapolis: University of Minnesota Press.

Hamano, Yasuki. 2004. "'Bunka' wa saikyō no maaketingu de aru" (Culture Is the Most Powerful Marketing). *Ekonomisuto* (Economist), May 25, 26–27.

Hannerz, Ulf. 1996. *Transnational Connections: Culture, People, Places*. New York: Routledge.

Hebdige, Dick. 1979. *Subculture: The Meaning of Style*. London: Methuen.

Hill, Peter B. E. 2003. *The Japanese Mafia: Yakuza, Law, and the State*. Oxford: Oxford University Press.

Hosokawa, Shuhei. 2002. "Blacking Japanese: Experiencing Otherness from Afar." In *Popular Music Studies*, ed. David Hesmondhalgh and Keith Negus, 223–37. New York: Oxford University Press.

Hosokawa, Shuhei, Hiroshi Matsumura, and Shun'ichi Shiba, eds. 1991. *A Guide to Popular Music in Japan*. Kanazawa, Japan: IASPM-Japan.

Iida, Yumiko. 2000. "Between the Technique of Living an Endless Routine and the Madness of Absolute Degree Zero: Japanese Identity and the Crisis of Modernity in the 1990s." *Positions* 8 (2): 423–64.

Inda, Jonathon Xavier, and Renato Rosaldo, eds. 2002a. *The Anthropology of Globalization: A Reader*. Malden, MA: Blackwell.

———. 2002b. "Introduction: A World in Motion." In *The Anthropology of Globalization: A Reader*, ed. Inda and Rosaldo, 1–34. Malden, MA: Blackwell.

Irvine, Judith T., and Susan Gal. 2000. "Language Ideology and Linguistic Differentiation." In *Regimes of Language: Ideologies, Polities, and Identities*, ed. Paul V. Kroskrity, 35–83. Santa Fe, NM: School of American Research Press.

Ishihara, Shintarō. 1991. *The Japan That Can Say No*. Trans. Frank Baldwin. New York: Simon and Schuster.

Itō, Satoru. 2002. "'Kyōsei' o kiiwaado ni tayō na ningen to tsunagareru jiko hyōgen o" ("Living in Harmony" is the Keyword for Diverse People to Express Themselves). *Blast*, August, 117.

Itō, Seikō. 1995. *Mess/Age* (CD liner notes, 23FRO31D). Tokyo: File Records.

Ivy, Marilyn. 1995. *Discourses of the Vanishing: Modernity, Phantasm, Japan*. Chicago: University of Chicago Press.

Iwabuchi, Koichi. 2002. *Recentering Globalization: Popular Culture and Japanese Transnationalism*. Durham, NC: Duke University Press.

Japan Foundation. 2005. "Korean and Japanese Hip-Hop and Contemporary Artists Perform Together in Seoul." *Japan Foundation Newsletter* 30 (5): 5.

Jenkins, Henry. 1992. *Textual Poachers: Television Fans and Participatory Culture*. New York: Routledge.

Jenkins, Henry, Tara McPherson, and Jane Shattuc. 2002. "The Culture That Sticks to Your Skin: A Manifesto for a New Cultural Studies." In *Hop on Pop: The Politics and Pleasures of Popular Culture*, ed. Jenkins, McPherson, and Shattuc, 3–26. Durham, NC: Duke University Press.

Kawabata, Shigeru. 1991. "The Japanese Record Industry." *Popular Music* 10 (3): 327–45.

Kelley, Robin D. G. 1997. *Yo' Mama's Disfunktional! Fighting the Culture Wars in Urban America*. Boston: Beacon.

Kelly, William W., ed. 2004. *Fanning the Flames: Fandom and Consumer Culture in Japan*. Albany: State University of New York Press.

Kelsky, Karen. 2001. *Women on the Verge: Japanese Women, Western Dreams*. Durham, NC: Duke University Press.

Kimoto, Rei-ichi. 2002. "Nihon ni okeru rappu jisseki o meguru ichi kōsatsu" (A Look at the Practices of Rap in Japan). *Sociology* 7 (2): 73–88.

Kinoshita, Mitsuru. 1999. "Rhymester." *Remix*, September, 16–19.

———. 2000. "Zeebra Recording Report." *Remix*, June, 14–15.

Kinsella, Sharon. 1995. "Cuties in Japan." In *Women, Media, and Consumption in Japan*, ed. Lise Skov and Brian Moeran, 220–54. Richmond, Surrey, UK: Curzon.

———. 2000. *Adult Manga: Culture and Power in Contemporary Japan*. Honolulu: University of Hawaii Press.

Kitwana, Bakari. 2002. *The Hip Hop Generation: Young Blacks and the Crisis in African American Culture*. New York: Basic Civitas.

Kobayashi, Masa'aki. 2004. "K Dub Shine: Rhyme and Reason." *Blast*, August, 30–31.

Koizumi, Katsumi. 1995. "Nihongo [kanji] ha nihongo [katakana] ni shinka shita" (Japanese has evolved into Japanese). In *Views*, 58–63. Tokyo, Japan: Kodansha.

Kondo, Dorinne. 1990. *Crafting Selves: Power, Gender, and Discourses of Identity in a Japanese Workplace*. Chicago: University of Chicago Press.

———. 1997. *About Face: Performing Race in Fashion and Theater*. New York: Routledge.

Kosaku, Yoshino. 1997. "The Discourse on Blood and Racial Identity in Contemporary Japan." In *The Construction of Racial Identities in China and Japan: Historical and Contemporary Perspectives*, ed. Frank Dikötter, 199–211. Honolulu: University of Hawai'i Press.

Koshiro, Yukiko. 2003. "Beyond an Alliance of Color: The African American Impact on Modern Japan." *Positions* 11 (1): 183–215.

Kosugi, Reiko. 2004. "The Transition from School to Work in Japan: Understanding the Increase in Freeter and Jobless Youth." *Japan Labor Review* 1 (1): 52–67.

Krush, DJ. 1998. *Japanese Hip-Hop History*. Tokyo: Chihaya Shobo.

Krush, DJ, and Yasumasa Sekiguchi. 1995. "DJ Krush." *Bad News*, December, 26.

Larkin, Brian. 2002. "The Materiality of Cinema Theaters in Northern Nigeria." In *Media Worlds: Anthropology on New Terrain*, ed. Faye D. Ginsburg, Lila Abu-Lughod, and Larkin, 319–36. Berkeley: University of California Press.

Leupp, Gary. 1995. "Images of Black People in Late Mediaeval and Early Modern Japan, 1543–1900." *Japan Forum* 7 (1):1–13.

Lie, John. 2001. *Multiethnic Japan*. Cambridge, MA: Harvard University Press.

Longhurst, Brian. 1995. *Popular Music and Society*. Cambridge: Polity.

Love, Courtney. 2000. "Courtney Love Does the Math." *Salon*. http://dir.salon.com/tech/feature/2000/06/14/love/index.html (accessed August 6, 2003).

Mankekar, Purnima. 2002. "Epic Contests: Television and Religious Identity in India." In *Media Worlds: Anthropology on New Terrain*, ed. Faye D. Ginsburg, Lila Abu-Lughod, and Brian Larkin, 134–51. Berkeley: University of California Press.

Marcus, George. 1995. "Ethnography in/of the World System: The Emergence of Multi-sited Ethnography." *Annual Review of Anthropology*, no. 24:95–117.

Marks, Jonathan. 1995. *Human Biodiversity: Genes, Race, and History*. New York: Aldine de Gruyter.

Martinez, D. P., ed. 1998. *The Worlds of Japanese Popular Culture*. Cambridge: Cambridge University Press.

Maxwell, Ian. 2003. *Phat Beats, Dope Rhymes: Hip Hop Down Under Comin' Upper*. Middletown, CT: Wesleyan University Press.

McGray, Douglas. 2002. "Japan's Gross National Cool." *Foreign Policy* no. 130: 44–54.

McLagan, Meg. 2002. "Spectacles of Difference: Cultural Activism and the Mass Mediation of Tibet." In *Media Worlds: Anthropology on New Terrain*, ed. Faye D. Ginsburg, Lila Abu-Lughod, and Brian Larkin, 90–111. Berkeley: University of California Press.

McLuhan, Marshall. 1962. *The Gutenberg Galaxy: The Making of Typographic Man*. Toronto: University of Toronto Press.

McRobbie, Angela. 1993. "Shut Up and Dance: Youth Culture and Changing Modes of Femininity." *Cultural Studies* 7 (3): 406–26.

———. 2002. "From Holloway to Hollywood: Happiness at Work in the New Cultural Economy?" In *Cultural Economy: Cultural Analysis and Commercial Life*, ed. Paul du Gay and Michael Pryke, 97–114. London: Sage.

Miller, Daniel. 1995a. "Introduction: Anthropology Modernity and Consumption." In *World's Apart: Modernity through the Prism of the Local*, ed. Miller, 1–22. London: Routledge.

———. 1997. *Capitalism: An Ethnographic Approach*. Oxford: Berg.

———, ed. 1995b. *Acknowledging Consumption: A Review of New Studies*. London: Routledge.

Miller, Laura. 2003. "Graffiti Photos: Expressive Art in Japanese Girls' Culture." *Harvard Asia Quarterly* 7 (3).

Miller, Roy Andrew. 1982. *Japan's Modern Myth: The Language and Beyond*. New York: Weatherhill.

Ministry of Justice (Japan). 2004. *Heisei 15-nenmatsu genzai ni okeru gaikokujin tōrokusha tōkei ni tsuite* (Regarding the Data on Registered Foreigners from the End of 2003 to the Present). http://www.moj.go.jp/PRESS/040611-1/040611-1.html (published June 11, 2004; accessed Jan. 25, 2005).

Mitchell, Tony. 2001a. "Kia Kaha! (Be Strong!) Maori and Pacific Islander Hip-Hop in Aotearoa-New Zealand." In *Global Noise: Rap and Hip-Hop Outside the USA*, ed. Mitchell, 280–305. Middletown, CT: Wesleyan University Press.

———, ed. 2001b. *Global Noise: Rap and Hip-Hop Outside the USA*. Middletown, CT: Wesleyan University Press.

Miyadai, Shinji. 1990. "Shinjinrui to otaku no seikimatsu o toku (zoku)" (Shinjinrui and Otaku Are the Key to the End of the Century [Pt. II]). In *Chūō kōron*. 214–234, Vol. 105.

———. 1994. *Seifuku shōjo tachi no sentaku* (The Choice of the School Uniform Girls). Tokyo: Kōdansha.

Miyadai, Shinji, Hideki Ishihara, and Meiko Otsuka. 1993. *Sabukarucha shinwa kaitai* (Dismantling the Myths of Subculture). Tokyo: Parco.

Mizuki, Shigeru. 1994. *Showa shi* (History of the Showa Era). Vol. 8, *Kōdō seichō ikō* (From the High-Growth Period On). Tokyo: Kōdansha.

Moeran, Brian. 1996. *A Japanese Advertising Agency: An Anthropology of Media and Markets*. Honolulu: University of Hawai'i Press.

Morris, Mark. 1986. "Waka and Form, Waka and History." *Harvard Journal of Asiatic Studies* 46 (2): 551–610.

Murakami, Takashi, ed. 2005. *Little Boy: The Arts of Japan's Exploding Subculture*. New York: Japan Society.

Muraoka, Kiyoko. 2004. "Ima no ongaku shōhisha wa, hatashite 'ongaku fan' na no ka?" (Are Today's Music Consumers Actually "Music Fans"?). *Data Watch*, Winter, 62–68.

Murata, Tomoki, ed. 1997. *Shibuya-kei moto neta disc guide* (A Record Guide to the Original Samples of Shibuya-Kei Music). Tokyo: Ohta Shuppan.

Napier, Susan J. 2001. *Anime from Akira to Princess Mononoke.* New York: Palgrave.

Nathan, John. 2004. *Japan Unbound: A Volatile Nation's Quest for Pride and Purpose.* Boston: Houghton Mifflin.

Neal, Mark Anthony. 2003. *Songs in the Key of Black Life: A Rhythm and Blues Nation.* New York: Routledge.

Neary, Ian. 1997. "Burakumin in Contemporary Japan." In *Japan's Minorities: The Illusion of Homogeneity.* M. Weiner, ed., 50–78. London: Routledge.

Negus, Keith. 1999. *Music Genres and Corporate Cultures.* London: Routledge.

"Nisen sannen bureeku suru aateisuto to jyanru" (The Artists and Genres That Will Break in 2003). *Oricon,* 23–24.

Nye, Joseph S., Jr. 2004. *Soft Power: The Means to Success in World Politics.* New York: PublicAffairs.

Ogasawara, Yuko. 1998. *Office Ladies and Salaried Men: Power, Gender, and Work in Japanese Companies.* Berkeley: University of California Press.

Ohmann, Richard, ed. 1996. *Making and Selling Culture.* Hanover, NH: University Press of New England.

Okamoto, Shigeko. 1995. " 'Tasteless' Japanese: Less 'Feminine' Speech among Young Japanese Women." In *Gender Articulated: Language and the Socially Constructed Self,* ed. Kira Hall and Mary Bucholtz, 297–325. New York: Routledge.

Perry, Imani. 2004. *Prophets of the Hood: Politics and Poetics in Hip Hop.* Durham, NC: Duke University Press.

Perullo, Alex, and John Fenn. 2003. "Language Ideologies, Choices, and Practices in Eastern African Hip-Hop." In *Global Pop, Local Language,* ed. Harris M. Berger and Michael Thomas Carroll, 19–51. Jackson: University Press of Mississippi.

Plath, David. 1969. *The After Hours: Modern Japan and the Search for Enjoyment.* Berkeley: University of California Press.

Potter, Russell A. 1995. *Spectacular Vernaculars: Hip-Hop and the Politics of Postmodernism.* Albany: State University of New York Press.

Prashad, Vijay. 2001. *Everybody Was Kung Fu Fighting: Afro-Asian Connections and the Myth of Cultural Purity.* Boston: Beacon Press.

Prevos, André. 1996. "The Evolution of French Rap Music and Hip Hop Culture in the 1980s and 1990s." *French Review* 69 (5): 713–25.

Radway, Janice A. 1991. *Reading the Romance: Women, Patriarchy, and Popular Literature.* Chapel Hill: University of North Carolina Press.

Raz, Aviad E. 1999. *Riding the Black Ship: Japan and Tokyo Disneyland.* Cambridge, Mass.: Harvard University Asia Center.

Recording Industry Association of Japan (RIAJ). 2003. *RIAJ Yearbook 2003: Statistics, Trends, Analysis.* Tokyo: Recording Industry Association of Japan.

Rhymester. 1999. Radio Interview. HMV Shibuya/ J-Wave Station, June 22.

"Risupekuto: Rappu de kataru kuukyo no rinri" (Respect: the Empty Morals Spoken of in Rap). 1999. *Asahi Shimbun,* December 11.

Ritzer, George. 2004. *The Globalization of Nothing.* Thousand Oaks, CA: Pine Forge Press.

Rivera, Raquel Z. 2003. *New York Ricans from the Hip Hop Zone*. New York: Palgrave Macmillan.

Robertson, Jennifer. 1998. *Takarazuka: Sexual Politics and Popular Culture in Modern Japan*. Berkeley: University of California Press.

Robertson, Roland. 1992. *Globalization: Social Theory and Global Culture*. London: Sage.

———. 1995. "Glocalization: Time-Space and Homogeneity-Heterogeneity." In *Global Modernities*, ed. Mike Featherstone, Scott Lash, and Robertson, 25–44. London: Sage.

Rose, Tricia. 1994. *Black Noise: Rap Music and Black Culture in Contemporary America*. Middletown, CT: Wesleyan University Press.

Ross, Alex. 2003. "Rock 101." *New Yorker*, July 14 and 21, 87–93.

Roth, Joshua. 2003. *Brokered Homeland: Japanese Brazilian Migrants in Japan*. Ithaca, NY: Cornell University Press.

Rugged Editorial Board. 1995. "Talk about Japanese Hip-Hop." *Rugged* 5: 6–7.

Russell, John. 1998. "Consuming Passions: Spectacle, Self-Transformation, and the Commodification of Blackness in Japan." *Positions* 6 (1): 113–77.

Saeki Kenzō, and Itō Seikō. 1988. " 'Ai shiteru' o kowasanakya nihongo wa kaerare-nai" (If We Don't Smash "I Love You," We'll Never Change the Japanese Language). *Music Magazine*, March, 78–83.

Sakurai, Riko. 2002. "Hip-Hop." *Asahi Shimbun*, March 30.

Sasaki, Shiro. 1996. " 'Ore wa kō da' to sakenda mono ga shōri suru: Kaisetsu ni kaete, Yutsuko san e messeeji" (To Be Successful, You Must Say "I'm This": A Message to Yutsuko). In *Wild Q*, ed. Yutsuko Chusonji, 146–49. Tokyo: Magazine House.

Savigliano, Marta E. 1995. *Tango and the Political Economy of Passion*. Boulder, CO: Westview.

Schein, Louisa. 1999. "Performing Modernity." *Cultural Anthropology* 14 (3): 361–95.

Schloss, Joseph G. 2004. *Making Beats: the Art of Sample-Based Hip-Hop*. Middletown, CT: Wesleyan University Press.

Sellek, Yoko. 1997. "Nikkeijin: The Phenomenon of Return Migration." In *Japan's Minorities: The Illusion of Homogeneity*, ed. M. Weiner, 187–92. New York: Routledge.

Shapiro, Carl, and Hal R. Varian. 1999. *Information Rules: A Strategic Guide to the Network Economy*. Boston: Harvard Business School Press.

Shibatani, Masayoshi. 1990. *The Languages of Japan*. Cambridge: Cambridge University Press.

Skov, Lise, and Brian Moeran, eds. 1995. *Women, Media, and Consumption in Japan*. Richmond, Surrey, UK: Curzon.

Spitulnik, Debra. 2002. "Mobile Machines and Fluid Audiences: Rethinking Reception through Zambian Radio Culture." In *Media Worlds: Anthropology on New Terrain*, ed. Faye D. Ginsburg, Lila Abu-Lughod, and Brian Larkin, 337–54. Berkeley: University of California Press.

Stanlaw, James. 1990. "Dancing in the Park: Takenoko Zoku, Rock and Roll Zoku, and Band Zoku." *World and I* 5 (9): 630–42.

———. 1992. " 'For Beautiful Human Life': The Use of English in Japan." In *Re-made in Japan: Everyday Life and Consumer Taste in a Changing Society*, ed. Joseph J. Tobin, 58–76. New Haven, Conn.: Yale University Press.

————. 2000. "Open Your File, Open Your Mind: Women, English, and Changing Roles and Voices in Japanese Pop Music." In *Japan Pop! Inside the World of Japanese Popular Culture*, ed. Timothy Craig, 75–100. Armonk, NY: M. E. Sharpe.

Steinhoff, Patricia J. 1992. "Death by Defeatism and Other Fables: The Social Dynamics of the Rengo Purge." In *Japanese Social Organization*, ed. Takie Sugiyama Lebra, 195–224. Honolulu: University of Hawai'i Press.

Sterling, Marvin. 2002. "In the Shadow of the Universal Other: Performative Identifications with Jamaican Culture in Japan." PhD diss., University of California, Los Angeles.

Tamanoi, Mariko Asano. 1990. "Women's Voices: Their Critique of the Anthropology of Japan." *Annual Review of Anthropology*, no. 19:17–37.

Tansman, Alan M. 1996. "Mournful Tears and *Sake*: The Postwar Myth of Misora Hibari." In *Contemporary Japan and Popular Culture*, ed. J. W. Treat, 103–33. Honolulu: University of Hawai'i Press.

Tate, Greg. 2003. "Introduction: Nigs R Us; or, How Blackfolk Became Fetish Objects." In *Everything But the Burden: What White People Are Taking From Black Culture*, ed. Tate, 1–14. New York: Broadway Books.

Thompson, Robert Farris. 1996. "Hip Hop 101." In *Droppin' Science: Critical Essays on Rap Music and Hip Hop Culture*, ed. W. E. Perkins, 211–19. Philadelphia: Temple University Press.

Tobin, Joseph J., ed. 1992. *Re-made in Japan: Everyday Life and Consumer Taste in a Changing Society*. New Haven, CT: Yale University Press.

————. 2004. *Pikachu's Global Adventure: The Rise and Fall of Pokémon*. Durham, NC: Duke University Press.

Tomlinson, John. 1999. *Globalization and Culture*. Chicago: University of Chicago Press.

Tonoshita, Tatsuya. 1993. "Senjitaiseika no ongakkai: Nippon ongaku bunka kyōkai no setsuritsu made" (Wartime Regulation of Musical Societies and the Establishment of the Japan Musical Culture Association). In *Bunka to fuashizumu* (Culture and Fascism), ed. S. Akazawa and K. Kitagawa, 91–128. Tokyo: Nihon Keizai Hyoronsha.

"Top 100 Albums: 2002 nendo nenkan chaato" (Top 100 Albums: 2002 Year-End Chart). 2003. *Oricon*, January 6, 103–15.

Treat, John Whittier, ed. 1996a. *Contemporary Japan and Popular Culture*. Honolulu: University of Hawaii Press.

————. 1996b. "Yoshimoto Banana Writes Home: The Shōjo in Japanese Popular Culture." In *Contemporary Japan and Popular Culture*. J. W. Treat, ed., 275–308. Honolulu: University of Hawaii Press.

Turner, Terence. 2002. "Representation, Politics, and Cultural Imagination in Indigenous Video: General Points and Kayapo Examples." In *Media Worlds: Anthropology on New Terrain*, ed. Faye D. Ginsburg, Lila Abu-Lughod, and Brian Larkin, 75–89. Berkeley: University of California Press.

Uchida, Yuya, et al. 1990. "New Rock." In *1970 nen dai hyakka* (Encyclopedia of the 1970s), ed. *Takarajina Magazine*, 84–85. Tokyo: JICC Publishing.

Uehara, Yoshihiro. 2000. "Tojō de hataraku myujishan Jin Back" (A Musician Who

Works in a Slaughterhouse Jin Back). In *Shūkan kin'yōbi* (Friday Weekly), Dec. 1, 30–33.

Uno, Roberta. 2004. "The Fifth Element." Theater Communications Group. http://www.tcg.org/am_theatre/at_articles/AT_Volume_21/at_web0404.html (accessed April 11, 2005).

Urla, Jacqueline. 2001. " 'We Are All Malcolm X': Negu Gorriak, Hip-Hop, and the Basque Political Imaginary." In *Global Noise: Rap and Hip-Hop Outside the USA*, ed. Tony Mitchell, 171–93. Middletown, CT: Wesleyan University Press.

Vogel, Harold L. 1994. *Entertainment Industry Economics: A Guide for Financial Analysis.* Cambridge: Cambridge University Press.

———. 2001. *Entertainment Industry Economics: A Guide for Financial Analysis. 5th ed.* New York: Cambridge University Press.

Waters, Malcolm. 1995. *Globalization.* London: Routledge.

Watson, James L., ed. 1997. *Golden Arches East: McDonald's in East Asia.* Stanford, CA: Stanford University Press.

Weiner, Michael, ed. 1997. *Japan's Minorities: The Illusion of Homogeneity.* London: Routledge.

Weiss, Brad. 2002. "Thug Realism: Inhabiting Fantasy in Urban Tanzania." *Cultural Anthropology* 17 (1): 93–124.

West, Cornel. 1990. "The New Cultural Politics of Difference." In *Out There: Marginalization and Contemporary Cultures,* ed. Russell Ferguson et al., 19–36. Cambridge, Mass.: MIT Press.

———. 2004. *Democracy Matters: Winning the Fight Against Imperialism.* New York: Penguin Press.

Wilk, Richard. 2002. "Television, Time, and the National Imaginary in Belize." In *Media Worlds: Anthropology on New Terrain,* ed. Faye D. Ginsburg, Lila Abu-Lughod, and Brian Larkin, 171–86. Berkeley: University of California Press.

Wolf, Eric. 1999. *Envisioning Power: Ideologies of Dominance and Crisis.* Berkeley: University of California Press.

Wood, Joe. 2000. "The Yellow Negro." In *Giant Steps: The New Generation of African American Writers,* ed. Kevin Young, 310–33. New York: HarperPerennial.

Woolard, Kathryn A., and Bambi B. Schieffelin. 1994. "Language Ideology." *Annual Review of Anthropology,* no. 24:55–82.

Wynter, Leon E. 2002. *American Skin: Pop Culture, Big Business, and the End of White America.* New York: Crown.

Yamamoto, Tsunetomo. 1979. *Hagakure: The Book of the Samurai.* Trans. William Scott Wilson. Tokyo: Kodansha International.

Yano, Christine. 2002. *Tears of Longing: Nostalgia and the Nation in Japanese Popular Song.* Cambridge, Mass.: Harvard University Press.

Zeebra. 1996a. "For the B-Boys Only: 'Mane' jya naku 'shōka ~ shōka' de aru koto o rikai shiro" (For the B-Boys Only: It's Not "Imitation" But "Absorption ~ Enlightenment" That One Must Understand). *Front,* Sept. 15, 94.

———. 1996b. "Word Is Bond, Vol. 7: Shōgen (Lamp Eye)." *Front,* July 15, 88–89.

INDEX

Ian Condry is an associate professor of Japanese cultural studies in Foreign
Languages and Literatures at the Massachusetts Institute of Technology.

Library of Congress Cataloging-in-Publication Data
Condry, Ian.
Hip-hop Japan : rap and the paths of cultural
globalization / Ian Condry.
p. cm.
Includes bibliographical references and index.
ISBN-13: 978-0-8223-3876-5 (cloth : alk. paper)
ISBN-10: 0-8223-3876-9 (cloth : alk. paper)
ISBN-13: 978-0-8223-3892-5 (pbk. : alk. paper)
ISBN-10: 0-8223-3892-0 (pbk. : alk. paper)
1. Rap (Music)—Japan—History and criticism.
2. Culture and globalization—Japan. I. Title.
ML3531.C66 2006
782.4216490952—dc22
2006010440